Reformation Thought

An Anthology of Sources

Reformation Thought

An Anthology of Sources

Edited and Translated, with an Introduction, by
MARGARET L. KING

Hackett Publishing Company, Inc.
Indianapolis/Cambridge

Copyright © 2016 by Hackett Publishing Company, Inc.

All rights reserved
Printed in the United States of America

19 18 17 16   1 2 3 4 5 6 7

For further information, please address
  Hackett Publishing Company, Inc.
  P.O. Box 44937
  Indianapolis, Indiana 46244-0937

www.hackettpublishing.com

Cover design by Rick Todhunter
Interior design by Elizabeth L. Wilson
Composition by Aptara, Inc.

Library of Congress Cataloging-in-Publication Data
Names: King, Margaret L., 1947– editor.
Title: Reformation thought : an anthology of sources / edited and translated, with an introduction by Margaret L. King.
Description: Indianapolis : Hackett Publishing Co., Inc., 2016. | Includes index.
Identifiers: LCCN 2016008622 | ISBN 9781624665172 (pbk.) | ISBN 9781624665189 (cloth)
Subjects: LCSH: Reformation—Sources.
Classification: LCC BR301 .R46 2016 | DDC 230/.04409031—dc23
LC record available at https://lccn.loc.gov/2016008622

The paper used in this publication meets the minimum requirements of American National Standard for Information Sciences—Permanence of Paper for Printed Library Materials, ANSI Z39.48–1984.

CONTENTS

Introduction	xi
Chapter One: In Search of Christ: Steps toward Reformation	**1**
The whole of holy Scripture is the word of the Lord. From John Wyclif, *On the Truth of Holy Scripture* (1377/1380)	3
Who is the church? From Jan Hus, *On the Church* (1413)	7
Here you have no real home. From Thomas à Kempis, *The Imitation of Christ* (1420/1427)	10
By faith we possess that which we do not have. From Marguerite de Navarre, *The Mirror of the Sinful Soul* (1531)	14
God's gift to us is Christ on the cross. From Benedetto da Mantova, *The Benefit for All Christians of Jesus Christ Crucified* (1543)	19
Chapter Two: Erasmus: The Egg That Luther Hatched?	**23**
All hope of safety rests in iron. From Desiderius Erasmus, *Handbook for the Christian Soldier* (1503)	25
Christianity itself is akin to Folly. From Desiderius Erasmus, *Praise of Folly* (1509)	27
May these be the stories we tell each day. From Desiderius Erasmus, *The Summons* (1516)	31
Spurned and rejected by all, Peace speaks out. From Desiderius Erasmus, *The Complaint of Peace* (1517)	34
Get ready to swim, for life or death. From Desiderius Erasmus, *The Shipwreck* (1523)	37
Chapter Three: Luther the Rebel	**42**
The believer's whole life should be one of repentance. From Martin Luther, *Ninety-Five Theses* (1517)	45
A free lord of all things, subject to no one. From Martin Luther, *On the Freedom of a Christian* (1520)	49
Faith alone justifies and fulfills the law. From Martin Luther, *Preface to the Letter of Saint Paul to the Romans* (1522)	53
Over the soul, God can and will grant authority to no one but himself alone. From Martin Luther, *On the Power of the State* (1523)	57

They live like dumb cows and unthinking pigs.
   From Martin Luther, *The Small Catechism* (1529)   60

Chapter Four: Luther's Lieutenants   64

Why else do we adorn them with golden crowns?
   From Andreas Bodenstein von Karlstadt, *On Extirpating Images* (January 27, 1522)   68

Not a woman's nonsense, but the word of God.
   From Argula von Grumbach, *Letter to the rector and council of the University of Ingolstadt* (September 20, 1523)   71

If works can justify, of what use is Christ and our regeneration?
   From Philip Melanchthon, *Defense of the Augsburg Confession* (1530)   74

Chosen by God for the reformation of the church.
   From Philip Melanchthon, *Funeral Oration for Martin Luther* (February 22, 1546)   77

The kingdom of Christ and the kingdoms of this world.
   From Martin Bucer, *The Kingdom of Christ* (1550)   80

Chapter Five: The Swiss Response   84

The freedom of the Gospel means freedom to eat.
   From Ulrich Zwingli, *On Choice and Freedom in Food* (April 16, 1522)   88

No woman ever sold Jesus or betrayed him, but a man named Judas.
   From Marie Dentière, *A Very Useful Letter to Marguerite de Navarre* (1539)   91

The intolerable blasphemy of the Mass, and a welcome conversion.
   From John Calvin, *Letters,* to Renée de France, duchess of Ferrara, and Jeanne d'Albret, queen of Navarre (1541, 1561)   94

Eternal election: The inscrutable profundity of God's judgment.
   From John Calvin, *Institutes of the Christian Religion* (1559)   97

Resisting tyranny—by force of arms if necessary.
   From Theodore Beza, *On the Right of Magistrates over Their Subjects* (1574)   100

Chapter Six: The Radical Reformation   103

The godless have no right to live, unless the Elect permit them to.
   From Thomas Müntzer, *Sermon to the Princes: An Exposition of the Second Chapter of Daniel* (Allstedt, July 13, 1524)   108

Hear, children, the instruction of your mother.
   From the martyr testaments of Maeyken van Deventer (Rotterdam, 1573) and Janneken Munstdorp (Antwerp, August 10, 1573)   111

All created things belong to all in common.
   From Peter Riedemann, *An Account of Our Religion, Teaching, and Belief* (1540–1541)   114

Do you think they were discussing hypostases?
   From Michael Servetus, *On the Errors of the Trinity* (1531)   117

Then we will know for sure just who are the real heretics.
   From Sebastian Castellio, *On Heretics: Whether They Should Be Punished, and How They Should Be Treated* (1554)   120

Chapter Seven: The English Compromise   **124**

They have gotten into their hands the third part of your realm.
   From Simon Fish, *A Supplication for the Beggars* (1529)   129

Who would refuse light in darkness? In hunger, food? In cold, fire?
   From Thomas Cranmer, *Preface to the Great Bible* (1540)   132

What did he take, and break, and give, but bread?
   From Lady Jane Grey, *A Certain Communication* (1554)   134

We shall either win you heaven, or die upon your pikes.
   From Edmund Campion, *Challenge to the Privy Council* (1580)   138

And I later returned to private examination and prayer.
   From Lady Margaret Hoby, *Diary* (1599–1605)   140

Chapter Eight: Catholic Reform and Renewal   **144**

A good bishop will not fail to perform this office.
   From Gasparo Contarini, *The Duties of a Bishop* (1517)   148

You have usurped this new and unprecedented honor.
   From Reginald Pole, *On the Unity of the Church* (1536)   152

The heretics have spread their false theology to the masses.
   From Ignatius of Loyola, *Letter* to Father Peter Canisius (Rome, August 13, 1554)   155

I took great care not to do anything against obedience.
   From Teresa of Ávila, *The Book of Her Life* (1565)   157

Devotion is to charity as the flame is to the fire.
   From Francis de Sales, *Introduction to the Devout Life* (1609)   160

Chapter Nine: The Expanding Reformation   **164**

The effect of religious discord is the destruction of religion itself.
   From Jacobus Arminius, *Oration 5: How to Settle Religious Differences among Christians* (February 8, 1606)   167

Horrible chains bind the soul during this earthly life.
   From Jacob Boehme, *Of True Repentance*, in *The Way to Christ* (1622)   170

The return of all things, when God will be all in all.
   From Johanna Eleonora Petersen, *Autobiography* (1718)   173

The power and spirit of the Lord Jesus was poured upon them.
From Margaret Fell, *Women's Speaking Justified, Proved, and Allowed of by the Scriptures* (1666) — 176

God is the joy of his heart, and the desire of his soul.
From John Wesley, *The Character of a Methodist* (1742) — 179

Chapter Ten: The Reformation Overseas — 182

War cannot force the Indians to believe, but only to pretend to believe.
From Francisco de Vitoria, *On the Indians of the New World*, First lecture, section two: *The false arguments for the subjection by the Spanish of the Indians of the New World* (1539) — 186

So many become Christians, my arms grow weary from baptizing them.
From Francis Xavier, *Letter* to his fellow Jesuits in Rome (Cochin, January 15, 1544) — 189

Are we not of all people on earth the happiest and most fortunate?
From Marie de l'Incarnation, *Letter to a lady of quality* (Quebec, September 3, 1640) — 192

I hear the cry of the whole earth, drunk with the blood of its inhabitants.
From Roger Williams, *The Bloudy Tenent of Persecution* (1644) — 195

More than three hundred souls were savingly brought home to Christ.
From Jonathan Edwards, *A Faithful Narrative of the Surprising Work of God in the Conversion of Many Hundred Souls in Northampton* (November 6, 1736) — 198

Texts and Studies — 202
Index — 219

For Paul Grendler,
a small tribute to a great scholar
for whose inspiration and encouragement I am ever grateful

INTRODUCTION

Reformations are recurrent in the history of Christianity. The Cluniac and Gregorian reforms of the tenth and eleventh centuries, and the Constantinian reform of the fourth, were notable episodes of that impulse. But the Reformation that extends from the fourteenth to the eighteenth centuries exceeds these prior episodes for the impact it had on the lives of believers and the course of later history. It featured the participation of the whole population, not just church leaders; a sharp critique of those in authority, both secular and clerical; and the remaking of institutions from the state to the family. So massive and fundamental a disruption produced no single conclusion but a diversity of ideas—not "Reformation thought," in fact, but rather "thoughts."

This volume explores that array of disparate and often contradictory ideas by making audible the voices of their authors: voices of yearning, vision, and conviction. The voices of forty-one authors are heard in the fifty texts presented here. By birth they are French, German, Czech, Dutch, Swiss, Italian, Spanish, English, and American. By occupation they are professors, pastors, cardinals, bishops, priests, and nuns; two are shoemakers, one is a physician, and one the founder of Rhode Island. Eleven are women, of whom two are royal princesses, two members of religious orders, and the rest married women of middling and noble rank. Fifteen are Catholic, while twenty-six represent the Lutheran, Reformed, and Radical streams of the Protestant movement.

The genres in which these authors write include treatise, lecture, pamphlet, letter, speech, devotional work, martyr testament, diary, memoir, and autobiography. The tones in which they speak are theoretical, polemical, didactic, meditative, and inspirational. Their works are presented in ten chapters that range over four hundred years. While most are from the sixteenth century, the first is from the late fourteenth, more than a century before Martin Luther broke with the Roman church, and the last two from the mid-eighteenth, when the Reformation culminated in Methodism in England and the Great Awakening in colonial Anglo-America.

Chapter One, "In Search of Christ: Steps toward Reformation," begins in the late 1300s with the English theologian John Wyclif, who pronounces a principle heard throughout the Reformation era: the primacy of Scripture, by which God, apart from the church, speaks to ordinary people. His follower, the Czech theologian Jan Hus, is similarly concerned with people of faith—and not the clerical hierarchy—who constitute the real church, a view for which, among others, he was burned at the stake in 1415. Writing soon afterwards, the German priest Thomas à Kempis offers in his *Imitation of Christ* a guide to the spiritual life identified with the suffering and sacrifice of Christ. Writing in the 1500s, more than a century later, both the remaining authors in this chapter were evangelicals,[1] reformers as yet detached from the Lutheran revolution that was even then underway. In 1531, the French princess Marguerite de Navarre reflects on God's gift of faith that fills her heart with an almost unbearably powerful love. In 1543, the Italian monk Benedetto da Mantova presents the doctrine of justification by faith that was also central for Luther: the righteousness that sinful souls acquire by faith in Christ, who had suffered and died for them.

Chapter Two, "Erasmus: The Egg That Luther Hatched?," is devoted to the thought of Desiderius Erasmus, the arch-humanist and reformer whose views seem to point to the Lutheran revolution but who declined to confront the institution of the church. In five works published between 1503 and 1523, Erasmus denounces the ignorance, corruption and hypocrisy of the clergy, the excesses of the cult of saints, and the warmongering of both secular and clerical leaders, while calling each individual to pursue a biblically based life of devotion to God and service to all.

Chapter Three, "Luther the Rebel," presents, like the previous chapter, five works by a single predominant author: Martin Luther, the pivotal figure who initiates the decisive break with Rome. His 1517 critique of the sale of indulgences insists that only an individual's relation to God mattered for salvation. His 1520 treatise *On the Freedom of a Christian* and 1522 preface to the translation of Paul's epistle to the Romans expound the fundamental doctrine of justification by faith. His 1523 treatise *On the Power of the State* bars any intrusion by secular government into matters of faith. *The Small Catechism* of 1529 presents Reformation doctrines in a concise format, enabling children to master the rudiments of faith and so transmit the Lutheran legacy to the next generation.

Chapter Four, "Luther's Lieutenants," looks at four persons from Luther's circle who in different ways executed the Lutheran agenda. In his 1522 tract *On Extirpating Images,* Andreas Bodenstein von Karlstadt defends the destruction of images of the saints in all the churches of Wittenberg, one of the extreme measures he introduced during Luther's absence that Luther later repudiated. In her 1523 letter to the officers of the University of Ingolstadt, the noblewoman Argula von Grumbach defends a young man charged with heresy for having distributed Lutheran literature. In his 1530 *Defense of the Augsburg Confession,* Philip Melanchthon expounds the doctrine of justification by faith, and in his 1546 *Funeral Oration* for Luther, he establishes the

---

1. Evangelicals emphasized the biblical basis of Christian faith and the centrality of Christ's crucifixion for the salvation of souls. Although evangelicals could be Catholic or Protestant, in the era discussed here, the term generally describes Catholics committed to church reform.

reformer's preeminence in the genealogy of the leaders of God's church from biblical times to the present. Martin Bucer, an early convert to the Lutheran program who later forged an independent path, defines in his 1550 treatise *The Kingdom of Christ* the proper relationship of church and state in a post-Reformation world.

Chapter Five, "The Swiss Response," considers the Reformation's progress in the cities and territories of the Swiss Confederation, beginning with Ulrich Zwingli's reform of Zurich in the early 1520s. In 1522, Zwingli's defense of the eating of meat during Lent, traditionally forbidden by the church, marks the moment of that rift. Soon Geneva entered the fray, where a 1539 episode sparks the plea for support made to Marguerite de Navarre by Marie Dentière, the French-born wife of a Reformed pastor. There follow two letters of 1541 and 1561 to high-ranking Frenchwomen by John Calvin who, having fled France and sought refuge in Switzerland, rose to head the Genevan church. In quite a different tone, in a passage from his massive compendium, the *Institutes of the Christian Church* (1559), he defends the doctrine of predestination essential to the international Reformed movement that he founded. Calvin's successor in Geneva, Theodore Beza, in his 1574 treatise *On the Rights of Magistrates over Their Subjects,* defends the right of French Calvinists, known as Huguenots, to resist their rulers.

Chapter Six, "The Radical Reformation," considers several facets of that complex movement that aroused the antipathy of both Protestants and Catholics. Unlike the German and Swiss Reformations, accomplished on the scaffolding of civic and princely institutions, or the English and Scandinavian, coterminous with whole kingdoms, the radical Reformation erupted from below and seethed in the interstices of the political system. Representing the Anabaptist experience are the martyr testaments of Maeyken van Deventer and Janneken Munstdorp on the eve of their executions in 1573, and Peter Riedemann's defense of the communal ownership of goods drawn from his 1540–1541 account of the Hutterite faith. Thomas Müntzer's 1524 exhortation to the princes of Saxony exemplifies a faith he believed to be directly inspired by the Holy Spirit, while passages from *On the Errors of the Trinity* (1531) by Michael Servetus, who was martyred for his anti-trinitarian views, represent the extreme rationalist pole of the Radical Reformation. Provoked by the execution of Servetus in 1553, Sebastian Castellio's 1554 polemic *On Heretics* marks the beginning of the end, in the Western world, of the prosecution of crimes of thought or belief.

Chapter Seven, "The English Compromise," traces the course of the Reformation in England, where King Henry VIII had renounced papal authority and made himself head of the church. The 1529 pamphlet of Simon Fish anticipates the royal program by detailing the cost of the Catholic establishment in England, which, he charges, had taken over one-third of that nation's wealth. In 1540, Thomas Cranmer, Archbishop of Canterbury, introduces the English translation of the Bible that the king ordered to be used throughout the nation, and urges all the people of England to read it. In 1554, four days before her execution by the Catholic Queen Mary, Lady Jane Grey defends her Protestant faith in a conversation, recorded by her own hand, with the cleric dispatched to convert her. Parrying the attempts of English Jesuits to restore the country to Catholicism, the Protestant Queen Elizabeth, Mary's successor, executed, among others, the eloquent Edmund Campion, who in his 1580 *Challenge to the Privy Council* boldly declares his intention to do just that. Yet not long after all this turmoil, in the first years of the next century, Lady Margaret Hoby, an Anglican Protestant raised in a Puritan household, calmly records in her diary accounts of her daily religious meditations alongside those of her household tasks.

Chapter Eight, "Catholic Reform and Renewal," considers the response of the Catholic church both to reform pressures from within and to the new crisis of the Lutheran rupture. In his 1517 treatise on *The Duties of a Bishop*, the Italian Gasparo Contarini identifies the bishop's role as crucial for the reform of the church, presenting a reform program that would eventually be enacted by the decrees of the Council of Trent. Meanwhile, in response to the Protestant threat, the English cardinal Reginald Pole confronts King Henry VIII, his kinsman, in his monumental 1536 defense of the unity of the church. The Spanish priest Ignatius of Loyola, later canonized, was the founder in 1534 of the Society of Jesus, whose stated objective was to defend the church and the papacy, and he wrote thousands of letters to advance that goal. His 1554 missive to Peter Canisius proposes a strategy of cultural warfare to counter Protestant propaganda in the German lands. The Spanish mystic Teresa of Ávila, later canonized, was less concerned with the Protestant threat than with the realization of genuine reform in the church, and is seen in her 1565 autobiography fiercely pursuing her mission to found the strictly reformed order of Discalced Carmelite nuns. Finally, the Savoyard bishop Francis de Sales, later canonized, proposes in his 1609 guide to the "devout" life a program of charity and service to be pursued not so much by the clergy as by laypersons of all ranks and occupations.

Chapter Nine, "The Expanding Reformation," explores the broadening currents of Protestant reform that unfolds in the seventeenth and early eighteenth centuries. It opens with the 1606 university oration of Dutch-born Jacobus Arminius reflecting on the past century of religious turmoil and calling for the settlement of religious differences—for the sake of religion itself. The devotional works of the German artisan Jacob Boehme, among them *The Way of Christ* (1622), introduce a new note: avoiding all discussion of doctrine, they call for personal regeneration as the only road to salvation. The Radical Pietist movement Boehme inspires is exemplified by Johanna Eleonora Petersen, a German wife and mother whose *Autobiography* (1718) looks to the ultimate salvation of all—even Jews, infidels, and the fallen angels—when at the end of time all creation returns to God. The Pietist impulse is expressed in England in the Quaker and Methodist movements, represented here, respectively, by Margaret Fell and John Wesley. In her 1666 pamphlet *Women's Speaking Justified, Proved, and Allowed of by the Scriptures,* Fell defends the right of women to speak in public, for they have been empowered by God to do so. With his invitation to a joyous and confident relationship with God, described in his 1742 tract *The Character of a Methodist,* Wesley breathes new life into Anglican worship.

Chapter Ten, "The Reformation Overseas," considers the divergent experiences of Reformation Catholics and Protestants as Europeans ventured onto the global stage. The Reformation challenge fueled the zeal of Catholics for global mission, reflected here in works by the Dominican theologian Francisco de Vitoria, the Jesuit priest Francis Xavier, and the Ursuline nun Marie Guyart de l'Incarnation. In 1539, Vitoria cautions the Spanish missionaries eager to convert the native peoples of the Americas: the Indians must not be coerced, he argues, for coercion would be not only unjust but also fruitless, yielding a mere pretense of belief. Francis Xavier, later canonized for his missionary work in Asia, does not coerce but rather persuades, guides, and teaches the multitudes he converts to Christianity, as evidenced in his 1544 letter to the Jesuit leadership in Rome. Marie Guyart, canonized in 2014, by her 1640 letter from imperiled Quebec describes the school for girls she has founded, and her attempts to bring the Christian faith and French civilization to the daughters of the Hurons and Algonquins.

The Protestant experience in Anglo-America was quite different from the Catholic, for the Protestants who came to the New World were seeking not converts primarily, but rather refuge from the depredations of the Old World. In 1644, the native Englishman Roger Williams rejects any limitation of the freedom of religious belief, a position that for him was not merely theoretical, for he had founded the colony of Rhode Island to embody that principle—a refuge for Jews and other nonbelievers, as well as every kind of Christian. Nearly a century later, the pastor Jonathan Edwards, in his *Faithful Narrative of the Surprising Work of God in the Conversion of Many Hundred Souls in Northampton* (1736), documents the recent resurgence of Christian enthusiasm in that Massachusetts town. On the edge of the wilderness, the European Reformation blossoms into the American Great Awakening.

The authors of the ideas presented in these ten chapters were persons whose commitment to the Christian church, in its many guises, was unstinting. Some of them suffered for their beliefs, and some were martyred. Their achievement is not one final truth, but a gallery of Christian perspectives reflecting the stormy experiences of the Reformation era. As a consequence of this intellectual and spiritual vitality, by the middle of the eighteenth century, with the Enlightenment underway and the modern age approaching, the Christian churches were primed and ready for new challenges—and not locked away and captive within an institution incapable of change. That is, in the end, the gift of Reformation.

A Note on Texts and Translations

Full citations of the sources of the fifty texts included in this anthology are given in the Texts and Studies section at the end of the volume. Thirty-eight of the fifty have been newly translated by the present author from Latin, French, German, Italian, and Spanish. Eight texts originally appearing in English editions of the sixteenth through nineteenth centuries (those by, in order of appearance, Fish, Cranmer, Grey, Campion, Fell, Wesley, Williams, and Edwards) have been modernized in spelling, punctuation, and diction, so as to make them more accessible to contemporary readers. In addition, the Hoby selection, based on a seventeenth-century English manuscript, and the seventeenth-century English translation of the contemporary German work by Boehme, are similarly modernized. Two texts are reprinted with permission from recent translations: that by Teresa of Ávila, and one of those by Martin Luther (*On the Freedom of a Christian*). In these cases, I have consulted but not reproduced the translator's notes; the annotations are mine. Biblical quotations in narrative and notes are given in New International Version (NIV) translation except when otherwise indicated.

Chapter One: In Search of Christ: Steps toward Reformation

The Reformation movement that exploded in the sixteenth century began in the fourteenth, and many of its central themes had already been articulated over the 150 years prior to Luther's rebellion. This chapter presents a sampling of the voices that were in the vanguard of reform, enunciating critiques of the church and exploring new dimensions of Christian belief. It is notable that four of these five advocates for reform—three priests and a monk—were themselves clerics. The reform impulse derived from within the church itself, and was not imposed upon it from without.

The English philosopher John Wyclif (c. 1330–1384) was both a parish priest and a professor closely associated with the University of Oxford, where scholasticism[1] reigned supreme. Yet in his theology, he turned against the scholastic consensus—precisely because, as a philosophical "realist," he believed that words meant what they said, and most particularly the word of God. That is the theme of his monumental work *On the Truth of Holy Scripture* (1378), excerpted here. Through the Bible, according to Wyclif, God communicated truth directly to ordinary people. For that reason, it should be translated into a language that they might understand, and not remain imprisoned in the Latin of the learned or the French of secular elites. After his death, his followers, called "Lollards,"[2] produced an English translation widely known as the "Wyclif Bible." For these views and others—including a thunderous critique of the doctrine of transubstantiation[3] and a defense of civil authority over church property and personnel—Wyclif's books were ritually burned in 1410 and 1413. In further repudiation, in 1428, his body was exhumed from consecrated ground, reduced to ashes, and scattered.

Resembling in some ways his forerunner Wyclif, Jan Hus (c. 1372–1415), a professor at the University of Prague in Bohemia (modern Czech Republic), led a cohort of young reformers energized by nationalist passions and popular religious currents. Preaching to large crowds in Czech, the language of the people

---

1. The philosophical system prevailing in European universities based on a fusion of Aristotelian metaphysics and logic and Christian thought.
2. A term of uncertain origin, possibly designating the place of origin or the manner of speaking of Wyclif's disciples.
3. The belief that bread and wine, the elements of the Eucharist, the commemoration of Christ's Last Supper, are transformed by priestly action during the celebration of the Catholic Mass into Christ's body and blood.

rather than the Latin of the professoriate, Hus denounced clerical corruption, arguing that the real church was the invisible gathering of all those—living, dead, or yet unborn—predestined by God for salvation. Such a frontal assault could not be tolerated. The pope and his agents excommunicated[4] Hus, and laid an interdict[5] on any place where he sought refuge. Finally, lured to the Council of Constance (modern Germany, 1414–1418), on the single day July 6, 1415, Hus was tried, condemned, and executed. He went boldly to the stake and, it is reported, sang hymns as the flames engulfed him. Galvanized by his martyrdom, his followers and their noble supporters launched the Hussite wars that achieved, by the peace settled in 1436 at the Diet of Jihlava (modern Czech Republic), some accommodation for Czech religious aspirations.

Unlike Wyclif or Hus, the German Thomas à Kempis (Thomas Hemerken von Kempen; 1379/80–1471) was not a theologian, nor a heretic or a martyr. He was a priest and a monk nourished by the *devotio moderna* ("new devotion"), a largely lay[6] reform movement that flourished in the fourteenth and fifteenth centuries. Its ideals are expressed in *The Imitation of Christ*,[7] written around 1420/1427. It is a set of instructions for the spiritual life, urging both clergy and laity to follow Christ by looking inward, and by identifying with his suffering and sacrifice. It frequently cites the Bible, which even when not cited is the substratum of nearly every statement. It does not name philosophers or theologians, except Aristotle once, to reject his message, and Saint Augustine twice, whose subjectivity prefigures Thomas' own. Its tone is incantatory, its limpid prose hauntingly arrayed with complex rhymes and rhythms, its simplicity compelling—and it compelled many. Measured by the number of surviving manuscripts (some 770 in Latin, and in Dutch, German, French, Italian, Spanish, and English translations), and an unbroken stream of printed editions in all subsequent centuries, it is one of the principal books of the Western tradition. It influenced, among others, the seventeenth-century Spanish Catholic saint Ignatius of Loyola (see Chapter Eight); the eighteenth-century English founder of Methodism John Wesley (see Chapter Nine); and the twentieth-century German theologian, pastor, and enemy of Nazism Dietrich Bonhoeffer.

In 1531 in France, a woman speaks of God in her own voice, candidly and intimately—more so than her predecessors Wyclif, Hus, or Thomas à Kempis.

---

4. By excommunication, the church excludes a person from communion or fellowship with the church, a severe penalty in this era.
5. The interdict forbids the performance of any religious services or sacraments, a decree that penalizes an entire community.
6. Lay persons, collectively the laity, were all those who were not clergy, the officials and functionaries of the church.
7. His authorship has been questioned, but most scholars credit the work to him.

But she could, because her rank allowed her to: for Marguerite de Navarre (1492–1549) was of royal blood, the sister of one king of France (Francis I, r. 1515–1547), and grandmother of another (Henry IV, r. 1589–1610). From 1521 to 1524, Marguerite joined a circle of reform-minded evangelicals and was imbued with views that at that very moment were fueling the rebellion of Martin Luther—but they would reach no such fruition in France. From 1524, French evangelicals were silenced: forced to recant, driven into exile, burned at the stake. As sister of the king, Marguerite could not resist his decrees; but as sister of the king, she tried to do so, nurturing within the truths she cherished, and protecting those who embraced them. *The Mirror of the Sinful Soul*, her first published work—and she would become one of the major female authors of the age—displays her evangelical beliefs. It draws on Catholic and mystical antecedents; reprises aristocratic conventions of courtly love; and anticipates reformist notions of faith as the pathway to God.

Like the circle of French evangelicals who nurtured Marguerite de Navarre, Italian evangelicals anticipated many themes of the Lutheran rebellion before their suppression by the Roman Inquisition, launched in 1542. One year earlier, the Benedictine monk Benedetto da Mantova had composed the work (subsequently revised for publication in 1543 by humanist poet Marcantonio Flaminio) that encapsulated the thought of the short-lived Italian Reformation: *The Benefit for All Christians of Jesus Christ Crucified*. This brief and impassioned work expounds the doctrine of justification by faith that would also be central for Luther, although phrased with a distinctively Italian spiritual tonality. It conveyed this message: Burdened by their sins and yearning for salvation, all those who believe in Jesus Christ receive the benefit of the atonement he made by suffering and dying on the cross. Their faith alone justifies them, conferring on them the righteousness of Christ himself.

By the time the principal Italian reformers had fled their homeland to seek asylum further north, the Protestant Reformation had begun. Its roots were long, reaching back at least to the generation of Wyclif, and watered since that time by lay pious and evangelical streams reflected in the texts presented in this chapter.

The whole of holy Scripture is the word of the Lord

from John Wyclif, *On the Truth of Holy Scripture* (1377/1380)

In chapter 15 of Wyclif's three-volume work *On the Truth of Holy Scripture*, a scholastic philosopher uses the logical methods that are the tools of his trade to prove that the Bible possesses a truth greater than the truth philosophers presume to discover. Since "the whole of holy Scripture" is the word of God, and God does not lie, and has made his word available to all in the words of Scripture, every Christian may be his own theologian and access that truth. Moreover, since every part of Scripture is equally informed by the mind of God, any part is superior to any decretal letter[8] or statute issued by the pope. True, the pope is the successor of Peter, Christ's disciple, and the vicar of Christ. But even Peter, like the other apostles, had no authority in himself, but only as one who communicated the word of God. So popes may govern the church and issue statutes, but they may not claim for these "human innovations" an authority equal to the Gospel. To do so would be to make the pope the equal of Christ, and would be—"of this I am certain," Wyclif interjects—a "manifest blasphemy."

Taking together all that has been said, it appears in sum that those who distort holy Scripture by twisting its meaning not only diminish its authority, but the more that they know what it properly means, the more do they try as best they can to weaken and wreck it.[9] For these adversaries have no evidence beyond their dialectical constructs to support their claim that a passage of holy Scripture can only mean what their dialectical constructs construe it to mean—a conclusion having no greater certainty than its antecedent. . . .[10]

Each Christian will arrive finally at the conclusion that the surest possible proof derives from the authority of holy Scripture, which is the proof deriving from faith; for from faith in Scripture, which commands faith, there comes no greater, no more certain, and no more efficacious proof. For since the whole of holy Scripture is the word of the Lord, how could there be any greater, more certain, or more efficacious testimony to its truth than that God, who cannot lie, has said so in his Scripture, which is the mirror of his will—and therefore it is true. . . . And as I said earlier, each person, with ready and willing spirit, must be his own theologian,[11] whereupon the truth will freely and frankly reveal itself to him. And so, just as all rivers flow into the sea, the truth contained in each created mind is communicated to it by the creator. . . .

---

8. Decretal letters: decisions on matters of church law issued by the pope.

9. Wyclif here criticizes contemporary scholastic philosophers, practitioners of an elaborate method of argumentation known as "dialectical," which defended or refuted ideas set in opposition to each other.

10. The terms "antecedent," "conclusion," and below, "demonstration," are all features of dialectical argumentation.

11. The term "theologian" is used here and below, as distinct from "philosopher," to speak of those who authentically pursue knowledge of the sacred.

The evidence [of Scripture] exceeds all the evidence from dialectic that a philosopher or layman derives from reasoning or the senses. . . . And lest these phonies pretend that they have received their understanding directly from God, God has provided his Scripture, common and accessible to all, so that all might grasp its Christian truth. For God cannot abandon his people, but rather always sheds his light on them. . . . And to ensure that Mother Church[12] continues to be so illuminated is the responsibility of the theologians, who must dutifully attend to their task, and not be tempted to foment fictions alien to the message of holy Scripture. . . .

Since what one apprehends in a true statement is the authority of the speaker, and since all the truths God utters are of this sort, who doubts that, as it must follow, every one of these truths possesses the same authority as any other? And further, since each truth is identical to that in the divine mind, it also follows, that it is not identical in greater or lesser degree, but absolutely the same . . . from which it is seen that all of Scripture is equally authoritative in every one of its parts. The entirety of holy Scripture, therefore, is the unique word of God, and those we call its authors are only scribes or messengers appointed to write down the law of God as he has dictated it to them, and are not really authors in comparison with God, but only secondarily so. . . .

Consequently, any part of holy Scripture possesses infinitely greater authority than any decretal letter: for while every decretal letter originates with some pope . . . every part of holy Scripture originates directly and immediately from God. . . . For all of the decretals are products of human innovations devised after the institution of the church in order to address any problems that might happen to arise.[13] But such is not the case with holy Scripture, since the word of God informed every part of it and immediately conveyed its truth to his scribes, who added to it no accretions of their own, but as was required of them faithfully recorded it. This is why the prophets so often declare, *Thus says the Lord.* . . .[14]

And this distinction between the pope's authorship and God's destroys the claim that the decretal letters have an authority equal to the Gospel's. That would be true if the Evangelists[15] had been the authors of the Scripture; but the Gospel is true not because some Christian wrote it, but because God has

---

12. The Catholic church, seated at Rome and headed by the pope—although at the moment Wyclif wrote, at the outset of the Great Schism of the church (1378–1415), papal authority and the pope's Roman residence were in contestation.

13. Wyclif refers here to the presumed donation by Roman Emperor Constantine of wealth and dominion to the church at Rome—for Wyclif, the moment at which the betrayal of original Christianity took root.

14. Isaiah 37:6, Jeremiah 9:23, Ezekiel 20:30, among other cases.

15. The writers of the four Gospels: Matthew, Mark, Luke, and John.

said it; nor are the words of the authors of holy Scripture valid because they spoke them, but because they have spoken what God instructed them to speak. In illustration, the apostle Paul witnessed in this way to the authority of Christ: *I want you to know, brothers and sisters, that the gospel I preached is not of human origin. I did not receive it from any man, nor was I taught it; rather, I received it by revelation from Jesus Christ.*[16]

For the apostles were inspired by the Holy Spirit, and consequently the words they speak are the word of the Lord, and what they proclaim has divine authority, and not merely their own. How then may the successor of Peter and vicar of Christ[17] presume today to possess greater authority than the apostle Peter himself dared to command? . . . Nonetheless, I do not deny but rather concede that the bishops of Rome, the vicars of Christ, may properly issue statutes for the improvement of the church—which statutes, whatever they may be, should be obeyed, unless they are invalidated because they either conflict with other statutes or contradict holy Scripture. But to claim that such statutes, because they have been issued by the pope, have an authority equal to that of the Gospel—of this I am certain—is a manifest blasphemy. . . .

For God bestowed the whole of his law through the scribes of the books of the Old and New Testaments, permitting nothing foreign to be added to it, nor anything removed. How then might any man presume to hold his own decree, in that it is his, equal in authority to holy Scripture? Lest he seem to do so, therefore, he should ground his statements in Scripture, as do many decrees and decretal letters that never presume, since their authors are human, that they are equal in authority to the word of the Lord, for that would be to blasphemously claim that those authors themselves are God. . . .

It appears from all that has been said, therefore, that no one who came after Christ can possess an authority as great as his. Accordingly, none of the decretal letters can possess the authority of the Gospel. . . . Otherwise, such authority might be ascribed to any of the papal bulls,[18] which is absurd, since in these matters the church has been deceived, deceitful, and mistaken . . . and so an emended letter is issued to abrogate the one previous, and there proceeds a parade of contradictory bulls, each later missive revoking the intent of the one that came before. . . . To say, therefore, that all papal bulls possess the same authority and the same certitude of truth as holy Scripture would be blasphemously to make the pope the equal of Christ.

---

16. Galatians 1:11–12.

17. The pope was considered to be Peter's successor and Christ's vicar, the terms used here instead of Wyclif's "priest of Christ and vicar of Peter."

18. Papal bull: an official papal letter sealed with a lead seal (*bulla*) to authenticate its origin.

Who is the church?

from Jan Hus, *On the Church* (1413)

Hounded into exile by excommunications and an interdict, Jan Hus responds to the churchmen who pursued him with his massive work *On the Church*. Its aim was not to placate his critics. Instead, where theologians had defined the church as consisting of the pope as its head and the cardinals, the highest-ranking prelates, as its body, Hus argues otherwise: Jesus Christ, he posits, is the only head of the church, and its body consists of the community of all those whom God has predestined to salvation—living, dead, and yet unborn. Such a notion, grounded in Scripture, was a deadly broadside: Who could prove that the swollen hierarchs of the church were numbered among the saved? And even if they were, they certainly did not constitute the whole but only a minuscule part of the Christian community. So disputing the claims of his enemies, Hus delegitimizes the church, and defangs it: Why should obedience be owed to an institution founded on false premises? And what power can reside in its armory of interdicts and excommunications? The brief excerpts below suggest the force of Hus's opposition.

Christ the only head of the church

Hus explains that the church does not consist of the pope, as head, and cardinals, as body, but rather of Jesus Christ, as its head, and as its body, all human beings predestined to salvation—past, present, and future.

From what has been said, it is concluded that Christ alone is the head of the universal church. . . . Accordingly, if any Christian[19] were to be, as Christ is, head of the universal church, given that the church cannot be a two-headed monster, . . . it would be necessary to concede that the Christian who was head of the church was himself Christ, or that Christ was subordinate to that Christian. . . .

So it is established that Christ alone is the head of the holy universal church, and that all those predestined to salvation, past and future, are his mystical body, and each one of them is a member of that body. Now we must see if the Roman church is that holy universal church, and the bride of Christ. And it seems as though it is, since there is only one holy catholic and apostolic church, which is none other than the Roman church. . . .

---

19. That is, the pope.

But now to argue the contrary: the Roman church is a church whose head is the pope, and whose cardinals the body, which are its component parts. But that church is not the holy catholic and apostolic church, and so the proposition put forward is false. . . .

Based on all that has been presented here, it is clear what must be said about the proposition stated at the outset of this chapter. . . . It is not the case that this church [made up of the pope and the cardinals] is the holy catholic and apostolic church. . . . Nor is the pope its head, nor the cardinals the whole body of the holy, universal, and catholic church. For Christ alone is the head of that church, of which those predestined to salvation are the body, and each one of them a member of that body, comprising a single person, the bride of Jesus Christ.

Obedience owed only to God

Obedience is owed only to those who themselves obey the law of God, Hus explains, and only those commandments that come from God should be obeyed.

The next matter to be discussed is this: To what extent is the Apostolic See[20] to be obeyed? . . .

Any mode of human life that is guided by charity is virtuous, and any that is not guided by charity is vicious. And so it follows that just as no person can be neutral in terms of virtue or vice, since a person must either be included within the grace of God or be outside it, so also no human interaction can be neutral. Therefore, if a superior commands what is virtuous, he is to be obeyed, but if he commands what is vicious, the command must be vigorously resisted. These things being so, every faithful Christian should be on guard lest the Roman pope, or any prelate, issue a command to be obeyed as if it were God's commandment—as though that prelate was incapable of error, when only Christ does not err. . . .

Furthermore, no command that is not reasonable or useful to the church of Christ is explicitly or implicitly made in Scripture. And if such a command were issued by the pope or any prelate, their subordinate would not be required to obey it, for that would be to violate God's freedom to determine what is lawful. For we ought to accept on faith that God causes nothing to be demanded of us that is not sound and reasonable, and thus profitable for our salvation. . . . Therefore no one should obey any man in any matter, however minor, that might contravene God's commandment. . . .

---

20. Apostolic See: in this context, the papacy, the See of Rome.

On excommunication and the interdict

Excommunicated for the last time in 1412, Hus promises to suffer patiently, while arguing that only God can excommunicate, and those who issue false excommunications, not mandated by God, in effect excommunicate themselves.

Now by this excommunication they subject me to trials and denunciations, excluding me from all contact with the human community. But thanks be to God, who did not empower this excommunication to rob an innocent man, while he humbly endures it, of virtue or righteousness, nor to impute to him sin that he did not commit. . . .

For he [who assigns the penalty of excommunication] should excommunicate the person whom God excommunicates, for a crime that he is known to have committed, and after three warnings, moved by his love of God and concern for the salvation of the man whom he excommunicates. . . . Having considered all this, the faithful Christian may come to recognize how many prelates, clerics, and laypersons have been excommunicated by God because they have not kept God's commandments; and how many excommunicate themselves, when they howl and hurl excommunications at others. . . .

Also in 1412, the pope issued an edict, or "bull," putting under a general interdict any locality where Hus resided for any length of time and for three days thereafter. Hus questions the justice of an interdict, which punishes the innocent as well as the one person who has offended the church, and speculates, mockingly, whether heaven itself will be placed under the interdict if Hus, on his death, is called there by God.

I always wonder about the basis or explanation of a general interdict, by which good people who have done no wrong are deprived of the sacraments, including communion, confession, and others, and even infants of baptism; and likewise, how it can be that the ministry of God is withheld from all the righteous because of an interdict imposed on account of just one man. Imagine if an earthly king were denied the service of all of his loyal subjects because of just one who was rebellious! . . . How is it then that a pope or bishop, without sanction of either Scripture or revelation, can with such insouciance withhold service from Christ the king? When a general interdict is imposed on a city or diocese, moreover, sin is not lessened, but increased.

And so, because I have preached Christ and his Gospel, and by desiring the clergy to live according to Christ's law, have exposed the Antichrist, the prelates and . . . the archbishop of Prague have, as a first step, secured a bull from Pope Alexander[21] ordering that the word of God not be preached in the chapels to the people. I have appealed this bull, and have not succeeded in gaining a hearing. . . .

But I ask where is this dictum found? "Every locale, city, town, village, or castle whatever, exempt or non-exempt, to which the forenamed Jan Hus may go, and for as long as he remains there, and for three whole days after his departure therefrom, by this decree we place them under ecclesiastical interdict and order the ministries of God halted."

Since, then, according to this curial message . . . that "to whatever locale exempt or non-exempt Jan Hus may go, and for as long as he remains there, we subject it to the ecclesiastical interdict," it follows that, as is highly possible given the absolute power of God, if Jan Hus on his death should reach the heavenly Jerusalem, that city, too, would be subject to the ecclesiastical interdict.

Here you have no real home

from Thomas à Kempis, *The Imitation of Christ* (1420/1427)

Persistently, searchingly, powerfully, Thomas à Kempis summons his listeners to find true life with Christ. These excerpts from the second book of *The Imitation of Christ* introduce three of the author's recurrent themes. First, the true life of the spirit is found within, apart from external things and even other people, for in that external world of things and events and conversations, there is no peace and no real home. Second, true joy is found in friendship with Jesus, who enters within the self and resides in the recesses of the soul. No other relationship can satisfy as does friendship, and union, with Jesus. Third, the seeker must share the suffering of Jesus on the cross. Only those who bear the cross as Jesus did can achieve salvation; and they will bear that burden joyfully as they ascend by the royal road of the holy cross to eternal life.

Chapter One: The conversation within

Thomas implores the Christian to turn within his own soul to find there the kingdom of God; it is not to be found without.

The kingdom of God is within you, says the Lord. Turn to the Lord with your whole heart, and flee this wretched world, and your soul will find peace.

---

21. Alexander V, antipope, 1409–1415. At times of crisis, a figure might be elected to the papacy in opposition to one already chosen; subsequently, church officials determined which had properly held the title of pope, deeming the other an antipope.

Learn to despise what is external, and give yourself to what is internal, and the kingdom of God will nestle within you.

For the kingdom of God is this: peace and joy in the Holy Spirit, a peace not given to sinners.

Christ will come to you offering to you his consolation, if you have prepared within yourself a fitting home for him.

All of his glory and splendor is found within, and there he will be pleased to reside.

Many are his visitations to that inward man, sweet is his conversation, pleasing his consolation, great is his peace, his friendship wondrous beyond imagining.

. . . . .

Here you have no real home; wherever you go, you are a wandering stranger; nor will you ever have peace, unless within you, you are united with Christ.

Why do you keep searching, when here there is for you no place of respite?

. . . . .

Chapter Seven: The love of Jesus above all things

Only the love of Jesus, Thomas promises, can bring solace to the soul.

Blessed is he who knows what it is to love Jesus, and to despise himself for Jesus' sake.

He must give up what he loves for the beloved, because Jesus wants to be loved alone above all other things.

The love of created things is deceitful and unstable; the love of Jesus, is loyal and enduring.

He who loves what is created flounders and falls; he who loves Jesus is forever steadfast.

Love him, and you will always have him as a friend; he will not let you go when all others leave you, nor permit you ever to perish.

One day, you will be parted from all others, whether you wish it or do not.

Living or dying, hold fast to Jesus; and trust in his faithfulness, for when all others leave you, he alone can bring you solace.

. . . . .

Chapter Eight: Close friendship with Jesus

Jesus is the only true friend, Thomas declares, without whom there is no fulfillment.

. . . . .

How dry and tough you are without Jesus! How foolish and useless, if you desire anything but Jesus!

What greater loss is there than to lose the whole world?

But what can the world give you, if you do not have Jesus?

To be without Jesus is dark hell, and to be with Jesus, sweet paradise.

If Jesus is with you, no enemy can harm you.

He who finds Jesus, finds a treasury of goodness, good beyond all goodness.

And he who loses Jesus, suffers loss beyond loss, more than the whole world.

He who lives without Jesus is wretchedly poor; and wondrously rich is he who lives with Jesus.

. . . . .

Chapter Eleven: How few are those who love the cross of Jesus

Christians pretend to love Jesus, Thomas observes, but few are willing to share in his suffering.

Jesus has many who now seek his heavenly kingdom, but few willing to bear his cross.

He has many who desire consolation, but few who welcome tribulation.

He finds many who wish to dine with him, but few who wish to fast with him.

All want to rejoice with him, few want to suffer for him.

Many follow Jesus to the breaking of the bread, but few to the drinking from the cup of his passion.[22]

---

22. A reference to the Last Supper, when Jesus broke the bread of his body and poured the wine of his blood, signifying the death he was going to suffer; the same cup that at Gethsemane he asked to be taken from him: cf. Luke 22:42.

Many marvel at his miracles, few share in the shame of the cross.

Many love Jesus, so long as no danger looms.

. . . . .

Chapter Twelve: The royal road of the holy cross

Only by bearing the cross of Jesus and sharing its shame and pain, Thomas insists, will the Christian come to eternal life.

. . . . .

Why then do you fear to bear the cross, by which you will gain the kingdom?

In the cross is salvation, in the cross life, in the cross protection from your enemies.

In the cross a stream of heavenly sweetness, in the cross strength of mind, in the cross spiritual delight.

In the cross, the highest virtue, in the cross, perfect holiness.

There is no soul's salvation, nor hope of eternal life, except in the cross.

So take up your cross and follow Jesus, and you will enter life eternal.

He has led the way for you, burdened by his cross, and for you he died on the cross; so that now you may bear your cross, and seek to die on the cross.

Because if you die with him, with him also you will live. And if you share his suffering, you will share his glory.

For in the cross is all that exists, and on your dying all depends; and there is no other road to life, and to true peace within, except the road of the holy cross, and the daily exercise of death.

Go where you will, see whatever you wish: and you will not discover a higher road above, nor a surer road below, than the road of the holy cross.

. . . . .

The cross then is always ready, and waits for you everywhere.

You cannot escape it, wherever you may run to, because wherever you may go, you bear it with you always, and you will always find it with you.

Look above, look below; look without, look within; and in all these places, you will find the cross.

You must everywhere endure all things if you are to have peace within and merit an eternal crown.

If you willingly carry the cross, it will carry you, and take you to the longed-for end which is the end of suffering, although here there will be no end to it.

If you bear the cross unwillingly, it will be a burden, and will weigh on you greatly; and yet you must bear it.

If you cast off one cross, you will surely find another one, and heavier perhaps.

Do you think you can evade what no mortal can escape? Which one of all the saints on this earth was ever without cross and tribulation?

Not even our Lord Jesus Christ was for even an hour free of the pain of his passion: while he still lived, he said: *Christ must suffer, and rise from the dead, and then enter his glory.*[23]

How then can you seek any other road than this royal road, which is the road of the holy cross?

By faith we possess that which we do not have

from Marguerite de Navarre, *The Mirror of the Sinful Soul* (1531)

Marguerite is in search of love—God's love—and tells us so in 1434 verse lines comprising 717 rhymed pairs of lines, or couplets, whose singsong wizardry charm the ear and vocalize her yearning.[24] But belying the tinkling verse, Marguerite's work is theologically complex and biblically anchored. She is unworthy to love God; but by his gift of faith, she is drawn to him; and in response, he descends to her, and inhabits her heart, filling it with a love of unbearable force and sweetness—and worse than unbearable, inexpressible. These themes recur, within a frame of biblical allusions and paraphrases that draw especially on the prophets and psalms of the Old

---

23. A conflation of two passages from Luke: and he said to them, "Thus it is written, that the Messiah is to suffer and to rise from the dead on the third day" (Luke 24:46), and "Was it not necessary that the Messiah should suffer these things and then enter into his glory?" (Luke 24:26).

24. The translation renders the French original into blank verse of five pulses per line, capturing to some extent the aural effect Marguerite sought.

Testament, and the epistles of the New. The excerpt given here consists of the last 155 lines, a little over 10 percent of the poem. It is notable for the poet's confession of insufficiency (she is "but dust and dirt," line 1427); her experience of fulfillment through divine grace (her heart "lives and breathes in rapture," knowing "it has received too much," lines 1348–49); her identification with Saint Paul's visionary experience on the Damascus road (lines 1382–1429); and her celebration of faith: "A faith that gives us hope of truth indubitable/engendering in us love unsurpassable" (lines 1415–16).

> If God wants me to come to him by faith,
> Can anything in all creation harm me?[25]   1280
> Faith, that is, as we must understand it,
> A gift from God, as it is rightly called:
> Faith that binds with flaming bonds of love
> The humblest servitor to her creator;
> Thus bound to him I know no longer fear,   1285
> Or pain, or labor, or distress, or sorrow;
> In unity with him, to bear the cross,
> To suffer, die, these are but consolation.
> Alone my strength is feeble, insufficient,
> And so I lean on him, who brings me comfort.   1290
> His love is so enduring and so certain
> That never does it ever wane or waver.
>   What is it then can cause my severance
> And separation from the grace of God?
> Certainly not the magnitude of heaven,   1295
> Nor the deep profundity of hell,
> Nor the great expanse of all the earth,
> Not death, not sin, though fiercely both besiege me,
> None of these can for a single day
> Deprive me of the all-embracing love   1300
> Of God my father, through Jesus Christ his Son;[26]
> For his love is that perfect kind of love
> That loves me, even if I love him not,
> And loves me doubly, though he is not loved.
> My love is too sparse to love, but his love   1305
> Loves for me, as though it were my own.[27]

---

25. For the next several lines, cf. Ephesians 2:4–9.
26. Romans 8:35–39, paraphrase.
27. For the next several lines, cf. 1 Corinthians 13:1–7.

Within my soul he loves himself for me,
And loving me, inflames my heart with love.
This love he causes loves himself so much
That it, not I, in consequence contents him. 1310
Contented thus in love, his love augments
And multiplies beyond the bounds of love.
　O true lover, the fount of heavenly love,
And of the treasure of heaven the one source,
May I think, and even dare to say 1315
It comes from you? and may I so write here?
Can a mortal being comprehend
The greatness of your goodness and your love?
And if you please to leave its mark deep
Within a heart, may that heart tell the tale? 1320
Certainly not; it is not large enough
To hold within the great immensity
That is your nature.[28] Reason tells us this:
Comparison cannot be made between
a finite thing and his infinitude. 1325
But when the heart is joined to him by love,
Its nothingness is so replete with fullness,
That all its finitude is overcome;
so filled with joy that can be scarcely borne,
Believing that the whole world dwells within. 1330
　A single ray of brilliance from the sun
Will blind the eye, and hide the greater radiance;
But ask the eye what it has seen, it says
"All of it"; but that would be a lie;
For blinded by just one ray of the sun 1335
It cannot see its magnitude of light;
And nonetheless, the eye is well content
Believing, as it seems, it has enough;
For it has not the power to endure
The sun's measureless intensity. 1340
　Likewise, by some subtle agency,
The heart perceives a scintilla of God's love,
And finds its flame so piercingly intense,
So sweet, so good, it is not possible
For it to say that it is love; the little 1345
It has felt so fully sates its hunger,

---

28. For this and following lines, cf. Ephesians 1:23; 3:18–19.

That satisfied, it longs for nothing more,
But seemingly it lives and breathes in rapture.
The heart knows it has received too much;
But that excess has wakened a desire,   1350
A powerful longing always to receive
What it cannot, nor is it worthy of it.
Ineffable that pleasure, it knows well,
Yet longs for what it does not understand,
Not comprehending what this true good is,   1355
Unable to express what it has felt. . . .
   Speech, then, is not within its power,
No more than comprehension of that flame.
The heart that holds the fullness of God's love,
Can find, in truth, how it may be described,   1360
And happy the one that has such great abundance
That it can say: "My God, I have enough."
But having it, does not dare to speak—
Fearing, perhaps, that it may dissipate—
Unless the words support the edification   1365
Required by one's neighbor, for her salvation.
   It is impossible; so I fall silent.
For there is none so perfect or so pious,
Who seeks to speak of the Almighty's love,
Its goodness, sweetness—however he describes it,   1370
Or how God's grace has touched him deep within,
Who will not avert his gaze, and hold his tongue.
   Then I, a slithering worm, a dead dog,
A heap of rotten dung, worth less than nothing,
Must speak no more of this love's celsitude;   1375
But neither may I show ingratitude,
For selfish it would be to have not written,
And so illumine some inquiring soul.
For to conceal the gifts of that good master
Would be a crime, for which no punishment   1380
Would be sufficient, except eternal pain.
So come, then, O blessed apostle Paul,
Who tasted this sweet honey to the full,
Blinded for three days, in heavenly rapture,
Satisfy my ignorance and dearth.   1385
What did you learn from that celestial vision?[29]

---

29. Acts 9:1–19.

Listen to what he says: O great immensity
And vastness of the treasure of God's wealth,
From this source does all human wisdom come,
From this fount does our sacred science flow,   1390
Incomprehensible are the workings of your mind,
Unfathomable, to us, the pathways that you take,
And by our senses undecipherable.[30]
O good Saint Paul, your words astonish us
We are perplexed that you who are so wise   1395
Do not reveal this secret that you know.
Again we ask about this love divine:
May we hope one day to gain possession of it?
  Listen to him; for here is what he tells us:
The eyes of mortal man have never seen,   1400
Nor with his ears ever understood,
Nor in his yearning heart has ever known,
What is prepared for us, and promised to all
Of those who love him at the end of time.[31]
  Have you nothing more to say? "No, nothing."   1405
What he has said, while he says no more, suffices
To waken our desire and expectation
For what he cannot name and explicate,
Drawing our hearts, our passion, and our hope
To long for that which cannot yet be seen.   1410
Do I say see? nor thought of, nor even felt:
The willingness to die a martyr's death.
  O giant gift of faith, this benefit bestowing
That we possess that which we do not have![32]
A faith that gives us hope of truth indubitable   1415
Engendering in us love unsurpassable.
And God is love, this well we know.
If love abides in us, so too does God.[33]
He is in us, and our whole being in him.
We are all of us in him, and he in all.   1420
Though by faith we do possess him, to put in words
What that possession is exceeds our power.
  Wherefore, since Saint Paul, supreme apostle,

---

30. Cf. 2 Corinthians 12:1–7.
31. 1 Corinthians 2:9, paraphrase.
32. Cf. Hebrews 11:1.
33. 1 John 4:16, paraphrase.

Chose not to speak of these matters further,
Following his injunction and example,   1425
I too fall silent. But trusting in God's promise
(Though I confess I am but dust and dirt)
I cannot fail to offer up thanksgiving
For all the blessings that I do not merit
That he has showered on me, his Marguerite.   1430
Now to the heavenly king, immortal, invisible,
The one omnipotent God, incomprehensible,
Be all honor, glory, praise, and adoration
For eons upon eons without end.³⁴
AMEN

God's gift to us is Christ on the cross

from Benedetto da Mantova, *The Benefit for All Christians of Jesus Christ Crucified* (1543)

For Christians desiring salvation, the high moral code set forth in the Hebrew Bible (Old Testament) is not a blessing but a curse: it is, in the language of the *Beneficio di Cristo*, "the malediction of the Law," an indictment of the seeker, showing all the ways he has sinned. For that curse, there is a remedy, the "benefit" or gift of Christ's crucifixion. For Christ atones on the cross for all the sins of the world; and all those who believe in him, reap the benefit of his suffering, are liberated of their sins, and may confidently hope for their salvation, knowing that "we have been made righteous not by our own works but by Christ's merits, we may live joyously in the certainty that the justice of Christ abolishes all of our injustice. . . ." A moving but straightforward statement of the *theologia crucis* (theology of the cross), drawn here primarily from Paul's letters to the Romans, Corinthians, Galatians, and Colossians, the *Beneficio di Cristo* brings to believers the certain hope of salvation.

Now that God, having sent that great prophet whom he had promised, who is his only-begotten Son, so that he might liberate us from the malediction of the Law and reconcile us with God, and by cleansing our free will enable us to do good works, and restore us to the likeness of the Creator³⁵ that we

---
34. 1 Timothy 1, paraphrase.
35. Cf. Colossians 3:10.

had lost through the sin of our first parents; and now that we, knowing that under the heavens there has been given to us no other name by which we can be saved except that of Jesus Christ;[36] so now powered by our living faith let us run into his arms as he invites us to do, calling *Come to me, all you who are weary and burdened, and I will give you rest.*[37] What solace, what joy can in this life be equal to that of him who, feeling himself oppressed by the intolerable weight of his sins, hears the sweet and soothing words of the Son of God, which promise so cordially to free him and relieve him of so great a burden? . . .

Since then by the Law's operation we know our infirmity, John the Baptist points out to us the physician who will heal us, saying, *Behold, the lamb of God, who takes away the sin of the world;*[38] which is to say, he liberates us from the heavy yoke of the Law, abolishing and annihilating its maledictions and fearsome menaces,[39] repairing all our infirmities,[40] reviving our free will, restoring us to our first innocence and renewing in us the image of God. Accordingly Paul says, *For as in Adam all die, so in Christ all will be made alive;*[41] for we do not believe that Adam's sin, which we have inherited through the body, can outweigh Christ's justice, which we have inherited through faith. . . .

And so the Law was given to us so that we might know that we sinned. Yet, at the same time, we know that sin is not stronger than Christ's justice, by which we are justified before God. For just as Christ is greater than Adam, so too is Christ's justice more powerful than Adam's sin; and if Adam's sin sufficed to make us sinners and children of wrath when we had committed no fault of our own, much more will Christ's justice suffice to make us righteous and children of grace without our having performed any good works—which have no quality of goodness unless before we perform them, we have already ourselves been made just and righteous. . . . So we see how greatly in error are those who, weighed down with their sins, doubt the benevolence of God, deciding that he will not remit, cover, and pardon the gravest sin, though he has already by his only-begotten Son atoned for all our sin and all our iniquity, having to that end issued a general pardon to the entire human race. From that pardon all will benefit who believe in the Gospel, that is in the joyous news that the apostles have proclaimed throughout the earth. . . .

O huge ingratitude! O what an abomination, if we, though professing to be Christians, and hearing that the Son of God has taken upon himself all

---

36. Cf. Acts 4:12.
37. Matthew 11:28.
38. John 1:29. (Revised Standard Version [RSV])
39. Cf. Galatians 3:13.
40. Cf. John 9.
41. 1 Corinthians 15:22.

of our sins, which he has completely blotted out with his precious blood, offering himself up to be tormented for us on the cross, yet we nonetheless pretend that we ourselves can become righteous and win the remission of our sins through our works—as though the righteousness, the justice, the blood of Christ was not enough to do these things. . . .

We therefore, beloved, do not embrace the foolishness of the doltish Galatians,[42] but rather the truth taught by Saint Paul, and we give the whole glory for our justification to the mercy of God and the merits of his Son, who with his blood has liberated us from the sovereignty of the Law and the tyranny of sin and death,[43] and has led us to the kingdom of God where he will bestow on us eternal joy. When I say that he has liberated us from the sovereignty of the Law, it is because he has given us his spirit, which conveys to us absolute truth, and has perfectly satisfied the Law, extending that satisfaction to all his members, that is, to all true Christians, so that they may appear without fear at God's tribunal, clothed in the justice of their Christ and freed by him from the malediction of the Law.

So the Law can no longer accuse or condemn us, nor can it arouse our passions and appetites, nor increase our store of sin; on this account, Saint Paul says that the contract that bound us has been canceled by Christ and annulled by the wood of the cross.[44] Our Christ having freed us from the sovereignty of the Law, he has thereby freed us from the tyranny of sin and death; for death can no longer reign over us, having been conquered by Christ's resurrection, and so also by us, who are the members of his body. . . .

This descendant of Abraham,[45] Jesus Christ, the most perfect fruit of God's promise, who has crushed the head of the venomous serpent—that is, the devil—so that all those who believe in Christ, trusting wholeheartedly in his grace, with Christ alongside them triumph over sin, death, Satan, and hell. This is Abraham's blessed seed who was to bring God's blessing, as he promised, to all the peoples of the earth. Before Jesus, each person individually had to confront that fearful serpent, and by his own efforts free himself from malediction; but this burden was so onerous, that the strength of everyone in the world, gathered together, was not sufficient to sustain it. God, therefore, father of all mercy, moved to compassion by our misery, gave us his only-begotten Son, who has saved us from the serpent's venom, and has accomplished our justification and salvation, so long as we accept him and repudiate all our other means of justification.

---

42. As described in Paul's letter to the Galatians, who though converted by Paul, in the latter's absence began to return to observance of Jewish and pagan ritual.
43. Cf. Romans 7:1; 8:2.
44. Cf. Colossians 2:14: "the charge of our legal indebtedness."
45. Cf. Genesis 22:17–18.

Beloved, let us embrace the justice offered us by our Jesus Christ, making it ours by means of faith, so that knowing we have been made righteous not by our own works but by Christ's merits, we may live joyously in the certainty that the justice of Christ abolishes all of our injustice, and makes us righteous, pure, and holy in the sight of God—God who, when he sees us incorporated with his Son by faith, will no longer consider us to be children of Adam, but his very own children, and will make us, together with his legitimate Son Jesus Christ, the heirs to all his riches.

Chapter Two: Erasmus: The Egg That Luther Hatched?

Was Erasmus indeed, in the words he imagined were used of him, "the egg that Luther hatched," the precursor of the Reformation?[1]

Certainly, Desiderius Erasmus (1466–1536) was influenced by the ideas of contemporary proto-reformers, and he developed strands of evangelical thought that would reappear in Luther's work and that of his colleagues and successors. First, he asserted the absolute priority of holy Scripture, a principle argued forcefully, as has been seen, by his predecessor Wyclif, and would become a fundamental Reformation doctrine. Second, he rated interiority above externalities: the inner state of the soul, its absorption in faith and love of God, rather than the performance of rituals, rites, and ceremonies, the idolatry of images and relics, and the cult of saints. Third, he valued the efforts of the individual alone in an unmediated approach to God, dispensing with clerical intervention—a view that correlated with his low opinion of members of all ranks and orders of priests, monks, friars, and prelates.

Yet as befitted this preeminent humanist thinker of northern Europe, Erasmus was steadfast in his valuation of the power of words to guide the human mind and spirit to good action. Inspired by words, especially the New Testament message that constituted the *philosophia Christi*, the "philosophy of Christ," the individual could unaided, employing his free will, lead the Christian life. This theology of words and deeds amounts to a profound critique of the church, to whose institutions and practices Erasmus is indifferent or hostile. Yet his critique neither challenges the ultimate authority of the church, nor calls for the kind of personal conversion and transformation that would characterize the Reformation already in formation during his lifetime.

A sampling of the Erasmian outlook is offered by excerpts given here from five of his works initially published between 1503 and 1523.[2] His *Enchiridion*, or *Handbook for the Christian Soldier* (1503), presents a guide to spiritual development for a man who had been a soldier, a master of slaughter and destruction, but now has renounced his trade and seeks to pursue the Christian life. Erasmus guides this convert step by step, building a new man concerned with interior, not exterior things. The *Enchiridion*'s exhortations

---

1. The source of this often repeated phrase is a letter Erasmus wrote in December 1524; see John C. Olin, *Desiderius Erasmus: Christian Humanism and the Reformation*, 16n35. Full citation in Texts and Studies.
2. Erasmus continually revised his works, which appeared in multiple editions after the first.

to the religious life may not suit modern tastes, but on its publication in 1503, it was an immediate best-seller, and soon appeared in many Latin editions and was translated into several vernacular languages, including English, Czech, German, Dutch, Spanish, and Polish.

Erasmus' most famous work, his *Praise of Folly* (1509), cleverly employs the figure of Folly, a clownish female abstraction, to probe the absurdity of the human condition. Both young and old live in illusion, which makes life tolerable; professionals foolishly vaunt their achievements; theologians and clerics, who should be servants of God, are too often corrupt, negligent, and hypocritical; and even genuine Christians, who choose to suffer in God's name, show themselves to be fools.

Erasmus invites Christians to the study of God's word in *The Summons* (1516), the preface to his edition and Latin translation (from the original Greek text) of the New Testament, correcting the translation, entitled the Vulgate, then in circulation. Merely reading and reflecting on the words and events contained in Scripture will turn heathens—those who have strayed from the faith—into Christians; whereas attending to rituals and ceremonies, or venerating icons or relics, will not. The learned are invited to turn from their philosophies to the philosophy of Christ, a message so plain and simple that ordinary people—laborers and artisans, unlettered women, and children—can understand it. All truth is revealed in the words of Scripture, and especially in the Gospels, which present Christ, the Son of God, "speaking, healing, dying, rising."

In *The Complaint of Peace* (1517), Erasmus unambiguously presents his view—in his mind, the Christian view—of war: war is the worst calamity that can befall human society. War means the slaughter of the innocent, and the breakdown of all human bonds. It defies the divine will, since Christ came to make peace between human and divine; at his birth, angels proclaimed "peace on earth"; and his last words to his followers before his passion and crucifixion were of peace: "my peace I leave with you." Churchmen disgrace themselves by taking sides and engaging in war, and secular rulers who do so pursue their own self-interest rather than the good of their people. In *The Complaint*, these arguments are made by Peace herself, who speaks her lament even as she is searching for some place of refuge, for war is everywhere.

Taking up the project, in his maturity, of composing dialogues for children, called "colloquies," that teach moral principles along with correct Latin, Erasmus encapsulates in witty stories serious messages about Christian faith. In *The Shipwreck* (1523), he contrasts the useless prayers made to saints by passengers on a ship about to break up and sink in a storm to the heartfelt prayer uttered directly to God by the true Christian faithful. In the end, it is these who survive the shipwreck while the others drown, just as in the drama of the Christian life: while all others face damnation, the truly pious are saved.

All hope of safety rests in iron

from Desiderius Erasmus, *Handbook for the Christian Soldier* (1503)

The two opening chapters of the *Handbook for the Christian Soldier* center on the ironic contrast between the target's profession of soldier and the godly life—seeming opposites; and yet the religious man is a soldier for Christ, and his *Enchiridion*, or handbook, is also his dagger, his forged-iron weapon, as the word (originally Greek) has both those meanings. The first chapter warns that we must be ever watchful, since to live in the world is to be engaged in continual warfare, in which one must be the soldier of God and not of his enemies. The second chapter defines the two principal "Christian weapons": prayer and knowledge. The apostle Paul had recommended constant prayer, and Erasmus sees knowledge, especially knowledge of the Gospel, as absolutely essential: he who commits himself to the study of holy Scripture, Erasmus assures, "will be armed and ready to face any enemy assault." Erasmus closes by advising his friend to always have with him this *Enchiridion*, a handbook that is also a dagger: for "all our hope for safety rests in iron."

In this life we must always be on our guard

> *Erasmus develops a warfare metaphor appropriate for the target of his* Enchiridion, *a retired soldier who must now become a Christian soldier, and engage in an unrelenting struggle against sin.*

First of all, as you know yourself, we must be aware that this mortal life is nothing but a kind of perpetual warfare. . . . in which ordinary people are easily destroyed, their souls entrapped by that trickster, the world, whose tentacles of seductive pleasures hold them fast. . . . Since we must all engage, therefore, in such a relentless and dangerous campaign against so many enemies, sworn to our utter destruction and armed to the teeth, so wary, so expert, so treacherous, would we not be insane if we did not seize our own weapons, stand on our guard, suspect everything?

> *To make peace with sin is to be estranged from Christ, and to break the covenant made in baptism—a betrayal unworthy of the Christian soldier, who must remain loyal to his king.*

Anyone who makes peace with sin violates the contract made with God in baptism. . . . Or did you not realize, O Christian soldier, that from the moment when you were initiated into the faith by that lifegiving stream, you gave yourself by name to Christ as your commander, to whom you owe your life twofold: Once when it was given to you at birth, and once when it was restored to you in baptism?—and so you owe more to him than you do to yourself. . . .

For what other purpose did he have the sign of the cross inscribed on your forehead than that, so long as you lived, you would follow him in battle under that banner? For what other purpose were you anointed with his sacred ointment than that you would ever afterward fight the eternal fight against sin? How great is the shame that befalls a man who deserts his lord and king, how great indeed his execration by all of humankind. Why do you disdain Christ your commander, neither compelled by fear of him, though he is God, nor restrained by love of him, who for your sake became man? . . . With what impudence do you dare to march with hostile standards against your king, who gave up his own life for you? . . .

You have not followed Christ, and your soul is distressed; but God can renew your spirit.

Innumerable are the enemies ranged against you, but he who stands for you can overcome them all. *If God is for us, who can be against us?*[3] . . . With God's help, no one fails to conquer, unless he chooses defeat. His generosity has never failed anyone; if you take care not to doubt him, you will prevail. He will fight for you, and he will impute to you the merit of his liberality. You should recognize that it is he who wins every victory, who, being first and solely free from sin, has destroyed sin's sovereignty. But he grants all this to you not without some effort on your part; for he who said, *Take courage, I have conquered the world*,[4] wants you to have a valiant, not a cautious spirit. In this way, we shall in the end, fighting as he has fought, conquer through him. . . .

The weapons of Christian warfare

The first principle of Christian warfare, I propose, is to have thought through and deliberated about what kind of weapons are best employed against the enemy that you will confront. Further, you must have them always at the ready, lest some cunning foe attack you when you are unaware and defenseless. In the kind of warfare with which you are familiar, there are often quieter moments, perhaps when the enemy takes to winter quarters, or when a truce is in effect. But in waging war while still in this mortal body, Christians must not permit themselves to be separated even by a finger's breadth, as they say, from their weapons. At no time do we step out of the line of battle, never do we fail to keep guard, because our enemy is relentless. . . .

---

3. Romans 8:31.
4. John 16:33 (New Revised Standard Version [NRSV]).

The weapons to be used in Christian warfare should be specified in turn. Two, to be brief, are especially valuable . . . : prayer and knowledge. The apostle Paul commands us to pray without ceasing, desiring us always to be armed by that means. Pure prayer rising up to heaven is a citadel no enemy can assail. Knowledge provides the mind with useful ideas. . . .

After a discussion of prayer, Erasmus turns his attention to knowledge as a formidable weapon against the spiritual enemy.

Believe me, most beloved brother, there is no enemy attack, however ferocious, nor incursion, however fierce, that a profound knowledge of holy Scripture does not easily repel; and there is no harsh adversity, that it does not make bearable. . . . For all of holy Scripture is divinely inspired and proceeds from God its author. It is modest: the language is simple, but embedded in its frankly plain prose are deep truths of faith. It is spectacular: for though what mortals know is never uncorrupted by some blot of error, the knowledge that comes from Christ alone shines as white as snow, wholly radiant, wholly pure. . . . If you dedicate yourself wholly to the study of holy Scripture, if you meditate on God's law day and night, you will not fear the terror that comes by night or by day, but you will be armed and ready to face any enemy assault. . . .

So now as you have wished, to satisfy your request, I have forged for you an *enchiridion*, that is to say, a kind of dagger, which you must never let out of your grasp, either in public or in private. Even when you must go about the business of this world, endure the weight of this righteous armor, so as to deny the enemy the chance to attack you when you are not fully armed. By no means should you hesitate to keep this dagger by your side, for it weighs little, and protects you greatly. For though it is small, if you artfully wield as well the shield of faith, you will easily withstand the furious assult of your enemy, and avert a deadly wound. But now the time has come to pick up and use that handbook, which if you diligently follow its instructions, I am confident that our commander Christ will lead you in triumph from this place to his heavenly Jerusalem, where there is no war, but only immortal peace and perfect tranquility. Meanwhile, all our hope for safety rests in iron.

Christianity itself is akin to Folly

from Desiderius Erasmus, *Praise of Folly* (1509)

When Folly, clad in jester's garb, bounds forth to take the pulpit and give her own eulogy—already an absurdity, before one word is uttered, because eulogies are not normally spoken by the person eulogized, and females do not, in 1509, normally speak in public—the stage is set for a multilayered comic exploration of everything in the world. Folly will expose the folly of all her worshipers, who are her worshipers precisely in that they imitate her, the most sincere form of worship. Why is no temple built to Folly, she asks? Because she has no need of one; the whole world is her temple, and everyone in it her acolyte.

Among the followers of Folly are old and young (a slobbering old man and a slobbering child are equally foolish); male and female; nobles and paupers; philosophers and poets; teachers and lawyers; and the whole parade of professional clerics: theologians, monks, priests, bishops, and popes. Here Erasmus, lurking behind Folly's skirts, in the final section comes to the fore: Christianity itself is folly. What fools Christians are, seekers of salvation amid a garden of delights! What a fool was Christ, who offered himself as a sacrificial lamb and embraced the cross! The whole Christian religion challenges the commonsense of everyday life, and so is foolish, if ultimately wise; *For the wisdom of this world is foolishness in God's sight*, as Paul the apostle writes.[5] This is more than wordplay. The madcap Folly is Erasmus' puppet, but he is the ventriloquist.

The following passages are taken from the sections of *Praise of Folly* critiquing the various orders of the clergy, and conclude with a statement of the ultimate folly, and consequently the wisdom, of the Christian religion.

The theologians. It might be better to say nothing about the theologians, an amazingly haughty and crotchety set, . . . lest they shout me down pronto as a heretic—since that's exactly the thunderbolt they use to terrify anyone who disagrees with them.[6] Meanwhile they forget all about the good things I've done for them, although they really owe me a lot, since they are so absurdly in love with themselves that they seem to inhabit some kind of heavenly realm from which they look down to sneer at all other mortals as though they were mere brutes plodding in the mud. . . .

And then they delight in dissecting theological minutiae, such as the principle by which the world was framed and founded, or the pathways by which Original Sin descended to posterity.[7] . . . At what precise moment was the Son born to the Father?[8] . . . Can it be argued that the Father hates the Son? Could God have come to earth as a woman, as the devil, as an ass, as a gourd,

---

5. 1 Corinthians 3:19.
6. The charge of heresy was exceptionally serious, and its threat could be used to control opposition.
7. Original Sin: the sin of Adam and Eve, who disobeyed God in the Garden of Eden.
8. This question and those following are absurd extensions of theological discussions of the doctrines of the Trinity and Incarnation.

or as a pebble? And if so, how could that gourd have preached from the pulpit, performed miracles, or been nailed to the cross? . . .

Innumerable are the niceties more subtle even than these, concerning instantiations, ideations, interrelations, formalizations, quiddities, haecceities,[9] undetectable by the eye unless, in absolute darkness, you can see things that do not exist. . . . Moreover, a host of scholastic[10] schools render these obscure obscurities still more obscure, such that you can more easily find your way out of a labyrinth than out of the web of arguments put forth by Realists and Nominalists, Thomists, Albertists, Occamists, and Scotists[11]—and I am not naming them all, just the principal ones. . . .

But in the meantime, they acclaim and applaud themselves, frolicking day and night in these jolly frivolities, allowing not an iota of time to reading even once the Gospels or the Epistles of Saint Paul. And at the same time, with their heads lost in the clouds, they think that . . . it is they who support the universal church, which would otherwise fall in ruins, by the tootling of their syllogisms. . . .[12]

Monks and mendicants.[13] Another group that considers itself very fortunate are those commonly called "monks." . . . Their lot would be truly wretched if I did not assist them in many ways; for everyone detests this breed of men, while they are completely satisfied with themselves. First of all, they think it the highest form of piety if they are so ignorant that they can't even read. Then they think that they delight the ears of God and his angels when in church they raucously bray out their psalms,[14] of which they know only a few, and understand not at all. And many of them profit from their filth and squalor, cruising through the public squares bawling mightily as they beg for bread, brazenly invading inns, carriages, and boats, while intruding on the turf of the truly needy. And by this behavior these slick operators, in their filth, ignorance, boorishness, and impudence, claim to personify the apostles! . . .

---

9. Quiddity and haecceity: (roughly) the "whatness" and "whichness" of any thing.

10. Scholasticism, the "thinking of the Schools," was not a unitary movement, but one consisting of many "schools" of thought, named for their key principles or their originators.

11. Erasmus names various schools of scholasticism, including those adhering to a particular view of the cosmos (Realists and Nominalists) and those named after an iconic figure (Thomas Aquinas, Albertus Magnus, William of Ockham, Duns Scotus).

12. Syllogism: the kind of logical argument characteristic of scholastic method.

13. Monks were required to remain in their monasteries, bound by vows and living under a "rule." The mendicant, or "begging" orders, in contrast, were itinerant, and often were popular preachers to urban audiences.

14. The principal duty of monks was to sing the psalms at seven daily worship services in the monastery church.

Just think: Is there a jokester or jester you would rather watch than these fellows giving their posturing sermons, while they pretentiously yet quite absurdly imitate what the masters of the rhetorical art have taught? God Almighty! How they wave their arms, how they shriek and mumble and croon, how they hurl themselves about and contort their faces, so that everything shakes with their howls. . . . Yet there are many who, when they see this performance, thanks to my good offices, believe they are watching Demosthenes himself, or Cicero. . . .[15]

Bishops, cardinals, priests, and popes.[16] Popes, cardinals, and bishops, the princes of the church, long since matched worldly princes in the extent of their folly, and just about exceeded them. What is signified, after all, if any of them thinks about it, by that linen vestment of strikingly brilliant whiteness, if not a wholly blameless life? Or what is signified by the bishop's two-horned mitre, its two peaks joined by a single knot, if not perfect knowledge of both the New and Old Testament? . . . These things, I suggest, and many others of the sort, require, do they not, if any of them thinks about it, a life of care and effort? But these fellows live pretty easily, amusing themselves. . . .

In the same way, the cardinals should view themselves as the successors of Christ's apostles; and, accordingly, should shoulder those responsibilities that they have inherited. They must not then act as masters, but as the caretakers of the gifts of spirit, for all of which they will be required in but a little while to give a meticulous accounting. . . . Whatever else is the purpose of all their wealth, since they are standing in for the impoverished apostles?

Then the popes, the vicars of Christ on earth, if they attempted to emulate his life, which is to say his poverty, troubles, message, cross, and sacrifice; or if they thought about what is meant by "pope," whose name means "father" and whose surname, "most holy"; then who on earth would be more overladen with sorrow? . . . How many comforts would they forego, if they ever were struck by the hammer of wisdom? . . . Such wealth, all those honors, all that power, all those triumphs, so many offices and dispensations and taxes and privileges, all those horses, mules, and servitors, so many delights. . . . Nor indeed should we fail to consider the consequences for all those scribes and copyists, notaries and lawyers, advocates, lobbyists, and secretaries; and all those muleteers and stablehands, loansharks and pimps—I would say something harsher here, but fear it would hurt your ears; that huge crowd of hangers-on who now strangle Rome (sorry, I mean to say "service Rome") would die of starvation.

---

15. The Greek Demosthenes and Roman Cicero were the two leading orators of antiquity.

16. The pope is the highest member of the hierarchy of the Catholic church, followed by cardinals and archbishops and bishops; priests serve the community of those who live in a local parish.

And then the mob of priests who think it wicked to fall short of the holiness of their superiors, behold! How fiercely do they battle for their share of the tithe with sword, sticks, and stones and all other possible armaments. . . . Nor do their shaved heads remind them that a priest should rid himself of all the appetites of this world, and think only of the other one. But these fine fellows believe they have performed their office well if they whisk through it fast, stuttering out their little prayerlets—which, by gum, I would be amazed if God can hear or understand, since they themselves neither hear nor understand the words that they bawl out. . . .

Christian folly. All that's been said leads to this conclusion: that if all mortals are fools, so, too, are the pious—as was Christ himself. Although he was the wisdom of the Father, yet he became a fool in order to heal the foolishness of mortals. For he assumed the nature of mankind, and walked about in the likeness of a man; and in the same way, he became sin, so as to redeem us from our sins, offering no other solution than the folly of the cross. With this folly he earnestly imbued his doltish and moronic apostles, steering them clear of wisdom, teaching them with stories about young children, the lilies of the field, tiny mustard seeds, and fragile little sparrows,[17] things without sense or reason, guided only by nature, living life without artifice or anxiety. . . .

And so that I do not chase after the infinite, I will sum up: the Christian religion, without a doubt, has some kind of kinship with folly, and very little with wisdom. . . . There are no greater fools than those who are wholly possessed by Christian ardor, so great that they give up their possessions, forgive injuries, suffer abuse, love enemies as friends, abhor pleasure, welcome fasts, vigils, tears, trials, and humiliation, disdain life and look forward to death—in short, they seem to have completely abandoned ordinary existence, as though their soul dwelled elsewhere, not in their body. What else can this be, but madness?

May these be the stories we tell each day

from Desiderius Erasmus, *The Summons* (1516)

In persuasive tones, and with a simplicity geared to reach a broad audience, Erasmus introduces his edition and translation of the New Testament with a "Summons" to embrace the one true philosophy, sent by God, and

---

17. Erasmus is naming some of the props of the stories, or "parables," recorded in the Gospels, that Jesus tells his followers to describe the kingdom of God.

superseding all that came before: the "philosophy of Christ." It should be communicated to all through translations into vernacular (popularly spoken) languages, a medium by which it could reach the unschooled: laborers, women, and children. Fittingly for the preface to the edition of a scriptural work, the message is centered on words. It is not by performing rituals and ceremonies, nor by idolizing images and relics[18] of Christ and his saints, Erasmus advises—these were common practices in his day—that the Christian grows in the love of God and progresses to salvation. Rather, for the educated, it is by reading the Bible; and for the poor and the very young, it is by hearing the stories told by nurses to children, by families at their table, or by travelers around the fire where they gather at each day's end. These are, in and of themselves, a bountiful and sufficient education.

I most ardently wish, if anything can come of such wishes, that I be given an eloquence far greater than that of Cicero . . . if it would enable me to summon all mortals, as though with a trumpet call, to the sacred and salutary study of Christian philosophy. . . . [Such an eloquence] does not so much delight the ears with a pleasure that will quickly pass, but with sharp thrusts leaves inscribed on the minds of the listeners a message that grabs them, transforms them, and sends them away quite changed from what they had been. . . . What is to be aimed for is this: that nothing can claim greater certainty than the truth itself, expressed in the simplest possible and thereby the most effective language.

Above all, it is not useful at the present moment to renew the charge . . . that while scholars are so deeply engaged in their studies, many ridicule, although they are Christians, specifically this philosophy of Christ, many dismiss it, and only a few consider it, but disinterestedly; I will refrain from saying insincerely. . . . How does it happen that we who call ourselves Christians do not wholeheartedly embrace, as we should, this one philosophy? Followers of Plato, Pythagoras, Epicurus, the Academy, the Stoics, the Cynics, or the Peripatetics,[19] not only have mastered the dogmas of these sects, but retain them in memory, and go to battle for them, like champions prepared to die rather than betray the cause. Why do we not commit ourselves even more to Christ, our philosopher and king? . . .

He alone, we know for certain, is the teacher who has come from heaven. He alone has taught things that are certain, since he himself is eternal wisdom. He alone, the one author of human salvation, has taught what is necessary for salvation. He alone embodies absolutely everything that he has taught.

---

18. Relics: material objects or body parts widely esteemed because of their association with Christ or the saints.

19. Erasmus names a series of prominent ancient philosophers and philosophical schools.

He alone can fulfill all that he has promised. . . . What a new and stupendous kind of philosophy this is! For so that it might be transmitted to humankind, he who was God was made man; he who was immortal was made mortal; he who dwelled within the heart of the Father descended to earth. What a great thing we must recognize it to be, and by no means trivial, that this extraordinary teacher came to teach us after so many sects of outstanding philosophers, and after so many eminent prophets. Why do we not with pious curiosity explore what can be known about this event, investigate and examine it? . . . The road ahead is simple, and available to all. You need only a ready and willing spirit equipped, above all, with a simple and pure faith. . . .

I disagree strongly with those who do not want the unschooled to read holy Scripture translated into the vernacular,[20] as though what Christ taught was so complex that it could be understood only by a handful of theologians, or as if the strength of the Christian religion consisted in its impenetrability. The mysteries of kings are better hidden, perhaps, but Christ wants his mysteries to be communicated to all. Would that everyone, in my view, even the humblest little woman,[21] read the Gospel and the letters of Paul. And would that these be translated into all the languages of humankind, so that they may be read and understood not only by Scots and Irishmen, but even by Turks and Saracens.[22] What is most important is that they be understood. No matter that many will laugh, so long as others are captivated. May the peasant at his plow sing out the words, may the weaver at his loom repeat them, may the traveler ease the tedium of his journey by telling these stories![23] May these be the stories that occupy all Christians. For Christians we will surely be, when these tales from scripture are the stories we tell each day. . . .

All of us, in every single act of baptism—if those presenting the infant make their pledge using the words of Christ, and if that pledge comes from the heart—immediately, as we are swathed in the embraces of our parents

---

20. Only boys destined for the church or the professions went to school, where the main goal was to learn Latin. A fraction of the "unschooled" were literate, but only in the language they used daily, the "vernacular." These would be able to read the Bible only if translated.

21. Women were generally viewed as unintelligent, and certainly as without learning. Erasmus here is broadening the audience of Scripture to include the unlikely population of ordinary women.

22. Again broadening the audience of those who might respond to Scripture, Erasmus includes people speaking different languages and of different and even hostile cultures, just as, below, he includes people practicing modest trades. "Saracen" referred to Arabic Muslims; the Turks were Muslims, but not Arabic, and in Erasmus' day at war with some Christian states.

23. Storytelling was a principal leisure activity for Europeans at this time, particularly at night, when in the absence of electricity, it was impossible to read or, of course, access any of the media that occupy people today. Erasmus approved of storytelling, but wanted the stories to be grounded in Scripture.

and the caresses of our nurses, we are infused with the doctrine of Christ. For the knowledge that the blank slate of the soul first imbibes is planted most firmly and holds fast tenaciously. May the child's first babblings be of Christ, and his earliest infancy shaped by the Gospels of Christ—who from the start should be introduced to children in such a way that they, too, will love him. For just as the harshness of many teachers cause children to hate learning before they can acquire it, so there are those who make the philosophy of Christ dull and dreary, than which there is nothing more sweet. May children, then, be immersed in these studies, as they naturally grow into full maturity in Christ. . . .

And happy is he who at the hour of his death meditates still on the Gospel of Christ. Let us thirst for this Gospel with our whole heart; let us embrace it, kiss it, probe its depths, dwell within it; let us be transformed by it, for what we study changes who we are. . . . When we are shown relics of Christ, how we Christians prostrate ourselves, how we worship them! Why do we not adore rather the living, breathing likeness of him found in the Gospels? . . . [Such relics and images] can only recall the form of his body—if indeed they do anything of the sort—whereas the Gospels convey to you the living image of the sacred mind of Christ, and present him to you completely—his words, his miracles, his death, his resurrection—so that you would not see him more clearly if you looked upon him with your own eyes.

Spurned and rejected by all, Peace speaks out

from Desiderius Erasmus, *The Complaint of Peace* (1517)

The condition of peace is for Erasmus self-evidently superior to the condition of war. And yet he sees war everywhere: fought for trifling causes, by those who profess to be followers of Christ, and even led by princes and prelates whose duty it is to seek and advance peace. What then is Peace herself to do? She is figured here, as Folly was previously, as a female abstraction. And she wonders why she is spurned and rejected by all, when a preference for peace appears to be inherent in nature, created by God, and when Jesus Christ his Son was a champion of peace, so that those who pretend to fight in his name are deceiving themselves. She calls upon the princes of nations and the leaders of the church to seek peace and not war, and so better the lives of those they serve.

> *Humans have driven Peace away, and so brought calamity on themselves, not understanding how great is the good that they have repudiated. The inclination*

for peace is inherent in nature, and the tools for peace-making, reason and speech, are specific capacities of human beings. Yet they persist in their hostilities, when Peace is what they really need. Here, Peace presents herself.

I am Peace, . . . the source, parent, provider, protector, teacher of all good things in heaven or on earth; without me there is nothing vital, wholesome, sound, or holy. War, on the other hand, is a boundless sea of all the evils ever set loose in the realm of nature, a vicious force that withers all that flourishes, crushes what has been created, topples what has been built, undoes what has been well founded, embitters all that is sweet. . . . I ask in the name of the everlasting God, who would believe that the human race would be so insane as to expel someone like me at such great expense, with so huge an effort, with such fierce endeavor, . . . and at such enormous risk, while rushing to pay an extortionate price for such a heap of horrors?

If wild beasts had spurned me in this way, I could bear it more easily, recognizing their hostility to me as natural, deriving from the savagery of their minds. . . . For the awkward and unavoidable truth is that nature has created only one animal possessed of reason, and capable of God-like intellectual activity, and so designed to live in kindly and peaceful community—that is, the human animal; and yet, I could more easily make a home among wild beasts and dim-witted flocks than among these bellicose humans. . . . For animals, even though lacking the faculty of reason, still somehow coexist in civility and concord. Elephants gather together in herds, pigs and sheep graze together, . . . dolphins help out other dolphins, and the well-oiled colonies of ants and bees are famous. . . . Even the fiercest beasts get along together. Lions do not fight among themselves, one boar does not threaten another with his mighty tusks, peace reigns between lynx and lynx, dragons do not terrorize dragons, and amicability among wolves is proverbial. . . .

Humans alone, though they are the species most suited to live in concord, and most require such comity, cannot be pacified by nature, . . . nor by education; nor does their awareness of the many benefits of agreement resolve their differences, nor does their actual experience of present evils persuade them to join in mutual affection. . . . Yet humans alone possess the power of reason, which is common to all and shared with no other living creature. And humans alone have the capacity for speech, the principal agent of friendly relations. In them are implanted the seeds both of knowledge and virtue, as is a gentle and kindly nature inclined to generosity to others, while they delight in being liked, and enjoy being of service to others—unless they are corrupted by depraved desires, and from the human condition degenerate to that of savage beasts. . . .

Not only is a longing for Peace rooted in nature and in human nature, but Peace is taught and modeled by Jesus Christ.

For what other purpose did the Son of God descend to earth than to reconcile the world to the Father? So that human beings might be bound together by mutual affection and enduring love, and joined to him in friendship? . . . When Christ was born, did the angels sound the trumpets of war? . . . No, the angels of peace sing quite a different song, . . . proclaiming peace not to those panting for war and slaughter, . . . but to those of good will, and inclined to concord.[24] . . . And when Christ became a man, what else did he teach, what else did he preach but peace? He greeted his followers always with the promise of peace, saying *Peace be with you*; and he recommended to them that form of salutation as the one truly worthy of a Christian. . . . And when he knew he was to die, note with what great care he bestows peace upon them, as he had throughout his life: *Love one another*, he said, *as I have loved you*. And again: *My peace I give to you, my peace I leave with you*.[25] Do you hear what it is he left to his disciples? His horses? His armed guard? His empire? His wealth? None of these. What then? He gives his peace, he leaves his peace: peace with his friends, peace with those who hate him. . . .

Leaving aside the horrors of wars long ago, Erasmus notes that just the last ten years have seen constant warfare, fought not only by princes of the world but even prelates of the church, who amid the slaughter bear the sign of the cross, as do the mercenaries they employ in fighting what they falsely call a holy war.

Little wonder that those born of war breathe the spirit of war. And what makes the evil harder to root out, they disguise their impiety with a mask of piety: their banners are adorned with the cross. The godless soldier, paid piles of cash to perform butchery and slaughter, bears the sign of the cross— making a symbol of war the one symbol that could undo war. What is the cross to you, unholy soldier? Such souls as yours, and such deeds, are better suited for dragons, tigers, and wolves. That sign belongs to him who conquered not by fighting but by dying, who saved and did not destroy; and more than any other sign, it could instruct you who are the real enemies—if you really are a Christian—and how they are to be overcome. You raise high the banner of salvation as you cruelly assail your brother, and by the cross destroy him who was saved by the cross? . . .

How is such war to be called holy, which on some pretext or other, with soldiers and weapons of this sort, Christians wage against Christians? . . . How wretched is the lot of the warrior! If he vanquishes, he is a murderer; if he is vanquished, he dies, no less a murderer than his killer, since he too desired to murder. Then they hate the Turks as heathens and as enemies of Christ, as if behaving as they do, they could possibly be considered Christians; or as if any

---

24. Cf. Luke 2:14.
25. Cf. John 20:21, 13:34, 14:27.

spectacle could be more pleasing to the Turks than to see Christians slaughtering each other.[26] The Turks offer human sacrifices to the demons, it is said; but since these demons are especially pleased when one Christian slaughters another—really, I ask you, how do Christians differ from Turks? . . .

> *More than enough blood has already been spilled. It is time to put an end to all of this posturing. Those who say they want peace must make the effort to secure it. Rulers must set aside their quarrels, not seeking to extend their realms with alliances and treaties that just lead to more war, but rather act for the common good, while churchmen should perform properly the duties assigned them.*

Princes, I call upon you, on whose mere nod mortal affairs depend, who on earth mirror the princely image of Christ: hear the voice of your King calling you to peace. . . . Priests, dedicated to God, I call upon you to show, in all you do, what you know is pleasing to God. . . . Theologians, I call on you to preach the Gospel of peace so that it rings always in the ears of the people. Bishops, I call on you and all those holding high church office to use your authority to bind us to peace with eternal bonds. Nobles and magistrates, I call on you to execute what is commanded by the wisdom of kings and the piety of popes. . . .

What has been attempted with our human strength has not succeeded; but Christ himself will further those genuine efforts that he sees are undertaken in his name and cause. He will stand at your right hand, he will inspire you, and aid you who are furthering the goal that he himself greatly favors, so that the good of all will triumph over individual grievances. . . . And so at last, each to each, and all to all will show love and kindness, and will be pleasing to Christ, to please whom is the height of happiness. I have spoken my piece.

Get ready to swim, for life or death

from Desiderius Erasmus, *The Shipwreck* (1523)

Written in schoolboy Latin, this brief dialogue yet raises some of Erasmus' principal criticisms of the contemporary church. The action takes place on a ship that is about to go down in a storm. On board are a variety of travelers, among them rich merchants, members of the clergy, a nursing mother and

---

26. The European states carried on intermittent warfare with the Ottoman Turks, an Islamic people who had seized Constantinople in 1453.

her baby, the ship's captain and sailors, and the two interlocutors: Adolph, a participant in the event, and Anthony, to whom he relates the details.

When the captain announces that the ship is going down, the passengers must face likely death, and betray in their actions their true feelings. Many try to buy their way out, bargaining with this saint or that one, promising large gifts if they escape with their lives—even prostrating themselves on the deck to pray to a saint whose name they do not know. This situation gives Erasmus a chance to mock the cult of saints that has, in his mind, sidelined the worship of God himself, or reverence for Christ, the Savior.

In contrast, Erasmus approves of the quiet and profound faith of the nursing mother; the direct approach to God made by Adolph, the narrator, who not only bypasses the mediation of the saints but dispenses even with the rite of confession; and the life-affirming actions of a priest, who urges his fellow travelers to strip down as he does in preparation for entering the turbulent waters and facing what might come, whether life or death. In the end, these three, and the nursing infant, are among the handful who survive the terrible shipwreck. This gemlike story, one of some fifty that Erasmus crafted, conveys both dramatically and efficiently the author's call to seek a genuine relationship with God by means of simple communication, rejecting formalism in worship, and what was in his view the superstitious worship of saints, images, and relics.

Interlocutors Anthony, Adolph

ADOLPH. The sailor turned to us saying, "Friends, the situation demands that we all commend ourselves to God, and prepare for death." Asked by some who had experience of the sea how long it might be before the ship could no longer be saved, he replied that he could not say exactly, but no longer than three hours. . . . This said, he commanded us to cut the ropes, and saw the mast down to its base, and throw it along with the rigging into the sea.

ANTHONY. What for?

ADOLPH. Because if the sail was torn to shreds, it would become worse than useless, a liability; at that point, the only hope is in the helmsman's rudder.

ANTHONY. So what did the others do in the meantime?

ADOLPH. If you had been there, you would have seen the face of wretchedness. Singing the *Salve Regina*,[27] the sailors called upon the Virgin Mary, calling her Star of the Sea, Queen of Heaven, Mistress of the World, Harbor

---

27. *Salve Regina:* "Hail, Holy Queen," a traditional prayer, sung or said, addressed to the Virgin Mary. The appellations of Mary that follow are also traditional.

Erasmus, The Shipwreck

of Salvation, and assigning her many other titles not to be found anywhere in holy scripture.

ANTHONY. What did Mary have to do with the sea—who so far as I can recall, never set foot on a ship?

ADOLPH. In ancient times, it was believed the goddess Venus, who had been born from the sea, took care of sailors; and when she ceased to do the job, the Mother who was a Virgin took the place of the mother who wasn't.[28]

ANTHONY. You're pulling my leg!

ADOLPH. Some passengers prostrated themselves on the deck and prayed to the sea, sprinkling whatever oil they had at hand onto the waves, anointing it much as we do to soften up kings.[29]

ANTHONY. What words did they use?

ADOLPH. O most merciful sea! Most benevolent sea! Most wealthy sea! Most beautiful sea! Have mercy on us and save us! With such words they serenaded the unhearing waters.

ANTHONY. What ridiculous superstition! What else did the passengers do?

ADOLPH. Some puked, and some prayed. One Englishman promised the Virgin of Walsingham that, if he survived, he would bring her mountains of gold. Others pledged gifts to the True Cross that is here, and others to the True Cross that is there. The same with the Virgin Mary, who reigns in many places; and the vow is considered worthless if you do not specify the place.

ANTHONY. Ridiculous! As if the saints do not live in heaven. . . . Did no one mention Christopher?[30]

ADOLPH. One of them really made me laugh. Bellowing, so the saint would be sure to hear, he promised the Christopher who is in the cathedral in Paris a wax candle as tall as he was—a mountain, really, rather than a statue. While he was roaring away, repeating the vow again and again, a companion standing nearby elbowed him in the ribs, and warned: "Watch what you say, because you would not be able to pay up even if you sold everything you have." The other answered in a whisper, lest Christopher hear: "Silence, fool,

---

28. Erasmus mocks but is correct: the figure of the Virgin Mary assumed some of the characteristics of the Greco-Roman goddess Aphrodite/Venus in the early Christian and medieval eras.

29. Holy oil was used in Christian ceremonies, while medieval kings were often anointed with holy oil as part of the ritual of coronation.

30. It would have made sense to invoke Christopher, the patron saint of travelers.

do you think I mean what I say? If I ever reach land, I won't even give him a cheap tallow taper."[31] . . .

ANTHONY. I'm surprised no one mentioned the apostle Paul, who used to go to sea himself, and when his ship was wrecked, was washed up on the land. A man familiar with the evils of the world, he could assist those suffering misfortune.

ADOLPH. There was not a word about Paul. . . .

ANTHONY. Meanwhile, what were you doing? Did you make any vows to the saints?

ADOLPH. In no way.

ANTHONY. Why not?

ADOLPH. Because I don't bargain with the saints. What is such a vow but a kind of contract: I will give you this if you do that, or I will do this if you do that; I shall make a gift of wax, if I make it to shore; I will go to Rome, if you save me. . . .

ANTHONY. Then what did you do?

ADOLPH. I went directly to the Father himself, praying *Our Father, who are in heaven.*[32] No saint hears more quickly than he does, or answers prayers more generously.

ANTHONY. But did your conscience not hold you back? Were you not afraid to call him "father" whom you had offended with so many sins?

ADOLPH. Frankly, my conscience did bother me; but I soon took heart, telling myself: there is no father so angry with his son who would not, if he saw the child drowning in a stream or lake, wouldn't grab him by the hairs on his head and pull him back to shore. Amid all of this uproar, no passenger remained so calm as one woman who nursed the infant she held in her bosom.

ANTHONY. What did she do?

ADOLPH. She was the only one who refrained from shrieking or crying or making vows; she just held on to the baby, and prayed quietly. At the same time, as the ship was driven by the waves upon the shoals, fearing that it would break apart, the captain had it lashed with ropes from bow to stern.

---

31. The contrast between the promise and the hidden intention is both in size and quality—a life-size candle made of expensive wax versus a meager one made of rendered animal fat.
32. The opening words of the prayer "Our Father," called in Latin the "Paternoster"; Matthew 6:9.

ANTHONY. A desperate measure!

ADOLPH. And then there jumped up an ancient priest, some sixty years old, named Adam, who stripped off his clothes down to his underwear, along with his shoes and leggings, and commanded us all to do the same, so that we would be ready to swim. And standing there in the middle of the ship, he delivered a sermon on Gerson's *Five Truths on the Usefulness of Confession*,[33] then urged us all to prepare for life or death. A Dominican friar was also present, and those who wished to do so, confessed to these two.[34]

ANTHONY. What did you do?

ADOLPH. Seeing that all was in chaos, I silently confessed to God, repenting to him for my transgressions and imploring his mercy.

ANTHONY. And to where do you think you would be sent for eternity, if you had died in that state?

ADOLPH. That decision I left to the judgment of God. For I did not wish to be my own judge; yet throughout, my soul was at peace and hopeful. While all this went on, the captain came to us, in tears, saying that we should be prepared, as the ship would go down within a quarter hour. It had already been ruptured in some places, and water poured in. Then a sailor, seeing a church tower in the distance, urged us to pray for the help of whoever the saint was to whom the church belonged. All prostrated themselves on deck, and prayed to the nameless saint.

ANTHONY. Perhaps he would have listened, if you had called on him by name.

ADOLPH. It was unknown. . . .

While those who rushed for the safety of the lifeboat were lost at sea, the nursing mother and her baby who had already been dispatched on a plank, and Adolph and the priest clinging to the same fragment of the mast, make it to shore. Of the fifty-eight passengers, only five survive, including these who alone are described as having had faith in God—rather than an assortment of saints—and having shown courage and self-reliance.

---

33. Jean Gerson: a French theologian of the previous century, so this energetic priest was not without learning—although Erasmus finds the sermonizing at this moment absurd.

34. It was especially important to confess one's sins when one faced imminent death. Those who died with sins unconfessed would be sent to hell. The Dominicans were a religious order of mendicant friars with a particular preaching mission.

Chapter Three: Luther the Rebel

The rebellion against the Roman church of Martin Luther (1483–1546), an Augustinian friar and university professor, was an event of world-historical importance. It changed the course of German history and Western thought; but above all, it challenged the claim of the papacy to represent Jesus Christ on earth, unleashing huge creative energies not only among the Christian communities that broke away from Rome, but also among those who remained loyal to the old church. New forms of belief, of church order, and of the conduct of daily life competed, thrived, and failed, in patterns inconceivable to earlier proponents of reform. Luther's particular challenge to the church constitutes only one phase of the enormous upheaval that would result from his actions. Yet it was no mere prelude. It was rather a complete and potent campaign in a war that would have many battles, but none more important or decisive.

That campaign began with the promulgation in 1517 of Luther's *Ninety-Five Theses* on the sale of indulgences. A thesis is a statement that can be challenged or defended, and a set of theses shapes a debate to be held on an issue by two persons of opposing viewpoints. Normally, such debates, or disputations, took place in university settings, and centered on issues important mainly to scholars. Luther's theses are different: they respond to events occurring in the public square that impinged on the lives of ordinary people.

This was the triggering event: a Dominican friar had been commissioned to sell letters of indulgence throughout the German lands—documents promising forgiveness of sins committed not only by the living but also those already dead—the profit from which was intended to fund a new basilica of Saint Peter, the pope's church, in Rome. Luther's theses challenged the efficacy of indulgences, the plausibility of the theory behind them, the motives of the pope and church hierarchy, and the injustice of draining money from the poor to support luxury consumption by a privileged class in a foreign land. The *Ninety-Five Theses* quickly circulated throughout Europe, and aroused a furor of unprecedented intensity that would power the unfolding Reformation.

Although they probe contradictions in contemporary church practice, Luther's *Ninety-Five Theses* imply but do not constitute a new theology. But he had already begun to formulate such a theology even before 1517, and by 1520, in three powerful treatises, he announces the fundamental principles of what was to become a reformed Christian church. The electrifying message of the third of these treatises, *On the Freedom of a Christian*,[1] is that faith in

---

1. An equally possible translation of the title contains the word liberty, as in *On Christian Liberty*.

God through Christ frees the individual from subjugation to the law: the law, rites, and pronouncements of the church and its clergy, certainly, but also, by implication, any law.

This message not only propels the Reformation of the church, but also echoes down far longer corridors, into centuries when political or personal liberty rise up as matters for discussion and action. Luther does not intend, of course, a reign of lawlessness, quite the opposite: the faith-possessed Christian will be, in his view, a meticulous and disciplined observer of secular and religious law. But he opens up the possibility that each individual may possess an existential freedom that supersedes all other claims on his conscience. This is the remarkable promise of the last and most stunning of Luther's three treatises of 1520, after which Europe would never again be the same.

Luther's *Preface to the Letter of Saint Paul to the Romans* (1522) forms a tiny part of his *magnum opus*, the translation of the Bible from its original Hebrew and Greek into German[2]—a work that would become the foundation not only of religious experience in the Germanic regions, but also of its eventual national language and literature. But it is an exceptionally important part. Romans is one of the apostle Paul's thirteen letters[3] that form the major part of the twenty-one letters, or epistles; these in turn, together with the four gospels, the Acts of the Apostles, and the Book of Revelation, constitute the New Testament; while the New Testament itself constitutes the sequel to the much larger Old Testament, or Hebrew Bible. As few Bible-reading Christians realize, the epistles, for the most part, predate the gospels, and are among the very earliest texts of the New Testament. And yet in these works written during the first decades after the crucifixion of Jesus Christ, the basic principles of Christian theology are already enunciated. No one enunciates them more clearly than Paul, and nowhere more completely and forcefully than in Romans. It is these ideas that Luther distills in his preface to Paul's letter, and in most concentrated form in its introductory section, as seen in the excerpt given below.

By the period of 1520 to 1522, Luther had established the foundations of his theology. But now it was necessary to put the Reformation into action, and that meant dealing with existing secular institutions and preparing for the long-term stability of the new church. These are the concerns of the two works *On the Power of the State* and *The Small Catechism*, written respectively in 1523 and 1529, from which are taken the final two excerpts presented in this chapter. The first describes the relations that are to prevail between the new church and the still existent and indispensable state. The second looks to

---

2. The New Testament was published in 1522, based on Erasmus' Greek edition; the whole Bible, in which Luther was assisted by other scholars, in 1534.

3. Those ascribed to him by the consensus of scholars.

the instruction of children in the new faith, so that the religious revolution Luther had instituted might be propagated to future generations.

If Christians who have been saved by faith in Christ are free from the law and judgment—this is the core of Luther's theology, explicated, as elsewhere, in his *On the Freedom of a Christian* and his preface to Saint Paul's letter to the Romans—what need is there then of the state? And if there is to be a state, what role do Christians have in it? And what authority can it exercise over Christians? In *On the Power of the State*, Luther answers these questions, providing, in effect, a new political theory suited to the age of Reformation. The state, he responds, is still needed. Genuine Christians will be only a handful in a sea of nominal or false Christians; and the latter, unless under the discipline of magistrates and judges, will be like wolves and wild beasts set loose among innocent sheep. Christians, in turn, should honor and respect the state, because by its power social order and harmony are maintained. They may even serve the state, if they wish, as magistrates, judges, and executioners: for these roles are essential, and Christians qualified to perform them will benefit their neighbors by doing so. But the authority of the state is limited: it may not rule in matters of belief, and it has no power over the conscience of Christians, which must remain unbound and free. At this peak moment of his career, Luther drew a vivid red line between church and state, and power and faith.

Just as it was essential to define the relationship of Christians to state power as the new Lutheran program unfolded, it was essential to plan for the instruction of the next generation of Christians. Luther's first followers were converts, who had accepted as adults their justification through faith, and so possessed the zeal of converts. But all subsequent generations would need to be inducted into the community of faith through the intervention of adults—parents, teachers, and pastors—who would guide them to commitment to the faith. Instruction in the essentials of Christian doctrine and the development of genuine conviction in a whole population were now paramount goals. Luther responded in 1529 with his two catechisms, or sets of questions and answers: first *The Small* and then *The Large Catechism*, the second an elaboration of the first. Powerfully compressed and concise, *The Small Catechism*, especially, equips young people with not only a basic theology, but also a set of attitudes on which to build a lifelong commitment to Lutheran, or Protestant, doctrine. It is still used for that purpose today.

In all, the works presented in this chapter span a mere dozen years, reflecting the earlier phase of Luther's career but not his souring mood as social turmoil and competing interests threatened to overcome his mission. That mission was to reestablish the Christian church on a whole new foundation: on faith, as each individual came to experience it, rather than on the authority of an institution that embodied the tradition of the church. Unlike all earlier critics of the church, Luther's confrontation demanded fundamental change—institutional, cultural, theological: change so fundamental that it could not eventuate without rupturing the fabric of the old system.

Could there have been a reform of the church—the abuses of power, the bureaucratic stasis, the accommodation of superstition and formalism—without a complete rupture? The earlier reformers pointed the way, and Erasmus had elaborated a complete reform program, based on the spiritual and intellectual elevation of each individual. But Luther understood, in time, that collectively, the resolution of all the matters that presented themselves for correction, improvement, and reformulation, would completely overturn the institutions, practices, and thinking of the church as it then was. Its reformation would require a revolution. And if what was needed was a revolution, he was willing to be its engine.

The believer's whole life should be one of repentance

from Martin Luther, *Ninety-Five Theses* (1517)

The issues Luther raises in his *Ninety-Five Theses* on the sale of indulgences range from some that are social or political in nature, to others that are profoundly theological. The complexity of his reasoning far exceeds the slimness of the work, which occupies only a handful of pages in a modern edition, while the forcefulness of his language attests to the intensity of his objections. A sampling of twenty-seven of the theses is given here, not quite one-third of the whole, which touch upon some principal themes.

Luther opens with a theological argument that questions the validity of indulgences—and if they have no sound basis in theology, he implies but does not state, surely it is improper to sell them? Indulgences cannot absolve sin, which can only be removed by God: God forgives the sinner who repents, whose whole life should be one of repentance. Selling indulgences can only encourage the greed of the salesman, while the Christian, rather than buying a promise that cannot be fulfilled, should instead give his money to the poor; for the pope himself (an ironic note here) would surely not permit his basilica of Saint Peter to be built with money squeezed from the purses of the poor. The real treasure of the church does not consist of the merits of the saints, which are drawn upon with the purchase of indulgences, but by the gospel of God's grace, which is freely given to all. The indulgence salesmen speak of "peace" and the "cross," but offer no peace, and do not follow the cross, which is the only true path to salvation—and not the "false assurance of forgiveness" that indulgences offer.

Luther's opening theses are concerned with repentance, a profound sense of remorse, which is not to be dispensed with by any empty ceremony performed by a priest.

1. When he said *Repent*, Jesus Christ, our Lord and master, wished the entire life of the believer to be one of repentance.[4]

2. This word "repentance" cannot be understood to mean the sacrament of penitence, comprising the rites of confession and satisfaction as administered by a priest.

3. Yet neither does it signal only an interior repentance, which really amounts to nothing, unless it is also enacted externally by some form of denial of the flesh.

4. So long as self-hatred endures (which is true inward repentance), punishment of sin remains, at least until we enter the gates of the kingdom of heaven. . . .

Only God, and not the pope, can relieve the faithful of the penalty for their sins.

6. The pope cannot remit[5] the guilt of any sin, but only declare and confirm that it has been removed by God. He may grant pardon, certainly, in cases reserved specifically for his judgment; but otherwise, the guilt absolutely remains. . . .

Luther turns in theses 13 to 16 to the condition of the dying and the dead, who are unaffected by church doctrine, but deeply troubled by their past and fearful about their future. In these theses, he gives notable attention to the psychological state of the person facing death and the afterlife, and strikingly casts the domains of the afterlife—hell, purgatory, and heaven—as psychological states.

13. Those still living will be freed from canon law[6] by death, and those who are already dead are no longer subject to it.

---

4. A critical point: the Latin Vulgate translation (from the Greek) of Jesus' command is *poenitentiam agite* (Matthew 4:17), which could be rendered as "do penance"; but after Erasmus' edition and translation of the New Testament, reformers argued that the sense was rather "repent," a command that did not indicate any specific rite or sacrament of the church.

5. Remit: "remove" or "pardon."

6. Canon law: the body of laws made by and pertaining to a church—in this case, the Roman Catholic church, where it still is operative today. Luther does not deny the validity of canon law here, but denies that it applies to the dead. If it did, those in the zone of the afterworld known as purgatory could be released from punishment for sin by ecclesiastical decree.

14. The dying necessarily fear death greatly if their lives have been lacking in piety or love; and the less pious and loving they have been, that much greater is their fear.

15. Such haunting fear is in and of itself as great (not to mention other things) as any punishment suffered in purgatory, since it approaches near to the horror of hopelessness.

16. Hell, purgatory, and heaven are related to each other as are the three conditions of hopelessness, fear, and the certainty of salvation. . . .

In theses 27 and 28, Luther responds to the claim for the efficacy of indulgences made by the jingle associated with their notorious purveyor, the friar Johann Tetzel, to which Luther alludes: "As soon as the coin in the coffer rings, the soul from purgatory springs." The claim, according to Luther, is absurd, as only God can judge the destiny of the immortal soul.

27. The notion is merely human that as soon as a coin clinks in the pot, the soul of a loved one is released from purgatory, and has no divine authority.

28. This much is certain: the coin clinking in the pot fuels avarice and greed; but the promises made by the church are solely God's to grant. . . .

In theses 32 and 33, Luther refutes even more forcefully the case for indulgences.

32. They are eternally damned, along with those who misguided them, who on the basis of letters of indulgence believe that their salvation is certain.

33. Beware, beware of those who say that these papal indulgences are equivalent to the inestimable divine gift by which man is reconciled to God. . . .

In theses 43 to 50, all but one opening with the ringing statement "Christians should be taught," Luther details behaviors and beliefs that are more meritorious than is the purchase of indulgences. His instructions crescendo to an implicit critique of the pope, who, Luther suggests, impoverishes his people in order to construct the lavish church of Saint Peter's in Rome.

43. Christians should be taught that giving to the poor or lending to the needy are deeds more worthy than the purchase of indulgences.

44. For by an act of charity, charity is increased, and the giver is made a better person; but the purchaser of an indulgence is not made a better person, but one, merely, who has escaped punishment.

45. Christians should be taught that the person who sees a pauper and passes him by, spending his money instead on indulgences, does not gain for himself the pope's mercy, but God's anger.

46. Christians should be taught that unless they possess more wealth than they need, they should preserve what must be kept for their household necessities, and not squander it on indulgences.

47. Christians should be taught that they are free to purchase indulgences, but they should not be required to do so.

48. Christians should be taught that, in granting indulgences, the pope both more greatly needs and more greatly wants their devout prayer than their ready money.

49. Christians should be taught that papal indulgences are useful only if no trust is placed in them, while they are most harmful if, because of them, they lose their fear of God.

50. Christians should be taught that if the pope only knew how the indulgence-preachers pillaged the buyers, he would prefer that the Basilica of Saint Peter's[7] be burned to ashes than built with the skin, flesh, and bones of his sheep.[8]

In theses 56 through 66 (56 and 62 are given here), Luther discusses the theory behind the issuance of indulgences, which pardon sins committed: they are atoned for by drawing on the "Treasury of Merits" stored in the church. But what is that treasure? Nothing temporal, Luther argues, nor the "merits" accomplished by Christ and the saints, which are always available to Christians; rather, they are the Gospel story of God's grace.

56. The treasures of the church, from which the pope grants indulgences, are not sufficiently known nor understood by the people of Christ. . . .

62. The true treasure of the church is the holy Gospel of the glory and grace of God.[9] . . .

In the last four theses of the ninety-five, Luther reminds readers of the fundamental goods of peace and the cross, which are mocked by the traffic in

---

7. The indulgences being sold in the campaign led by Tetzel were meant to raise funds for the building of a new basilica of Saint Peter.

8. The Christian people are the "sheep," whose pastor, which means "shepherd," is the pope.

9. The word "gospel" means "news" or "announcement"; the four gospels of the New Testament collectively present the "news" or narrative of Jesus' birth, mission, and death. God's "grace" is his generous care for humankind, illustrated in the Gospel.

indulgences, and exhorts the faithful to follow Christ through pain and suffering, rather than grasp the false confidence that indulgences provide.

92. Farewell then, farewell to all those prophets who say "Peace, peace" to the people of Christ, where there is no peace.

93. Welcome, welcome to all those prophets who say "The cross, the cross" to the people of Christ, where there is no cross.

94. Christians are to be exhorted to follow Christ their head zealously through punishment, death, and hell.

95. For through these many tribulations they will more surely gain entrance to heaven than by trusting in a false assurance of forgiveness.

A free lord of all things, subject to no one

from Martin Luther, *On the Freedom of a Christian* (1520)

In November 1520, culminating an extraordinary year—the year in which he broke decisively with the Roman church—Luther wrote *On the Freedom of a Christian*. In it he defines two possibilities for the human condition: freedom or servitude. His categories, notably, do not refer to social or political circumstances as they would have for many thinkers before or since, but to a spiritual state. A person is free, and ipso facto a Christian, if he has by God's grace attained faith in Jesus Christ as savior; and a person who has not done so is neither free, nor a Christian, but a slave to sin and death. This absolute distinction between members of the same community on the basis of receptiveness to divine grace is both shocking and exhilarating. It inaugurates an original religious movement that would marshal mass support and release extraordinary energies.

But what do freedom and servitude mean for Luther? Presenting his case with the same symmetry that he presents his two propositions at the outset, he defines freedom as freedom from law—for a believing Christian is saved by faith, and not by obedience to the law; and servitude as subjection to the law, and a fruitless pursuit of innocence by acts of will that are forever doomed to be insufficient. Yet, Luther argues paradoxically, the Christian, though freed from the law, will fulfill the law. He successfully fulfills its requirements precisely because he does so not in order to achieve salvation, but out of love of God by whose grace he is already saved and free.

Introduction

1. So that we might thoroughly discern what a Christian is and the nature of the freedom that Christ obtained for and gave to him, about which Saint Paul has written so much,[10] I shall posit these two conclusions:

A Christian is a free lord of all things and is subject to no one.

A Christian is a dutiful servant in all things and is subject to everyone. . . .

2. To resolve these two contradictory statements on freedom and servitude, we shall consider that every Christian has a double nature: a spiritual and a physical. In regard to the soul, he is called spiritual, new, internal man;[11] in regard to flesh and blood, he is called a physical, old, and external man. And it is because of these differences that, as I have just said, he is mentioned in the Scriptures both in terms of freedom and servitude, one directly contrary to another.

The Internal Man

3. When we consider the interior, spiritual man in order to see what would be necessary for him to be, and to be called, a pious,[12] free Christian, it becomes clear that no external thing, of whatever name, can make him either free or pious; for his piety and freedom, or, on the other hand, his wickedness and imprisonment, are neither physical nor external. How does it help the soul if the body is unbound, fresh, and healthy, and eats, drinks, and lives however it likes? On the other hand, how does it damage the soul if the body is imprisoned, sick, and feeble, and hungers, thirsts, and suffers against its wishes? None of these things reach the soul, either to free or imprison her, or to make her pious or evil.[13]

4. Thus there is no help for the soul if the body puts on holy garments, as do the priests and clergy; nor if the body is in churches and holy places; nor if it is occupied with holy matters; nor if it physically prays, fasts, goes on a pilgrimage, and does every good work[14] that might only ever happen through and in the body. It must then be something entirely different that brings and bestows piety and freedom to the soul. For an evil man, a hypocrite and fraud,

---

10. Luther alludes to 1 Corinthians 9:19.
11. "Man," as Luther uses the term in this treatise, refers to an individual human person.
12. "Pious" throughout this work suggests not merely a sincerely religious person, but also one who has been "justified" and made righteous by God.
13. The word "soul" in the Latin original, *anima*, is feminine in gender.
14. The performance of "good works" such as those named here were generally considered to be the pathway to salvation; but it is this notion that Luther fundamentally challenges.

may also possess or practice all of these above-mentioned objects, works, and manners. In this way, furthermore, people become nothing more than pure hypocrites. On the other hand, it does not damage the soul if the body wears unholy garments, is in unholy places, eats, drinks, does not go on a pilgrimage, and omits all the works that the above-mentioned hypocrite performs.

5. There is nothing, either in heaven or on earth, through which the soul can live and be pious, free, and Christian, besides the holy gospel, the word of God preached by Christ. . . .

7. Thus the only work and exercise of all Christians should rightly be that they establish the word and Christ within themselves, continuously exercising and strengthening such a faith. For no other work can make a Christian. . . .

The External Man

19. Now enough has been said of the internal man, of his freedom, and of the principal righteousness, which requires neither laws nor good works, and which can indeed be harmed if someone presumes to be justified in this way. Now we come to the second part, to the external man. Here we wish to answer all those who are vexed by the previous discussion and who are in the habit of saying: "Well, so then faith is all things and is alone sufficient to make one pious. Why then are good works commanded? For we would be in good shape without doing anything." No, my dear man, not so. It would indeed be fine if you were solely an internal man and became completely spiritual and internal, but this will not happen until Judgment Day. On earth there is and will continue to be, only a beginning and an increase, which will be completed in the next world. . . . Therefore here should be repeated what was said above: "A Christian is a dutiful servant and is subject to everyone," or in other words, where he is free, he has to do nothing; where he is a servant, he must do all manner of things. How this happens we shall now see.

20. Although through faith a man is sufficiently justified internally, in regard to the soul, and has everything that he should have (though this faith and sufficiency always ought to increase until the next life), nevertheless he still remains on earth during this physical life and must rule his own body and interact with people. Here now works begin. He must not be idle; indeed, his body must be disciplined and trained with fasts, vigils, labors, and with every reasonable correction, such that it becomes obedient and in conformity to the internal man and to faith, rather than that it hinder or resist them, as is its way when it is not constrained. For the internal man is one with God, happy and merry for the sake of Christ, who has done so much for him, and all of his pleasure consists in also serving God in return, gratuitously and freely out of love. Yet he finds in his flesh a recalcitrant will which wants to serve the

world and seeks only what pleases it. Faith cannot tolerate this, and gladly seizes it by the throat to subdue and bridle it. . . .

21. But these same works must not be done in the opinion that man thereby becomes pious before God. Faith cannot tolerate this false opinion, for it alone is, and must be, the source of piety before God. Instead, works must be done in the opinion that thereby the body is made obedient and purified of its evil passions. . . . And yet works are not properly good, nor make him pious and righteous before God, rather he does them gratuitously and freely out of love, in order to please God; thereby not seeking or attempting anything else from them, than that they please God, whose will he gladly does to the best of his abilities. . . .

23. Thus these two sayings are true: "Good, pious works never make a good pious man, but a good pious man does good pious works. Evil works never make an evil man, but an evil man does evil works." Therefore, the person must always be good and pious first, before all of his good works, and good works follow and proceed from the pious, good person. . . .

Just as works do not make one believing, neither do they make one pious; but just as faith makes one pious, so it also makes one do good works. So then works make no one pious, and a man must first be pious before he works. Thus it is clear that faith alone, by sheer grace and through Christ and His word, makes a person sufficiently pious and saved. And that no work, no commandment, is necessary for a Christian's salvation, rather he is free of all commandments; and everything he does, he does out of sheer freedom, gratuitously, not seeking from it any benefit or salvation but only to please God; for he is already satisfied and saved through his faith and God's grace. . . .

25. From all this it is easy to understand the ways in which good works are to be condemned and not condemned, and how one should understand all doctrines that teach good works. For where these contain the false stipulation and the perverse opinion that we become pious and saved through works, then already such works are not good and are completely damnable, for they are not free and blaspheme the grace of God, who alone makes us pious and saved through faith. . . .

30. From all of this the conclusion follows that a Christian does not live within himself, but in Christ and his neighbor; in Christ through faith, in his neighbor through love. Through faith he rises above himself into God; from God he descends once again below himself through love, and yet remains always in God and divine love. . . . Behold, that is the proper, spiritual, Christian freedom, which makes the heart free of all sins, laws, and commandments, and which surpasses all other freedom as heaven surpasses the earth. May God grant that we properly understand and uphold this freedom. Amen.

Faith alone justifies and fulfills the law

from Martin Luther, *Preface to the Letter of Saint Paul to the Romans* (1522)

"This Letter is the true foundation of the New Testament, and the purest statement of the Gospel." Characteristically, Luther does not hesitate to make a claim of the highest magnitude: that here, in this letter that Paul wrote c. 56–57 CE from Corinth to the infant church in Rome, are presented succinctly all the major themes of the Christian message. The excerpt that follows consists of the larger part of Luther's preface within his preface: his definition of the terms Paul uses that Luther identifies as critical to an understanding of Christian faith and life. He explains that what is required of a Christian is not the mere outward observance but a vibrant inner acceptance of God's law; that sinfulness, likewise, is not constituted by external and superficial behaviors of the "flesh," but by internal and spiritual rebellion against God's will; and that the necessary profound and inward openness to God is acquired not by human decision but by God's grace. The linchpin is faith: by faith in God, that God bestows by grace, the Christian is made righteous, or just, and absolved of all sin.

More striking even than the coherence and daring of Luther's theology, derived from Paul's letter to the Romans, is the simplicity of the language in which these complex thoughts are stated. Like an artist whose palette offers only a few colors, Luther writes with only a few words, a minimal vocabulary. But the words are like boulders on the road: massive, dominating, unmistakable; Law, Sin, Grace, Faith; and "heart," "word," "will"; and "work," "inner," and "outer." The meanings are complex and abstract. The language is from the earth.

This Letter is the true foundation of the New Testament, and the purest statement of the Gospel. As such, it is essential not only that a Christian understand it thoroughly, each and every word, but that he daily return to it: for it is daily bread for his soul. It can never be read too often or studied too much, and the better it is known, the more precious and profitable it becomes. And so I want to do it due service by providing this Preface as a guide, . . . so that everyone can understand it fully. Before now, its message has been obscured by commentaries and useless chatter; but stripped of these, it is in itself a brilliant lamp, quite bright enough to illumine the whole Bible.

To begin, we must become familiar with the language Paul uses in this letter, and know what he means by these words: Law; Sin; Grace; Faith; Righteousness; Flesh; Spirit; and more. Otherwise, nothing can be gained from reading it.

Law

Law, a little word, must not here be understood as it is used in the world, as something that instructs you what to do or what not to do. This is how the law works on earth, where you do enough if you do what you are told to do, whether or not your heart is in it. But God looks deep into the heart; and his law, likewise, judges what is in your heart. So God is not so concerned that you have done the right thing, but that you have done it sincerely—and if it has not been, he will punish you all the more harshly as a liar and a hypocrite. . . .

For outwardly, you keep the law by doing good works, out of fear of punishment or hope for reward. All this you do without any desire to do so or from love of the law, but rather unwillingly and by force, as though you would behave quite differently if the law did not exist. From which it appears that you, in the depths of your heart, are an enemy of the law! . . . How can anyone hope to make progress through good works when he performs those works with an unwilling and unloving heart? How will you please God by works that proceed from a sullen and resentful heart? . . . .

But to fulfill the law is to do its work with joy and love, and freely, unburdened by the force of law, to live a godly and goodly life as though there were neither law or punishment. It is the Holy Spirit that implants such joy and unforced love in the heart. . . . But the Spirit is only given in, with, and through faith in Jesus Christ . . . And so it comes about that faith alone justifies, fulfilling the law. . . . And it is only from faith that good works proceed. . . .

Sin

Sin in the Bible means not just the external actions of the body, but rather all the forces that direct and impel those external actions, namely the potent impulses of the innermost heart. . . . For indeed, no external sinful act is effected unless a man applies to its accomplishment all the force of body and soul. And the Bible especially probes within the heart to seek out the root and matrix of all sin, which is unbelief lying deep within the heart. In the same way, therefore, that faith alone justifies us, readying our spirit and will to do outward works that are good, so also unbelief alone engenders sin, inciting the body and its desires to do outward works that are evil . . . .

Grace

Grace . . . signifies both the loving kindness that God feels for us, and the benevolence that moves him to pour into us Christ and the Holy Spirit with its gifts. . . . Daily must we receive these gifts and the Spirit, and even so they are not complete, since evil desires and sins persist within us that strive against the Spirit. . . . Because of our unslain flesh we are still sinners, but because we have faith in Christ, and have begun to live in the spirit, God shows us such kindness and mercy that he disregards our sins and does not condemn them. Instead, he accepts us on the basis of our faith in Christ until our sin is slain.

Faith

Faith is not the stuff of human dreaming and seeming that is often mistaken for true faith. And when people see that there results from that false faith neither virtuous living nor good works, then given what they have seen and heard, they fall into error, and say: "Faith is not enough; if one wishes to live righteously and reach heaven, one must do good works." And so when they hear the Gospel, they go so far afield that they conjure up in their own imagination a notion in their heart that claims, "I believe." And they are convinced that this notion is real faith. But since it is a human construct and contrivance that never really touches the depths of the heart, it is useless, and goes nowhere.

But faith is God's work in us, that changes us, and gives us new birth from God. . . . Oh, what a living, striving, building, mighty thing is faith, which cannot ever cease to generate good. Faith does not ask whether there be good works waiting to be done, but before the question is asked, it has already done them, and is always doing them. But the man who does not act like this is a man without faith. He grabs and gropes for faith and good works, but knowing neither what faith is, nor works, he blathers and babbles endlessly about faith and good works.

Faith is an unfailing, unmoving confidence in God's grace, a confidence so sure that one would die for it a thousand times. . . . Uncoerced, willingly and joyfully, the man who is grounded in faith will do good to everyone, serve everyone, suffer any harm for the love and glory of God who has shown him such grace. It is as impossible, assuredly, to separate works from faith as it is to separate light and heat from fire. . . . Pray to God to work faith in you. Otherwise, you will be forever without faith, no matter what you wish or will to try or to do.

Righteousness

Now Righteousness stems from this kind of faith, for it is understood as the "righteousness of God": that is to say, the righteousness that God himself issues, as is the will of Christ our Mediator, giving it to us and counting it as righteousness. In this way, he so changes us that we give to every man what is his due, since through faith we become sinless, and so eager to obey God's commands. In consequence, we render to God the honor due him, remitting to him all that we owe; and so too we serve all men willingly, as best as we are able, and remit to every man what is owed him. . . .

Flesh

Flesh and Spirit must also not be misunderstood here, so that Flesh pertains only to unchastity, and Spirit to what is in the heart. Rather Flesh, according to [the apostle] Paul, connotes all that is born of the flesh: the whole human being, including body and soul, reason and senses, since all these of our components are bound up with the flesh. . . . [Paul] says that the law is weakened by the flesh:[15] not by the sin of unchastity alone, that is, but by all sins, especially that of unbelief, which is of all the sins the most spiritual.

Spirit

Similarly, a person may be spiritual who is concerned with doing works that are external, like Christ when he washed his disciples' feet, and Peter, when he took his boat out to fish.[16] So a person is "flesh" when both inwardly and outwardly he lives and acts to benefit the flesh and serve his worldly existence; but he is "spirit" when both inwardly and outwardly he lives and acts to benefit the spirit and serve the life that is eternal. [*Luther now reasserts the importance of these definitions.*] Unless you understand these words as they have been explained here, you will never understand this letter of Saint Paul's nor any other book of the Holy Bible. Stay away, then, from any teachers who use these words in any other sense, whoever they may be, whether Jerome, Augustine, Ambrose, Origen, or any other such, and any even more famous than these.[17] Now let us examine the letter itself.

. . . . .

A chapter-by-chapter explication of the letter follows, concluding:

So this letter, in sum, gives us the richest possible guide to what a Christian should know: namely, the meaning of Law, Gospel, Sin, Punishment, Grace, Faith, Righteousness, Christ, God, Good Works, Love, Hope, and the Cross. . . . The whole letter is solidly grounded in scripture and illustrated by

---

15. Romans 8:3: "For what the law was powerless to do because it was weakened by the flesh, God did by sending his own Son in the likeness of sinful flesh to be a sin offering."
16. John 13:3–5; Matthew 4:18–20.
17. Luther names four of the greatest late-ancient Church Fathers.

examples from Paul's own life and the words of the prophets, so that nothing whatever is lacking. So it seems as though Saint Paul wished in this one letter to sum up in brief the whole of Christian and evangelical teaching. . . . Each and every Christian, therefore, should read this letter closely and often. May God grant his grace to do so. Amen.

Over the soul, God can and will grant authority to no one but himself alone

from Martin Luther, *On the Power of the State* (1523)

Luther's substantial treatise *On the Power of the State* describes the delicate balance that is to be maintained between a society of Christian believers and a secular state whose main role is to maintain order and punish defiance of the law. Its three parts deal with distinct issues. The first defines in six carefully reasoned arguments the proper relationship of Christians to the state. Although Christians are by their faith free of the law and have no need of the state, the state is nonetheless required to provide order and punish wrongdoing in a wider society where, in fact, Christians are few. Christians are not to undermine the state, therefore, but to respect and support it as best they can. The second part of the treatise asks how far the authority of the state may extend, and argues emphatically that it may only regulate the material and external lives of Christians; it must not impinge on the soul, or heart, or conscience of a Christian, which is subject only to God and must remain absolutely free. The third part admonishes the ruler of the state to behave in a Christian manner, continuing a long tradition of princely advice literature that culminated in Erasmus' works, especially his *Education of a Christian Prince* (1516). Excerpts from the first two parts are given below.

Part One: To what extent is obedience owed to the state?

> . . . . First: We must investigate the basis of worldly power and dominion, so that no one may doubt that it has been established on earth by God's will and direction. . . . *[The previous point is developed at length, and concludes as follows.]* And so it is sufficiently certain and clear that it is God's will that worldly power and dominion have been established to punish evildoers and to protect believers. . . .
>
> Second: Against this view weighty arguments can be made. . . . *[A series of New Testament passages are cited that advocate nonviolence and forbearance in*

response to wrongdoing.] These and similar statements appear to say clearly that the New Testament envisioned a Christian society undisciplined by any secular power. . . .

Third: In response to this critique, we must recall that Adam's children, who make up humankind, are of two sorts: those who belong to God's kingdom, and those subject to earthly power. . . . Clearly, those of the first sort need neither the power nor dominion of a secular state. And if the whole world was filled with genuine Christians, who truly believed, no princes, kings, or lords, no law or punishment, would be necessary or useful. What purpose would these have? For Christians possess in their hearts the Holy Spirit, which teaches them and guides them to harm no one, to love everyone, and willingly and cheerfully to suffer any injury, even death, inflicted on them by anyone. . . . And so it is impossible that earthly power and dominion can have any work to do among Christians, since they do on their own more than is required by any machinery of law and punishment. . . . But the unrighteous do nothing that is right, so are in need of the law to instruct, compel, and coerce them to obedience. . . .

Fourth: All those who are not Christians belong to the earthly kingdom, and are under the law. For since few believe, and even fewer live as Christians, . . . God has placed them outside of the Christian community of the kingdom of God and constructed for them another kingdom that exercises power over them. In that condition, however much they want to, they cannot perform their evil deeds; or if they do, they do so in fear, anxiety, and wretchedness. . . .

If anyone tried to rule the world according to the Gospel, dispensing with all worldly power and dominion, on the grounds that everyone was baptized and a Christian whom the Gospel exempts from the sway of Law and Sword, as these would not be necessary—friends, consider, what would be the outcome? He would release from their chains and cages wild, savage dogs to rip and rend their victims' flesh, while maintaining these were fine, gentle, harmless little puppies. But my aching wounds would tell the real story. Thus would evildoers, posing as Christians, abuse the freedom of the Gospel. . . .

To avert this end we must say: It is certainly true that Christians in and of themselves are not subject to worldly power and dominion, and do not need to be. But before instituting a Christian and evangelical regime, you must first take care to fill the world with real Christians. In truth, you will never do so, for the world's masses are and remain unchristian, however much they have all been baptized and go by the name of Christian. . . .

Fifth: Then you might say, if as you say above Christians have no need of worldly power and dominion, why then does Paul instruct all Christians in Romans 13:1 that *Everyone must submit to governing authorities,* and in

1 Peter 2:13: *Submit yourselves for the Lord's sake to every human authority*,[18] etc.? To which I answer: As I have already said, Christians by, among, and for themselves need no worldly power and dominion over them, as it is neither useful nor necessary for them; but since a true Christian while on this earth lives and cares not for himself alone, but rather for his neighbor, so as directed by spirit dwelling within him, he acts not to meet his own needs, but to do what is useful and necessary for his neighbor. And since the power of the state is a greatly needed force throughout the world to preserve peace, punish sin, and control evildoers, so he submits himself willingly to that power, pays his taxes, respects those in authority, serves, helps, and does whatever he can to support that power, so that it will be respected, obeyed, and feared. . . .

Sixth: Next you ask whether then a Christian may exercise state power and so punish evildoers. . . . To which I answer, . . . that you are obliged to serve and promote public authority as much as you can, with your body, possessions, respect, and soul. . . . And you should, if you see that there is need of hangmen, jailers, judges, lords, or princes, and you deem yourself to be qualified, apply for and secure that position, so that the necessary power of the state is not undermined, weakened, or allowed to fail. For the world cannot and dare not do without it. . . .

Part Two: How far does the power of the state extend?

Now we come to the main issue of this treatise. For now that we have established that a secular state is necessary on this earth, and we have seen how it is to function in a fair and Christian manner, we must now inquire how long its arm and how wide its hand may extend, so that it does not reach too far and impinge on the sovereignty and power of God. . . .

For every state must have its laws and authority, and without law, no state can stand. . . . But the laws of a secular state pertain only to the body and to possessions and such external things of this earthly life. For over the soul, God can and will grant authority to no one but himself alone. Accordingly, when worldly power extends itself to exercise authority over the soul, God's sovereignty is injured, and souls are corrupted and destroyed. . . .

When a man-made law addresses the soul—that it should believe this or that—it is a human mind that issues the decree, and that decree is not the word of God. And if it is not the word of God, then it may not be God's will. For we cannot know whether what God has not commanded is pleasing to

---

18. Romans 13:1 and 1 Peter 2:13.

him; and indeed, we know that it is not. For it is God's will that our faith be grounded solely and purely on God's word alone. . . .

No one should or can command the soul unless he is able to show it the way to heaven. But that no man can do, but only God alone . . . Now tell me, how can a mortal man see, understand, assess, discern, or change the human heart? These powers are reserved for God alone. . . .

They live like dumb cows and unthinking pigs

from Martin Luther, *The Small Catechism* (1529)

In a masterful act of compression, Luther provides in *The Small Catechism* a concise statement of Lutheran belief that is uncompromising in its adherence to doctrine but accessible even to the very young. It is preceded by an injunction to pastors and parents to prepare children adequately as Christians: this, not the observance of theological niceties or attending to administrative trivia, is the goal of their ministry. Of paramount importance for Luther is that children understand the elements of faith. They must first master the words of key texts, but then proceed to comprehend their significance. This is the road not only to their own salvation, but that of multitudes, for it is from those who have been carefully instructed as children that future leaders will come. Following the preface, eleven brief chapters present texts essential for an understanding of Christian doctrine and their exposition in question and answer form. Strikingly, the father of the family is directed to instruct the whole of his household using *The Small Catechism* as his tool. He is made thereby, along with the pastor, responsible for the propagation of the faith. Given here are excerpts from the preface "To all faithful and godly pastors and preachers," and from the sections on the Ten Commandments and the Lord's Prayer.

Preface: To all faithful and godly pastors and preachers

The miserable, woeful dereliction that I recently observed when I visited our parishes have pushed and driven me to prepare this little, plain, simple Catechism, or guide for Christian instruction. Help me dear God, what awful wretchedness did I see! The common folk especially in the villages, know absolutely nothing of the Christian faith, and sad to say, many pastors are wholly ignorant and incompetent to teach. As a result, though they are all called Christians, who have been baptized and admitted to the holy sacraments, they know neither the Lord's Prayer, nor the Apostles' Creed, nor the Ten Commandments,[19] and live like dumb cows and unthinking pigs. . . .

O you bishops, how will you answer one day when you stand before Christ that you have so shamefully neglected the people, and have not for even a moment performed your duty? . . . It concerns you not at all whether the people you serve know the Our Father, the Creed, the Ten Commandments, or any particle of the word of God. Woe to you, woe forevermore!

Therefore I entreat you all, my dear friends and brothers who are pastors and preachers, for God's sake, perform your duties with diligence, have compassion on your people who have been entrusted to you. Help us to bring this catechism to all people, and especially to the young, and if you can do no more at least do this: take up this guide and teach it to the people word for word, as follows.

First: Preachers should above all things set aside the many and various texts and versions of the Ten Commandments, the Lord's Prayer, the Apostles' Creed, the sacrament of the Lord's Supper, and so on. Rather, they should adopt and adhere to one version only, to be taught year in and year out. . . .

Second: When the people have mastered the text, then teach them also what it means, so that they may understand its significance. . . .

Third: When you have taught them this Small Catechism, then take up the Large Catechism, and so impart to them a richer and broader understanding. . . .

You should make a special effort to urge magistrates and parents to instruct the children well and send them to school. You must explain to them that it is their duty to do so, and that it is a damnable sin if they do not, by which they wreck and ravage the kingdoms both of God and of the world, making themselves the fierce foes of both God and humankind. And make it clear how they gravely harm the children if they do not help them to become pastors, preachers, teachers, and so on, for which neglect God will punish them terribly. . . .

So get busy, pastors and preachers! The responsibility we bear now is different than previously under the pope: it has become serious and essential. Now there is more trouble and effort, more risk and struggle, but less praise or thanks. But Christ himself will be our reward, if we labor faithfully. . . .

The preface to pastors and preachers is followed by eleven chapters of basic lessons in Christian doctrine. The first chapter presents the Ten Commandments, to each of which Luther adds an explanatory note in question and

---

19. The Lord's Prayer, taught by Jesus to his disciples (Matthew 6:9–13), is frequently recited by Christians alone and in congregations. The Apostles' Creed (documented from the fourth century) is one of the earliest formulations of essential church doctrine and is confessed by many Christian churches. The Ten Commandments (Exodus 20:1–17, Deuteronomy 5:4–21) contain moral laws central in both Jewish and Christian traditions.

answer form, as illustrated in this excerpt containing commandments seven through nine (Exodus 20:15–17).

From *The Ten Commandments*

The father of the family should explain them simply in this way to all in his household. . . .

THE SEVENTH COMMANDMENT

You shall not steal.
Question: What does this mean?
Answer: We should so fear and love God that we do not take our neighbor's money or goods, nor acquire them by deceitful dealing or bargaining, but rather help him to protect and improve his possessions and livelihood.

THE EIGHTH COMMANDMENT

You shall not give false testimony against your neighbor.
Question: What does this mean?
Answer: We should so fear and love God that we do not falsely lie to our neighbor, or trick, slander, or defame him; rather we should defend, praise, and think well of him.

THE NINTH COMMANDMENT

You shall not covet your neighbor's house.
Question: What does this mean?
Answer: We should so fear and love God that we do not seek by deceit to usurp his ownership of house or patrimony, pretending that usurpation to be just, but instead support and assist him in holding title to those properties.

In the third chapter of The Small Catechism, *Luther presents the Lord's Prayer, with some words of explanation following each phrase, as seen here for the first two verses (Matthew 6:9–10).*

From *The Lord's Prayer*

The father of the family should explain it simply in this way to all in his household.

ADDRESSING THE LORD

Our Father in heaven.
Question: What does this mean?

Answer: With these words God invites us to believe that he is our true father, and we his true children, and so we may turn to him in trust and confidence as loving children do their beloved father.

THE FIRST PETITION

Hallowed be your name,

Question: What does this mean?

Answer: God's name itself is holy; but in this petition, we ask as well that we may know and embrace his holiness.

Question: How does that happen?

Answer: When the word of God is taught plainly and purely, and we as the children of God respond by leading holy lives. Help us to do so, dear Father in heaven! . . .

THE SECOND PETITION

Your kingdom come,

Question: What does this mean?

Answer: The kingdom of God will surely come even without our asking; but we ask in this petition, that it come also to dwell within us.

Question: How does that happen?

Answer: When the heavenly Father gives us his Holy Spirit, so that we may by his grace believe his holy Word and lead holy lives, here now on earth and in heaven beyond for eternity.

THE THIRD PETITION

Your will be done, on earth as it is in heaven.

Question: What does this mean?

Answer: God's good and gracious will is surely done even without our asking; but we ask in this petition that it also be done within us.

Question: How does that happen?

Answer: When God assails and defeats every evil thought and desire of the devil, the world, and the striving of our flesh, that would cause us not to revere God's holy name or welcome his kingdom; and when he strengthens and maintains us in his word and faith until the end of our days, as is his good and gracious will.

Chapter Four: Luther's Lieutenants

Although reform had been in the air for years, indeed centuries, before Luther broke with the Roman church, the Protestant Reformation surely began in Wittenberg, its program carried out by Luther himself and a circle of friends and associates—Luther's lieutenants. Four of these figures are presented in this chapter, contemporaries born between 1486 and 1497, and dying between 1541 and 1560. Each represents a different kind of participation in the reform movement, and a different relationship to its instigator.

Andreas Bodenstein von Karlstadt (1486–1541),[1] one of Luther's first associates, was in 1512 Luther's sponsor for the doctoral degree in theology at the University of Wittenberg. Subsequently, the two together elaborated the fundamental ideas of the Lutheran reform movement. Both debated the papal advocate Johann Eck at Leipzig in 1519, and both were condemned by the papal bull of 1520 that marks Luther's break with the Roman church. But they would soon become enemies.

From May 1521 to March 1522, when after his appearance at the Diet of Worms Luther took refuge in the Wartburg Castle, his associates in Wittenberg supervised that city's evolution from the old to the new church. That transformation involved, for the most part, an effort of persuasion, conducted from the pulpit. But Karlstadt, with some colleagues, demanded more visible and structural reforms. On Christmas Day, 1521, at Karlstadt's direction, the Eucharist (the sacrament of Communion or the Lord's Supper) was for the first time celebrated in German rather than Latin, with the communicants partaking of both the bread and wine: for it was now to be understood that faith alone, and no ritual act or clerical posture, made the sacrament effective. The next month, the city council ordered images of saints, to which parishioners were most devoted, to be removed from the churches. Karlstadt's tract *On Extirpating Images*, explaining the rationale for that action, was published just days later, on January 27, 1522. Meanwhile, these changes provoked outbursts of popular violence. Alarmed, some of Luther's supporters urged his return.

On March 5, 1522, Luther returned to Wittenberg. He reversed Karlstadt's initiatives and restored order in the city, establishing, in eight magisterial sermons delivered between March 9 and 16, a more moderate agenda for the Wittenberg Reformation. Luther, too, opposed ecclesiastical images and paraphernalia, but he viewed Karlstadt's methods as disruptive and, still more

---

1. The surname "Karlstadt" designates not a noble seat but the city of his birth.

intolerable, a threat to the Christian freedom of the worshiper: "I will constrain no man by force, for faith must come freely without compulsion."[2]

Humiliated, Karlstadt left Wittenberg. Eventually, driven from the German lands altogether, he settled in Switzerland, where he joined the leadership of the Swiss Reformation. In the end, his drive to demystify the church was realized, and Karlstadt's way, more than Luther's, became established in modern Protestantism.

Argula von Grumbach (1492–c. 1554), an aristocrat by birth and outlook, was a more polished agent of Lutheran reform than Karlstadt, though equally determined. Like her contemporary Katharina Schutz, wife of the Strasbourg[3] reformer Matthew Zell, a second prominent female advocate of the early Reformation in Germany, Grumbach did so to defend someone else: in this case, an adolescent compelled to renounce his evangelical faith.

In 1522, the eighteen-year-old Arsacius Seehofer had journeyed to Wittenberg, returning to staunchly Catholic Ingolstadt as a convert to the new faith, with Lutheran books in hand. Arrested, examined, and pressured by threat of imprisonment and death at the stake, he recanted in the presence of the officials of the university, and was sentenced to the lesser penalty of exile.

This violent suppression of conscience outraged Grumbach. Over the next months, from September 20, 1523, to June 29, 1524, she wrote four letters in protest: one to the rector and faculty of the University of Ingolstadt, of which sections are given here; one to Duke William IV of Bavaria, whom she had known since childhood; and one each to the magistrates of the Bavarian cities of Ingolstadt and Regensburg.

None of her letters elicited a response, meeting "a wall of disdain."[4] Yet they aroused a furor nonetheless. An unidentified male reformer of some stature—several candidates have been suggested[5]—supplied a preface to her letter to the university officials, followed it with the charges made against Seehofer, and published the compilation, a conspicuous early use of the printing press in the service of the Reformation. It caught on, circulating in fifteen editions published before the end of 1523.[6]

---

2. Luther's second *Invocavit* sermon, March 10, 1522, as quoted in Sider, *Karlstadt's Battle with Luther*, 24. Full citation in Texts and Studies.

3. Strasbourg: now in modern France, but a German imperial city at the time of the Reformation.

4. *Argula von Grumbach: A Woman's Voice*, 44. Full citation in Texts and Studies.

5. *Argula von Grumbach: A Woman's Voice*, 56–61.

6. A sixteenth appeared early in 1524, two later in the sixteenth century, and two in the nineteenth before Matheson's authoritative 2010 edition in Argula von Grumbach, *Schriften*. For the print history, see Matheson's analysis at 38–48.

Despite this flicker of fame, Grumbach herself soon departed the stage. She remained in contact with both Luther and Spalatin,[7] by letter and in person, but those letters do not survive, and she is not heard from after 1530. She died in 1554, survived by only one of her children, Gottfried—a Protestant.

Meanwhile, in Wittenberg, Luther held sway with the able support of Philip Melanchthon (1497–1560),[8] his younger friend and loyal colleague, who expounded, systematized, and publicized Luther's theology. Following in the footsteps of the renowned humanist Johann Reuchlin, brother of Melanchthon's maternal grandmother and surrogate mother, Melanchthon raced to the top of the academic ladder. In 1518, he assumed the post of professor of Greek at the University of Wittenberg, just months after Luther had posted the ninety-five theses that sparked the Reformation. Melanchthon quickly joined the circle of those who forged a new theology grounded in Scripture and centered on the concept of justification by faith.

Primarily a scholar, Melanchthon differed markedly from Luther in temperament: he was quiet and restrained where Luther was bold and passionate. These qualities equipped him to serve as Luther's spokesman to high prelates, statesmen, and scholars, for whom he formulated concise statements of the new faith. In 1521, he published the first edition of his *Loci communes* (literally "Commonplaces," but more accurately "Fundamental Principles"), a manual of Lutheran thought based on the close reading of Saint Paul's letter to the Romans that had also been essential to Luther's theological evolution. In 1530, utilizing materials earlier compiled by Luther, he composed a brief statement of the Lutheran position for presentation to Emperor Charles V, which is known as the Augsburg Confession; this was followed by Melanchthon's longer explications of that document, in German and in Latin, as "Apologies" or "Defenses." An excerpt from the Latin *Defense of the Augsburg Confession*, which focused on the crucial doctrine of justification by faith, appears below. Meanwhile, Melanchthon had begun to construct a new pedagogy, reaching from the primary to the university level, that would marry Lutheran principles to humanist methodology—jettisoning scholasticism, seen as too closely identified with the theology of the Roman church. In both domains, the theological and the pedagogical, Melanchthon pursued a long strategy, preparing the materials by which key Lutheran principles might be transmitted to future generations, as indeed they have been.

In these and other ventures, Melanchthon's loyalty to Luther was unwavering. That loyalty achieved particular expression in his biography of Luther

---

7. Georg Spalatin, Latinized pseudonym of Georg Burkhardt (1484–1545), native of Spalt, a humanist, priest, and adviser to the Lutheran party in the early Reformation.

8. The unusual name is Greek for "black earth," the literal meaning of his German birth name, Schwarzerdt.

(1548), and in his Latin funeral oration delivered four days after Luther's death (1546), excerpts of which follow below. In that tribute, he places his lifelong friend among the sequence of patriarchs, prophets, apostles, and saints who have been and continue to be the leaders of the church.

Martin Bucer (1491–1551) was an early convert to the Reformation, having first been persuaded by Luther's arguments pronounced at the Heidelberg Disputation of 1518, which he attended. Although he was not one of the Wittenberg circle—as were Karlstadt, later disaffected; or Grumbach, a distant supporter; or Melanchthon, who succeeded to its leadership on Luther's death—he remained committed throughout his career to the core Lutheran doctrines of justification by faith and the paramount authority of Scripture as the word of God. In 1523, he joined the circle of Strasbourg reformers, where he labored especially to develop principles of church organization and promote unity among reform advocates. He remained in Strasbourg for more than twenty years, influencing John Calvin[9] during the latter's stay in 1538 to 1541, and leaving only in 1549, when the Strasbourg council, in the face of imperial pressure, wavered in its allegiance to reform. Invited to Geneva by Calvin and to Wittenberg by Melanchthon, Bucer accepted instead the invitation of the reforming Archbishop of Canterbury, Thomas Cranmer,[10] and took refuge in England, where he spent his last three years.

In Strasbourg, even as he engaged in lively discussion of theological matters with Erasmus, Melanchthon, and Calvin, and sought cooperation among the increasingly diverse Reformation churches, Bucer's main concern was to put Reformation doctrine into practice, molding local congregations into Christian communities. He brought his program of church-building with him to England, which was a kingdom not a city, and where the process of reform was directed from the top by leaders close to the center of power.

In this context, Bucer proposed in his treatise *De regno Christi* (*The Kingdom of Christ*), addressed to the young King Edward VI, a partnership of church and state in the construction of a Christian society. Like Luther, who had first aroused his zeal to reform the church, Bucer saw secular power as necessary to secure the peace and control the wayward, so that Christians could safely pursue their path to salvation. But Bucer went further, proposing a model of church-state unity that was, in terms of Luther's vision, ultimately repressive. However much he was a friend of princes, Luther would not allow the state to hold authority over conscience, for that would be to destroy Christian freedom, a principle that was for him sacrosanct: "For over the soul, God can and will grant authority to no one but himself alone."[11]

---

9. For Calvin, see Chapter Five.
10. For Cranmer, see Chapter Seven.
11. As Luther wrote in his treatise *On the Power of the State*; see Chapter Three above.

Touched by Luther in different ways, the four early followers who appear in this chapter were vehicles of the Reformation he launched—lieutenants in the sense that they entered the Reformation movement as followers of Luther, although Karlstadt and Bucer soon followed different pathways, and the noblewoman Grumbach was in no position actively to engage in a leadership role; only Melanchthon remained a lifelong companion and collaborator. Karlstadt eagerly sought to enact reform in the churches of Wittenberg, to be rebuked by Luther for his intemperance and driven not only from Wittenberg but eventually from Germany. Luther's disciple Grumbach fiercely rose to the defense of a young man who had imported to Catholic Ingolstadt Lutheran writings from Wittenberg. Bucer, a convert to the Lutheran cause even before the break with Rome, labored to establish churches and communities of Christians that embodied new Reformation ideals, an endeavor that led him some distance from Luther's original formulations. Melanchthon, the youngest of Luther's lieutenants, was the most tenaciously loyal to his mentor's ideals. He not only made Wittenberg the Rome of Lutheran reform, but inscribed Lutheran thought and doctrine in academic curricula adopted throughout the German lands and neighboring region, thus enlisting young minds for the new church over many generations to come.

Why else do we adorn them with golden crowns?

from Andreas Bodenstein von Karlstadt, *On Extirpating Images* (January 27, 1522)

Our deeds themselves declare how much we love images and idols, Karlstadt thunders: we adorn them and cherish them. It is because we love them that they must be destroyed and stripped utterly from the houses of God, for God requires us to love and worship only him. This is the simple and inarguable case Karlstadt makes against the deep-rooted custom of reverence for the images of saints that was the backbone of medieval religious practice. He further refutes arguments made in favor of images—that they instruct the common people who cannot read books; that they comfort the ill and dying; that they are prohibited by the Old Law (i.e., the commandments of the Old Testament) but not the New (the Gospels of the New Testament). In sum, images appeal to the flesh, while the truth of Christ is of the spirit. Images must be stripped from the altars of the churches, therefore, and taken down from the walls, so that Christians may worship God, as he has commanded, in spirit and in truth. Karlstadt's appeal is direct, dramatic, and compelling. It would be countered by Luther, but not because his essential points were incorrect.

Arguments:
1. It is impious, and in violation of the First Commandment, to have images in our churches and houses of God: *You shall have no other gods before me.*[12]

2. More harmful still, and diabolical, are the carved and decorated idols that sit on our altars.

3. It is, therefore, good, necessary, laudable, and righteous to destroy them, and confer instead all power and authority to scripture.

The houses of God are houses in which God alone should be praised, petitioned, and adored. . . . Images are frauds, bringing death to all who worship and love them. . . . It cannot be denied that we installed these so-called holy things in our churches out of love. If we had not loved them, we would not have set them in a place where God alone may dwell and reign. If we had known they were our enemies, we would have shunned, not welcomed them.

Our actions declare how we have loved images: Have we not bowed down before them as much as we bow to princes? Why else have we allowed them to be painted and bedecked with robes of velvet? Of damask? Of silver and gold? Why do we adorn them with golden crowns? With precious gems? And why show them all this honor and love that we do not readily show our children, wives, parents, rulers, and great lords?

Who could possibly believe us if we say: "We have not loved these idols, these carved and painted images"? When our own deeds say otherwise? God hates and despises these images, as I will explain, and regards them as abominations; and [given that] considers that we each become in his eyes the thing it is that we love. [Since] images are abominations, so we who love them have become abominable. . . .

This is why God said, right after he had given the commandment "You shall have no other gods before me": You must make no carved or graven images; you must make no likeness of anything that is in heaven above or on the earth below, or in the water; you must not worship them; you must not serve them. . . .[13]

With these words, God forbids any recourse to images, and routs the tomfoolery of the papists,[14] who by their clever trickery are always mangling

---

12. Exodus 20:3.
13. These statements paraphrase Exodus 20:4–5.
14. Papist: a term used by early reformers to denote supporters of the Roman church and pope.

scripture, turning white into black, and wrong into right. So one of them might say, "Of course, I do not worship images; I do not reverence them for themselves, but for the saints whom they represent." God's answer is brief and his words are clear: you shall not worship them; you shall not serve them; construe it however you may, this is my unshakeable command, you must not worship them, you must not bend your knee to them, you must not light a candle to them. If I had wanted you, God declares, to worship pictures of me or my saints, I would not have told you to not make images or likenesses. . . .

Nor is it true that images are the books of the common people;[15] for they cannot learn from them the way to salvation, since images offer no help whatever for gaining salvation, and nothing necessary for living a Christian life. . . .

Further, you must also understand this: I strongly urge those who are dying not to put their trust in a carved or painted crucifix. Such trust is misplaced: it can only bring those who are ailing to the bodily pains Christ suffered, which is of no use.[16] . . . But our image-lovers want the common people to experience the fleshly Christ, which benefits them not at all. They want them to feel how Christ suffered, rather than why he suffered. So they talk about his body . . . and his wounds;[17] but of the power of Christ, they say nothing. Yet without Christ's power, no one will be saved. . . .

Whereupon I say, even if images appear to be a good thing, yet we must not permit them in our churches and in the presence of believers. . . . If someone comes and argues that images inform and instruct the common people just as books do the learned, you must answer: "Since God has forbidden me to reverence images, I want to learn nothing from them." If another comes and argues that images call to mind the pains Christ suffered—so prompting the beholder to offer an "Our Father,"[18] and to think about God, who otherwise would neither pray to God nor think about him—to this person, Christian, you must respond: "God has forbidden images." Moreover, Christ says that God is a spirit, and that all who truly worship him, worship him in

---

15. The argument had been put forward by Gregory the Great (540–604) and others that images were the *biblia pauperum,* "Bibles of the poor." "Laity," here and henceforth, is translated as "common people," a phrase closer to the apparent meaning of the text.

16. Here Karlstadt references John 6:63 (Vulgate 6:64): "The Spirit gives life; the flesh counts for nothing."

17. The text reads "body, beard, and wounds," but "beard" is probably an error, and so is deleted here.

18. The Lord's prayer, also Paternoster, based on Matthew 6:9–13, often recited by believers in the Middle Ages—as it is today.

spirit;[19] but all those who worship God through images, worship him with lies, seeing only an illusory and external representation of God. . . .

So this, God says, is what you must do [to those who worship images]: Tear down and topple their altars, smash their icons, shatter their wooden idols, and burn their carved effigies.[20] . . . For we have no godly altars, only heathen or human ones. . . .

Often image-lovers say that the Old Law prohibits images, but not the New; and we follow the New, not the Old Law.[21] . . . To these opponents I make this answer: Dear friend, you say that the Old Law prohibits images. Will you therefore give them a place in the houses of God, and will you disregard that commandment? Why do you not also say that we need not honor our father and mother, since it is the Old Law that commands we do so? Murder, adultery, theft, and similar crimes, moreover, are forbidden on the same tablets[22] of the law that also prohibit images. And the prohibition against images is the first and principal one, while the prohibitions of adultery, theft, and so on, are given later, and are lesser. Why do you not also say: We will permit adultery, theft, murder, and such crimes, because the Old Law forbids them? But I say to you that God has forbidden images as much, and with equal force, as he has prohibited murder, theft, adultery, and the like. . . .

Not a woman's nonsense, but the word of God

from Argula von Grumbach, *Letter to the rector and council of the University of Ingolstadt* (September 20, 1523)

Born into the high nobility, Argula von Grumbach had the requisite prestige to challenge, though a woman, the leaders of the University of Ingolstadt, who had forced young Arsacius Seehofer to repudiate his Lutheran books and sent him into exile. She invites them to debate the matter, arguing that they had not proved that a single statement in those books was in fact hereti-

---

19. John 4:24: "God is spirit, and his worshipers must worship in the Spirit and in truth."
20. Karlstadt here paraphrases Deuteronomy 7:5, and in the next sentence, alludes to Exodus 20:4.
21. The Old and New Law: respectively, the commandments of the Hebrew Bible, known to Christians as the Old Testament, and Christ's life, teachings, and resurrection.
22. The Ten Commandments, the succinct statement of the Old Law, were engraved on two stone tablets; see Exodus 31:18.

cal: rather, they all were grounded in scripture, and so conveyed the word of God.

In her letter, Grumbach approves the works of Luther, whose German works she had read; recalls her father's gift to her, at age ten, of a Bible in a pre-Reformation German translation; and speaks movingly of her present experience of reading scripture. She lays out three sets of dualities that are the framework of her religious and cultural vision: the word of God as opposed to the church of Rome; the German as opposed to the Latin language; and the insurgence of the young and female (herself and Seehofer) against the old and male (the officials of the University of Ingolstadt). The latter are portrayed as tyrants who terrorized an adolescent with threats of imprisonment and death by fire—and were readying the same weapons to use against her. The German tongue is seen as a natural medium of discussion available to all members of the community, as opposed to Latin, the private preserve of university inmates. And the word of God, accessible to all Christians both male and female, is presented as an invincible force poised to vanquish the church of Rome.

Such words,[23] spoken by God himself, ring always in my ears: for they embrace women as well as men. And so, as one compelled by Christ himself, I write to you. . . .

My God, how do you expect to overcome this, you and your university, when you have so stupidly and despotically abused the word of God, making someone hold the holy Gospel in his hands and on the spot renounce it, as you have done with Arsacius Seehofer? Compelling him with the threat of imprisonment and death by fire to swear such an oath and sign such a testimonial, and so renounce Christ and his word? . . .

Show me by what authority you act, you mighty masters! I find it nowhere written in the Bible that either Christ, or his apostles, or any of the prophets imprisoned anyone, or sentenced anyone to exile or to death by fire or any other means. . . .

We all know well how much we owe obedience to our rulers. But over the word of God, they have no authority—not the pope, not the emperor, nor the princes. . . . But by God and the salvation of my soul, I declare that for me to renounce the writings of Luther and Melanchthon would be to renounce God and his word—which may God forbid forever. Amen.

. . . . .

How often I have heard your preacher, waving his decretals, screech at our women "Ketzer! Ketzer"—"Heretic! Heretic!" Pretty awful Latin that is!

---

23. Grumbach has just cited Luke 9:26: "Whoever is ashamed of me and my words, the Son of Man will be ashamed of them when he comes in his glory. . . ."

I could do as well myself, and I have never gone to university.[24] I have long been inclined to write to ask him to show me just what were the heretical dogmas that Martin Luther, that faithful servant of the Gospel, had taught. But I suppressed that impulse, and heavy-hearted, failed to act, recalling Paul's instruction that women should keep silent in church.[25] But now that I see no man ready to take up this matter and make himself heard, I am taking action.

. . . . . If commands could make people believe, why was belief not mandated to all unbelievers long ago? But this is the problem: it is the word of God that compels us, not the words of those composed of flesh and blood. You'll get nowhere by trotting out Arsacius Seehofer, putting in his mouth the oath you wrote for him, while puffing him up as an expert in the seven liberal arts. However much you wish to forget that he is only eighteen years old and still a child, no one else will forget. Already in this short time, from the news I hear on every side, everyone knows what fools you have made of yourselves. . . . . .

Are you not ashamed that Seehofer was made to renounce all the writings of Martin [Luther], who merely put the text of the New Testament into German? As a result, you have denounced as heretical the holy Gospel and the Epistles and the Acts of the Apostles.[26] And so there is no use arguing with you. . . . I haven't heard that any of you ever refuted from Scripture a single article of what [Luther] wrote. . . .

I beg you for the sake of God . . . to indicate to me just what it is that either Luther or Melanchthon has written that you find heretical. I find nothing in the German writings that seems heretical to me. A great deal of their work has been published in German, and I have read it; Spalatin sent me a complete list of the titles.

I have always sought to know the truth, although lately I have not been reading such books much, being immersed in the Bible, which all of Luther's work addresses anyway, so that everyone will read it. My beloved lord and father wished so much for me to read it, that he gave me one when I was ten

---

24. The German "Ketzer," derived ultimately from "Cathar," the name of one of many medieval heresies, was colloquially used for anyone deemed to be a heretic. Heresies, further, especially appealed to women, as Grumbach implies here, while mocking the learned accusers for dropping, in their accusatory frenzy, the propriety of Latin terminology. This is one of several occasions when Grumbach observes that she knows no Latin, not having received an advanced education, though she is literate in German.

25. Paraphrasing 1 Corinthians 14:34, while citing 1 Timothy 2, a similar injunction to silence.

26. Grumbach here names the components of the New Testament, omitting only the Book of Revelation.

years old.²⁷ But sadly, I did not obey him, dissuaded by my confessors,²⁸ especially the Observants,²⁹ who said that I would fall into error. Ah, but how splendid it is when the spirit of God teaches us and, more, helps us understand first this passage then that one, God be praised! revealing to me the real, true light shining forth.

. . . . .

I am not afraid to come before you, to hear what you have to say, and even to respond. For I can hear and respond to questions in German, and read them as well, by the grace of God. . . . May God grant that I may discuss these matters with you in the presence of our three princes and the whole community. . . . I am not afraid, so long as you wish to persuade me with words, and not, like tyrants, with threats of prison or the stake. . . .

I have no Latin, but you know German, the language in which you were born and reared. I have not written nonsense, like a woman, but like a Christian, the word of God, which the gates of Hell cannot withstand. But they can well withstand the Roman church! Just look at it—how could a church like that overcome the gates of Hell? . . . . .

By my hand,
Argula von Grumbach,
by birth von Stauff³⁰

If works can justify, of what use is Christ and our regeneration?

from Philip Melanchthon, *Defense of the Augsburg Confession* (1530)

Melanchthon is generally recognized as the primary author of the Augsburg Confession, a succinct statement of fundamental principles of Lutheran

---

27. A German Bible, apparently, of which there were some in circulation prior to Luther's.
28. Church officials opposed the reading of vernacular bibles by laypersons, suspecting they would be confused or deceived.
29. The Observants of whom Grumbach speaks belonged to the principal group of Franciscan friars, or "Friars Minor." She is being ironic, however; they were Observants, but they did not observe, in her mind, the truth that was vividly apparent in Scripture.
30. Grumbach's natal family were the von Stauff, a prominent family of the Bavarian nobility. As their name was more prestigious than her marital name von Grumbach, she sometimes used it to add distinction to her messages.

reform. After it had been attacked by opponents and rejected by Emperor Charles V, whom it was essential to persuade, Melanchthon further wrote two defenses of that Confession: one German, and briefer; the other Latin, and more extensive. The passage excerpted here, from the second defense, is a concise and precise exposition of the core Lutheran doctrine. Lacking even a glimmer of Luther's verve or passion, it is executed to meet the high professional standards of the day: it is systematic, highly-structured, and technical, for here Melanchthon speaks to the intellectual elite, combating scholastic theorists on their own ground. It centers on the two possibilities for "justification" (becoming "just," or "righteous") made available in Scripture: by fulfilling the commandments of the Old Testament; or by accepting the freely-offered promises of the New, by having faith in the atonement made for sins by Jesus Christ. But no one can fulfill the commandments of the Law, Melanchthon demonstrates; if that were possible, there would be no need of Christ. Instead, our justification, our regeneration, our salvation comes only through Christ, as a gift freely offered as was his death on the cross.

Article IV (II): On justification

Our adversaries condemn us for teaching that sins are forgiven not because of any merit of the sinner, but freely because of Christ, by faith in Christ. They condemn us, on the one hand, for denying that sinners may be forgiven their sins on account of their merits, and for affirming, on the other, that forgiveness of sins is accomplished by faith, and that through faith in Christ, sinners are justified. Now since this debate concerns an essential principle of Christian doctrine, which rightly understood enhances and amplifies Christ's glory . . . , we ask your Imperial Majesty kindly to listen to our views on this important matter. Since our adversaries understand neither the forgiveness of sins, nor the nature of faith, nor of grace, nor the meaning of justice, they wretchedly misconstrue this principle. . . . In order to clarify our position, and counter our opponents' objections, certain points must be made at the outset so that the bases of both sets of arguments, both theirs and ours, may be understood.

All of Scripture should be divided into these two parts: into law, and promises. . . . Of these two, our adversaries focus on the law—because in some way human reason naturally understands the law, having justice somehow divinely inscribed upon the mind—and seek to find by means of the law forgiveness of sins and the justification of the sinner. Yet the Decalogue[31]

---

31. Decalogue: the Ten Commandments.

requires not only external civil works[32] that could be effected in any case by reason alone, but it also demands other works, that derive from impulses beyond the rational: that is, genuinely to fear God, deeply to love God, sincerely to turn to God, truly to accept that God hears us, and to expect God's help at the hour of death and amid all afflictions; and it demands, finally, our obedience to God at our end and in our sorrows, lest we flee from, or resist, those burdens God has placed upon us.

Here the scholastics[33] . . . teach only a compliance with law empowered by reason, that is to say, civil works, and so pretend that reason, in the absence of the Holy Spirit, can love God above all other things. For so long as the human soul is apathetic, unaware of either God's anger or his judgment, it can believe that it wants to love God and perform good works for his sake.

Accordingly, these scholastics teach that humans can attain forgiveness for their sins merely by "doing what is in them"[34]—that is, if their remorse over their sinfulness elicits some act of love of God, or some good work performed for his sake. And this teaching, flattering humankind as it does, naturally has produced and proliferated many [flawed] practices in the church, such as monastic vows and abuses of the Mass. . . . And so as to foster and inflate people's confidence in such works, these scholastics announce that God necessarily bestows grace on anyone doing them—necessary not because God is compelled to do so, but because his ordinances are unchanging.

This view is riddled with many and pernicious errors, which would be tedious to enumerate. It is sufficient for the wise reader to consider this question: If this is Christian righteousness, what difference is there between philosophy and Christianity? If we merit the forgiveness of sins because of acts we have performed, how is Christ not diminished? If we can be justified by our reason, and the operations of reason, of what use is Christ or our regeneration? . . .

We have heard that some preachers, in their sermons, have set aside the Gospel and preach Aristotle's *Ethics*—nor are they wrong to do so, if the things our adversaries claim are true. . . . We see books that compare sayings of Christ to those of Socrates, Zeno, and other philosophers[35]—as though Christ had come for this purpose, to propose certain laws by which we might merit the forgiveness of sins, as though we do not receive that forgiveness

---

32. "Civil works": good works, motivated by compassion, performed within earthly communities.

33. Scholastics: the members of university faculties who had elaborated a complex theological system combining Aristotelian metaphysics and logic with the received tradition of Scripture and the Church Fathers.

34. A scholastic formulation, used to defend the free will efforts of humans to perform good works and atone for sin.

35. Socrates, the teacher of Plato, who first used the term "philosophy"; and the pre-Socratic philosopher Zeno of Elea, the presumed inventor of dialectic, a method of logical reasoning.

freely, because of his merits. If we accept, therefore, this doctrine of our adversaries, . . . then there is no difference between the justice conceived by philosophers . . . and Christian justice. . . .

But in fact, humans cannot by their own strength fulfill the law of God, and all are subject to sin, and to the punishment of eternal wrath and everlasting death. Therefore we cannot be freed from sin through the law, and justified, but we have instead been given the promise of the forgiveness of sins, and justification, on account of Christ, who was given for our sake to atone for the sins of the world, and appointed our Mediator and Propitiator.[36] And this promise is not conditioned on our merits, but freely offers the forgiveness of sins and justification. . . .

So this faith, which freely receives forgiveness for sins, employing its Mediator and Propitiator Christ to defeat God's anger—and does not employ our merits nor our love to defeat it—this faith is the true knowledge of Christ, and receives the benefits Christ offers, and regenerates our hearts, and enables the fulfillment of the law. And of this faith not a syllable is found in the teaching of our adversaries. Consequently, we fault our adversaries for teaching only the justice achieved through law, while they do not teach the justification offered in the Gospel, which preaches the justification achieved in Christ. . . . Nor do they see that by rejecting that faith, they annihilate entirely the promise of the free remission of sins, and justification through Christ.

Chosen by God for the reformation of the church

from Philip Melanchthon, *Funeral Oration for Martin Luther* (February 22, 1546)

In his funeral oration for Luther, given four days after the reformer's death, Melanchthon validates his mentor's career, identifying him as the key figure in the reconceptualizing and refounding of the church. In a spectacular image of the church of all the ages as a procession of its principals from Adam to Luther, Luther is envisioned as the heir to the patriarchs, the prophets, the apostles, the Church Fathers,[37] and the most acceptable of

---

36. "Mediator" because he is the intermediary between humans and God; "Propitiator" because he atones for, or satisfies, the requirements of the law.

37. Church Fathers: the theologians of the early Christian church, among them many bishops and saints, whose writings are, after the Bible itself, the foundation of Christian thought and doctrine.

medieval Christian thinkers—with not one scholastic philosopher, not even the acclaimed Thomas Aquinas, among their number.

Melanchthon further identifies Luther's main doctrinal contributions: the primacy of the Gospel as the word of God; justification by faith in Jesus Christ, and not by the works of the Law;[38] the confidence possessed in the faith of death by those so justified. He notes Luther's intellectual accomplishments as translator of the Bible, author of treatises and sermons, and director of the insurgent reform movement. Defending Luther against the charges of harshness and contentiousness, Melanchthon dwells on his affability, integrity, and courage. Finally, he reaffirms Luther's pivotal role in the whole of Christian history as the one chosen by God to restore his church, and so preserve the patrimony of his Son Jesus Christ. Melanchthon's oration, composed in Latin, was immediately translated into German and circulated in multiple editions, to be read as the final summation of Luther's achievement.

Though many godless men bitterly hated [our dearest father and teacher Martin Luther], yet we who know he was a God-appointed minister of the Gospel love and celebrate him. And we can demonstrate that his teaching did not consist, as these Epicureans[39] charge, of seditious opinions wildly hurled about, but that it was the expression of God's will, a guide to right worship, the exposition of Holy Scripture, and the declaration of the word of God, that is to say, the Gospel of Jesus Christ.

In orations delivered at times like these, it is customary to speak primarily of the private virtues of those who are eulogized. But I shall set that model aside, so that I may speak especially of this supremely important matter: Luther's service to the church. . . .

[God] raises up prophets, apostles, teachers, and pastors, . . . who read, hear, and love the writings of the prophets and apostles. . . . And it is a pleasant and worthwhile spectacle to behold the church of all the ages, and to consider the goodness of God, who has arrayed these worthy leaders one after the other in a continuous parade, so that as soon as those in the first ranks fall, immediately others march up to follow in their footsteps.

Melanchthon's lengthy enumeration of these worthies is given here in abbreviated form.

---

38. "Justification" also means, and is often translated as, the attainment of justice, or righteousness. The Law refers to God's commandments, communicated in the Old Testament. For Luther and his followers, the justification, or righteousness, obtained by obeying the Law is political in nature, tantamount to the just actions of those who obey the law of the state, whereas the justification obtained through faith in Christ is spiritual.

39. Epicureans: denotes an ancient school of philosophical materialists, whom Melanchthon along with other thinkers of this era anachronistically considered to be atheists.

Observe first the patriarchs Adam, Seth, . . . Methusaleh, Noah . . . who were succeeded by Isaac, Jacob, and Joseph . . . then by Moses, Joshua, Samuel, and David . . . and after them by [the New Testament prophets] Simeon, Zacharias, and John the Baptist, [then by] Jesus Christ and his apostles. It is a delight to behold this unbroken series of forebears, the visible witness of the presence of God in the church.

The procession continues also after the apostles, which although it is a somewhat lesser spectacle, yet it is adorned by witnesses to God: [the saint and martyr] Polycarp, . . . [Church Fathers and saints] Basil [of Caesarea], Augustine, . . . [medieval mystical writers] Hugh [of Saint Victor], [Saint] Bernard of Clairvaux, [Johannes] Tauler, and many others. And even if this last era has been less productive, yet God has always preserved a few. And now there has appeared a more splendid flame to light the Gospel sparked by the voice of Luther. . . .

What then were the great and worthy things that Luther accomplished, which make his career laudable? For many charge that he threw the church into disorder, and aroused a tangle of controversies—to these I respond that these troubles were caused by the church leadership. For when the Holy Spirit enlightens the world, the stubbornness of the impious provokes disorder, and the fault lies with those who will not listen to the Son of God, of whom the heavenly Father says: "Listen to him."[40]

Luther laid out the true and essential Christian doctrine. He examined the teaching about penitence, blatantly mired in utter confusion, and showed what true penitence was, and what was the way, with firm confidence of mind, to conquer the fear of God's anger. He expounded the teaching of Paul, that it is by faith that people are justified. He made clear the difference between Law and Gospel: between the justice attained by the Spirit, that is, and the justice demanded by the state.

He showed, too, how God is truly to be worshiped, recalling the whole church from its pagan frenzy, and the illusion that God can be worshiped even as minds turn away from God, tortured by doubts raised by some technicality. He taught us to worship with faith and good conscience, relying on the one mediator, the Son of God, sitting on the right hand of the eternal Father, and interceding for us—and not on statues of dead men. . . .[41]

And so that this splendid heavenly doctrine might be transmitted to posterity, he translated the prophetic and apostolic Scriptures[42] so lucidly,

---

40. Matthew 17:5; Mark 9:7; Luke 9:35.
41. A reference to the cult of saints.
42. Melanchthon refers to the Old Testament prophets and the New Testament, those sections of scripture the Lutherans especially prized; but in fact, Luther translated the whole of both testaments of the Bible.

that his translation by itself offers more clarity to the reader than a pile of commentaries. . . .

All who knew him, knew him to be kind, cordial to his friends, and not at all contentious or combative. . . . Of these things we ourselves, and many besides, are witnesses. To his sixty-third year, he spent his life in deep and serious study of religion and all the liberal arts. . . . No unsettling passions ever troubled his soul, no seditious counsels. . . . He never allowed religious matters to be contaminated by any ambition for power for himself or for his friends. . . . Amid frequent and serious crises, he exhibited enormous strength of spirit, never faltering, never vanquished by any terrors. . . .

The acuteness of his mind was such that amid confusion, he alone saw what was to be done. . . . And while his own mental powers were exceptional, yet he avidly read both ancient and recent ecclesiastical works and all kinds of history, from which with great dexterity he selected examples and applied them to our present situation. Of his eloquence, of course, we have enduring monuments, which have no equals, as the power of his oratory is unsurpassed.

That such a man has been taken from us—a man of supreme intellect, profound learning, honed by long experience, adorned with splendid and heroic virtues, chosen by God for the reformation of the church, who embraced all of us with his paternal love—this loss we for our part mourn deeply. . . . But we rejoice that now he enjoys that close and precious fellowship with God and his Son, our Lord Jesus Christ, . . . which by his faith in the Son of God he always both sought and expected. . . .

And we give thanks to you, almighty God, . . . that from the human race you have secured for your Son an inheritance, and sustain the ministry of the Gospel which you have now also reformed by Luther's hand. . . . And may we always persevere in our belief that so long as we hold firm to the pure teaching of the Gospel, and hear it, teach it, and love it, we ourselves shall be the house and church of God. . . .

The kingdom of Christ and the kingdoms of this world

from Martin Bucer, *The Kingdom of Christ* (1550)

My kingdom is not of this world, Jesus told his disciples.[43] But as Bucer outlines seven resemblances between the kingdom of Christ and the kingdoms

---

43. John 18:36.

of this world, he argues in effect that they are very much alike. In both kingdoms, power is concentrated in one person; the subjects of both are guided to live good and worthy lives; and people, gathered into smaller communities in which they find guidance, are assured the basic necessities of life. Both kingdoms, furthermore, are in a sense subject to each other: the worldly kingdom, necessarily, to Christ's, and Christ himself, when incarnate, to the kingdom of this world—though when seated in heaven at God's right hand, Christ rules his kingdom and is subject to no one. In the end, therefore, despite their many resemblances, worldly kingdoms and the kingdom of Christ are dissimilar, since only the kingdom of Christ can redeem souls and promise eternal life. Yet, despite this assertion of the preeminence of Christ's reign, Bucer here offers the case for the close bond between secular and divine governance, or church and state, describing a model that would pertain for England and the Scandinavian kingdoms, and many principalities of the Holy Roman Empire.

In what way are the kingdom of Christ and the kingdom of this world alike, and how different? (Book 1, chapter 2)

The first similarity between the kingdom of this world and the kingdom of Christ is this: that all power resides in the hands of only one person. In this they differ, however: the kings of this world, since they cannot act everywhere at once, nor foresee and provide for all things necessary for the welfare of the republic, set up . . . overseers, deputies, and delegates, . . . to assist in the administration of the state. . . . But our heavenly king, Jesus Christ, . . . foresees, provides, and establishes all things that are useful for our salvation. . . .

Secondly, the kingdoms of the world and of Christ have this in common, that kings also must guide and govern their domains so that their subjects are made godly and good, rightly knowing and serving God, and truly helping their neighbors in all their actions. To this end, the kings of this world must be ready to risk any perils, even exile or death itself. . . .

But however much the kings of this world intend to accomplish these things, . . . yet they are unable themselves to purge from the souls of mortals their innate impiety and injustice, nor make them truly pious and just. . . . For it is only [Christ our king] who can give his subjects new birth, leading those dead in sin to a life of righteousness. . . .

Third, in both the kingdoms of this world and that of Christ, . . . evildoers who openly display their impiety and injustice, and are not reformed when corrected, are rooted out. . . . They differ, however, in that the kings of this world, to correct the criminous, and expel the incorrigible, employ, by God's command, fines, beatings, imprisonment, exile, and various means of execution. . . . In the kingdom of heaven and of Christ, however, if they are curable, sinners are disciplined only by the word and by the Spirit, and chained by deeds of penitence, are led back to the road of salvation from which they had strayed. . . .

Fourth, the kingdoms of the world and of Christ are similar in that . . . [both] want their subjects . . . to be gathered into congregations, . . . and ruled by their ministers. Our king, however, also purifies his subjects from sin by his sacraments according to the secret mandate of his eternal election, and gives them new birth into eternal life—neither of which the kings of this world have the power to do. . . .

Fifth, our heavenly king further provides and ensures that his people are abundantly supplied with the necessities of life, lest any one of them be in need. . . . Above all, as is also a responsibility performed by worldly kings, he directs that every one of his subjects, from their very childhood, learn those arts and acquire those skills for which he has himself equipped and perfectly suited each one. . . .

Also, Christ our king breathes his Spirit into those [joined in Christian marriage], so that they may with utmost care teach and form the children he has given them to perfect godliness, holiness, and justice. In this way, having in baptism consecrated their children to the Lord, they may think of themselves as teachers more than parents; for they know that those whom they generated in the flesh are subject to death, but that those whom Christ has regenerated in baptism are destined for eternal life. . . . For if the souls of children, from the first moment at which they can understand anything at all, are not formed and accommodated to Christian obedience, there will sprout in them from Original Sin, as though from a root, the thorns and brambles of those sorts of vices that either bar the seed of the word of God from entering their hearts, resisting and repelling it, or if it is admitted, they suffocate and destroy it. . . .[44]

Sixth, the kingdoms of Christ and of this world are alike in that both are forever at war with both evil men and evil spirits. Yet they are different in that the kingdoms of this world may fight evil men with carnal weapons, while the kingdom of Christ fights only with spiritual weapons against enemies both carnal and spiritual. . . .

Seventh, the kingdoms of Christ and of this world are alike in this, that just as worldly kingdoms are subject to the kingdom of Christ, so also is the kingdom of Christ in its way subject to the kingdoms of this world. Yet although Christ our king, now ruling his kingdom while seated at the right hand of the Father, is subject to no one, but rather are all things in heaven and earth necessarily subject to him, nonetheless, when he walked on this

---

44. Cf. Matthew 13:21: "But since they have no root, they last only a short time."

earth, he was obedient unto death,[45] suffering an unjust death at the hands of those powers to which he himself had committed the sword. And likewise he commands his own, as well, to give their wholehearted obedience not only to the legitimate kings and just princes of this world to whom authority has been given, but even to vicious lords and brutal tyrants,[46] not only paying legitimate taxes and fees, but patiently enduring whatever decrees they impose, accepting their unjust judgments, and dutifully performing in every case whatever services are required. . . .

For this indeed all the holy martyrs and [Church] Fathers have always understood, that it is the supreme gift of divine mercy when legitimate kings and princes rule over human affairs, which is to say, those who honor the kingdom of Christ above all, and strive every day to foster and advance it more broadly among their subjects. Accordingly, the people of Christ . . . should look for their welfare only to Christ their king, and not be dismayed if savage tyrants are allowed to rule their worldly domains, but rather to pray constantly to the Lord that he choose as rulers of states legitimate kings and princes who will manage all things according to his own heart. . . .[47]

If what has been said here is dutifully considered, and the scriptural passages cited diligently reviewed, it will readily be understood what are the similarities between the kingdom of Christ and the kingdoms of the world, and what is proper to the kingdom of Christ, and how they are interrelated, so that they may mutually serve and support each other.

---

45. Philippians 2:8: "And being found in appearance as a man, he humbled himself by becoming obedient to death—even death on a cross!"
46. Cf. 1 Peter 2:13–17: "Submit yourselves for the Lord's sake to every human authority," etc.
47. Cf. Jeremiah 3:15: "Then I will give you shepherds after my own heart, who will lead you with knowledge and understanding."

Chapter Five: The Swiss Response

In the Swiss Confederation of cantons and cities, a semi-autonomous entity within the Holy Roman Empire, the Reformation would follow a different trajectory than in the German lands. It begins in the 1520s in German-speaking Zurich, very soon after Luther's break, under the leadership of Ulrich Zwingli. Considered the third great reformer—after Luther and Calvin—Zwingli's reform precedes Calvin's in Geneva by two decades. Under his guidance, some key features of the Swiss Reformed church, distinct from the German Lutheran, were already delineated well before the French refugee Calvin emerged in Geneva to take charge of the Swiss Reformation and shape the international Reformed movement.

In 1519, not long after Luther published his *Ninety-Five Theses,* Ulrich Zwingli (1484–1531) took up his post as "people's pastor" at the Great Minster (cathedral) in Zurich. For twelve years, he led the city toward reform, supported by the city council and in tandem with other Swiss cities that opted for the Reformation, especially Basel and Bern. Zwingli shaped a distinctive course, navigating several controversies that gave rise to authoritative statements of principle. In 1522, he addressed the controversy over Lenten fasting, rejecting in the expanded sermon excerpted in this chapter traditional Catholic prohibitions concerning food. Also in 1522, Zwingli challenged the principle of clerical celibacy, marrying a woman by whom he would have four children. In 1524, he advocated the removal of the images of saints from churches, the matter that had catapulted Karlstadt's conflict with Luther in 1522. In the same year, with an eye to putting an end to the Catholic Mass, while challenging as well the Lutheran doctrine of the "real presence" of Christ in the elements of bread and wine, he introduced a new Eucharistic liturgy—celebrated at ordinary tables set with plain wooden implements—conceived as a memorial of Christ's sacrifice.

From 1524 to 1525, Zwingli further grappled with Anabaptist[1] reformers opposed to the custom of infant baptism, which he forcefully defended. In 1529, he met with Luther along with other German and Swiss reformers at the Marburg Colloquy, which ratified fourteen of fifteen articles concerning the Eucharist—the fifteenth being the critical article affirming Christ's real presence. Two years later, at age forty-six, he fell on the battlefield at Kappel along with five hundred citizens of Zurich engaged in a futile religious conflict among the cantons of the Swiss Confederation. His successor, Heinrich Bullinger (1504–1575), declared Zwingli a martyr, and reaffirmed

---

1. For the Anabaptists, see Chapter Six.

the principles of Zwinglian reform in Zurich, even as the center of gravity of the Swiss Reformation shifted from Germanic north and east to the French-speaking west. The reformers here, while much in association with Zurich and German Strasbourg, were mostly refugees from neighboring France.

Born to a family of the minor nobility in Tournai, France, Marie Dentière (1495–1561) entered an Augustinian convent at a young age. Here she acquired her education, later evidenced by her knowledge of Scripture and theology. Here, too, she was exposed to Lutheran ideas then circulating in the region, and most likely in her own convent, for Luther had been an Augustinian himself, and that order was initially open to his critique of the Roman church. She apparently participated in the same kind of French evangelical discussions that also attracted Marguerite de Navarre, the author of *The Mirror of the Sinful Soul* discussed in Chapter One. It was perhaps at this point that she developed an acquaintance with Marguerite, a relationship that resurfaces in 1539, when Dentière would address to Marguerite the letter excerpted in this chapter. Well before that time, however, Dentière had left the convent and attached herself to the reform movement in Strasbourg. She married and had several children by one of the French-born Reformed leaders; and on his death in 1533, she married a second, whom she followed to Geneva in 1535, the year that city decisively joined the Reformed camp.

Meanwhile, in France, the evangelical movement came to a sudden end, as King Francis I—the brother of Marguerite de Navarre (see Chapter One)—struck out against religious agitation that had begun to threaten his own authority. As many reform leaders fled (including Calvin), Marguerite retreated to her own lands and her own thoughts. She remained outwardly observant of the old church, while inwardly venturing beyond its borders.

When in 1538, the Genevan city council expelled the two Reform leaders Calvin and William Farel, Marguerite turned to her old acquaintance Dentière to learn the circumstances of the fracas. Dentière responded in April 1539 with what she entitled her *Very Useful Letter to Marguerite de Navarre*. Though it offered in passing an account of in-fighting among the reformers, its main thrust was a plea for Marguerite's support: to avow and defend the Reform movement; to approve the role of women in the reform of the church; and to embrace the principal doctrines of the unfolding Swiss Reformation.

Addressed to Marguerite, whose name lent the work exceptional prestige, Dentière's book was intended for a much larger audience, and it circulated widely until censured and suppressed. Marguerite died in her private retreat in 1549, having had no further known contact with Dentière, who was still engaged in controversies within the Reformed party until her own death in 1561. By that time, Geneva had become the center of a dynamic international network of Reformed churches, the work of Dentière's compatriot, John Calvin.

Born in Noyon, France, the humanist, jurist, and theologian John Calvin (1509–1564) fled to Switzerland in 1533, propelled by the persecution of evangelicals launched by the French king. By 1542, at the still youthful age of thirty-three, he had settled permanently as the head of the Reformed church in the strategic city-state of Geneva, an enclave of France perched on the French-Swiss border, where a new belief system engendered a new kind of social order. Geneva now became the capital of the Swiss Reformation and the epicenter of the Reformed, or Calvinist, movement that would spread throughout Europe, from Scotland to Poland, the Netherlands, and France.

Calvin directed the Reformed network by training new pastors in Geneva and sending trusted emissaries abroad. In addition, he kept in touch with a broad community of reformers and statesmen through his letters. At the same time, he pursued his own theological work, summed up in his *Institutes of the Christian Religion*, first published in Latin in 1536 and finally in 1559, by which time it had appeared in five editions; French versions appeared from 1541 to 1560. Excerpts from both poles of Calvin's literary production are given in this chapter: from his letters, two missives to French noblewomen; and from the *Institutes*, Calvin's famous discussion of the doctrine of predestination.

Calvin reached out through correspondence—more than four thousand letters are extant, directed to more than three hundred addressees—to encourage, exhort, and sometimes reprimand friends, associates, and wielders of power who could advance the Reformed cause. Among those correspondents are more than eighteen women, nearly all French noblewomen. Excerpts from letters to two of them are given here. The first is directed to Renée de France (1510–1575), daughter of Louis XII, king of France (r. 1498–1515); Renée was also known as Renata, duchess of Ferrara, by her marriage to Ercole d'Este, duke of that Italian city. The second is directed to Jeanne d'Albret (1528–1572), queen of the tiny kingdom of Navarre by inheritance from her father; the wife of Antoine de Bourbon, first "prince of the blood"; and by that connection, mother of the future king of France, Henry IV (r. 1589–1610).[2] Viewing the enlistment of these noblewomen in the Reformed cause as profitable for its spread in France, Calvin hastens to guide the former in her newfound commitment, and celebrates the recent conversion of the second.

In contrast to his letters, concerned with pressing issues of the moment, Calvin's *Institutes* present a systematic and comprehensive theology, arguably

---

2. Jeanne herself had royal blood, moreover, through her mother, Marguerite de Navarre, sister of king Francis I (r. 1515–1547), encountered previously in Chapter One as a proto-reform author, and in this chapter as an acquaintance of Dentière. Renée was also strongly influenced by Marguerite, who had been her protector when she was a child and orphan at the court of Francis I.

the most important compilation of Reformation thought. Luther himself had written no comprehensive work, a task performed in his stead by Melanchthon (see Chapter Four), whose *Loci communes* (*Commonplaces,* or *Fundamental Principles*) were published in 1521, with three subsequent editions through 1559. Both Melanchthon's and Calvin's works evidence the need for the systematization of Reformation thought that presented itself almost as soon as the movement began, and both are written by inspired scholars and trained theologians. Calvin's work stands out, however, not only for its scope—in its final format, it is three times the length of Melanchthon's—but for its incisive and elegant prose. The section excerpted in this chapter on the doctrine of predestination, a central one in the Reformed faith, shows Calvin at his best: insisting on a doctrine repellent to many but essential, in his view, to a full understanding of God's nature and action that is grounded in Scripture.

Calvin's designated successor, Theodore Beza (1519–1605), one of the company of pastors Calvin gathered around him in Geneva, had been born in France to a distinguished family of the minor nobility. Trained in the law and expert in Greek, his theological works would guide the pastors who oversaw the broadening tide of Reformed churches. He was a capable administrator as well, and a practiced diplomat. His great mission, however, was to advance the cause of the French Huguenots, as his co-religionists there came to be known.

Despite the campaign of repression begun in the 1530s, the Reformed movement grew, attracting the support of great noble clans of the south, a region historically in tension with royal authority. By the 1550s, adherents of the Reformed church, or Huguenots, as they were now called, had grown to number some one-eighth of the French population. With armed noble advocates on both Catholic and Huguenot sides, war broke out in 1562, reaching a hideous peak in August–October 1572, when Catholic sympathizers killed thousands of Huguenots in the Massacre of Saint Bartholomew's Day. The conflict eased in 1589 when Henry of Bourbon, the Huguenot leader, succeeded to the French throne, and accepted Catholic conversion in 1593. In 1598, he issued the Edict of Nantes, which granted French Huguenots some degree of autonomy. The matter was settled for not quite eight decades.

When Calvin died in Geneva in 1564, and Beza acceded to leadership of the Geneva church, the French Wars of Religion had recently begun. Though Beza had journeyed often to France to support the Huguenot cause during the 1550s, hereafter his efforts would be exercised from the Swiss side of the border; but they were assiduous nonetheless. In 1574, following the St. Bartholomew's Day Massacre, he published in French the treatise *On the Right of Magistrates over Their Subjects,* a treatise later translated and circulated also in Latin. It raised a fraught question: whether Christian subjects may in good conscience resist a ruler who has become a tyrant—by force if necessary. Beza concludes that they may.

Beza's work is a major statement, and arguably the first, setting aside some theoretical discussions in Greco-Roman texts and by some scholastic philosophers, of the right of the people to oppose and overthrow the tyrant. His discussion would be followed by other works by Huguenot authors, and would reappear in justifications of two seventeenth-century rebellions: the Dutch Revolt and the English Revolution. It underlies, as well, the thinking behind the American Revolution of 1776. The professor of Greek who issued advice from Geneva would perhaps have been surprised at the power and reach of his quietly phrased but profoundly provocative words.

The Swiss Reformation, begun on the margins of Luther's titanic revolt in Germany, and intersecting with the struggle for religious freedom in France, is not lesser than the German, but rather its robust equal in significance, and ultimately of greater geographical reach. It gave birth to Calvinism, a dynamic alternative to Lutheranism within Reformation Europe, whose Reformed churches brought the new faith and a new way of life to regions far beyond Wittenberg or Geneva.

The freedom of the Gospel means freedom to eat

from Ulrich Zwingli, *On Choice and Freedom in Food* (April 16, 1522)

It had long been Catholic custom to observe a partial fast on Ash Wednesday and Fridays during Lent (the period of approximately forty days preceding Easter), when, in March 1522, friends of Zwingli defied the practice by the conspicuous consumption of a meal of sausages—Zwingli himself abstaining, but not disapproving. The sausage incident provoked a storm of criticism, to which Zwingli responded in a sermon on March 23, expanded and issued on April 16, 1522 as *On Choice and Freedom in Food*. Given here are excerpts from the first section of Zwingli's work, in which he meticulously cites and expounds nine New Testament passages taken from the gospel of Matthew, the Acts of the Apostles, and several of Paul's epistles. The accumulation of texts powerfully makes the case that the New Testament does not prohibit the eating of any kind of food at any time or under any particular circumstances: Christians may eat whatever they wish, so long as they do so in a spirit of thanksgiving.

On Choice and Freedom in Food exemplifies Zwingli's reliance on Scripture in the development of his theology and, no less important, the education of his congregants. It was not his first published work, but it was the first to enunciate the principles of a Reformed Christian alternative to Catholic orthodoxy. And the events it documents may be said to mark the beginning of the Swiss Reformation, originating the second major stream of Protestant belief to develop in the sixteenth century.

To all the godly Christian folk of Zurich, I, Ulrich Zwingli, a plain spokesman of the Gospel of Jesus Christ, wish you God's grace, love, and peace.

Now that you, beloved in God, for these past four years have so thirstily listened to the Gospel and the teaching of the holy apostles, which almighty God has mercifully delivered to you through my small skill, most of you have become wonderfully enflamed with the love of God and neighbor. Having accepted the Gospel truth and embraced and wholly adopted its freedom, and having now tasted and enjoyed the sweetness of that heavenly bread that sustains humankind, you have been unwilling to eat any other food of mere mortal doctrine....

[And to make full use of that Christian freedom,] ... some have written verses in their own German tongue, some have had lively discussions in homes and public gatherings, and some now during this recent fast—thinking no one would be offended—in their own homes, among themselves, have eaten meat, eggs, cheese, and other foods, formerly forbidden during fasts....

[In response to the discord that has on this account arisen], what should I do, entrusted as I am with the care of souls and of the Gospel, other than closely to examine the Scriptures, eliciting from them some light in this darkness of error, so that no one comes to suffer because of ignorance or confusion? ... I have therefore fashioned this sermon on the merits of choosing different kinds of foods, using no texts but the holy Gospel and the teaching of the apostles, which most wonderfully delight those who hear them, and set them free.... So let us read and understand, opening the eyes and ears of our hearts to hear and see what the spirit of God says to us....

First, as Christ says, *Don't you see that whatever enters the mouth goes into the stomach and then out of the body? But the things that come out of a person's mouth come from the heart, and these defile them.*[3] These words show that no food, so long as it is taken in moderation and with thankfulness, can defile a person.... Christ's meaning is that all foods are the same with regard to defilement: they cannot in any way at all defile.

Second, as is written in the Acts of the Apostles, when Peter was in Joppa, ... and wished to eat, ... [he had a vision of a great cloth lowered from the heavens by its four corners, teeming with all kinds of beasts, reptiles,

---

3. Matthew 15:17–18.

and birds, that were prohibited to the pious]: *Then a voice told him, "Get up, Peter. Kill and eat." "Surely not, Lord!" Peter replied. "I have never eaten anything impure or unclean." The voice spoke to him a second time, "Do not call anything impure that God has made clean."*[4] Now God has made all things clean and does not forbid us to eat, as these last words of his make perfectly clear: So why then do we willfully burden ourselves with forbidden foods?

Third, Paul writes to the Corinthians: *"I have the right to do anything," you say—but not everything is beneficial. "I have the right to do anything"—but I will not be mastered by anything.*[5] . . . Which is to say that I am free to do whatever I wish, although I may not always do so, for fear of too greatly offending my neighbor. . . . No one, then, can deprive me of my freedom and subject me to his power. . . .

Fourth, Paul goes on to say in the same epistle that *food does not bring us near to God; we are no worse if we do not eat, and no better if we do.*[6] Paul is speaking of food that had been sacrificed to idols, not ordinary food. . . . Even if one eats the food offered to idols, he is no less worthy before God; nor is he more worthy than one who does not eat it; and the one who does not eat it, equally, is no better. . . .

Fifth, Paul says in the same epistle: *Eat anything sold in the meat market without raising questions of conscience.*[7] These words are self-explanatory. . . .

Sixth, Paul writes in his letter to the Colossians: *Therefore do not let anyone judge you by what you eat or drink.*[8] . . . Once again you hear that you must judge no one to be good or evil on account of food or drink; he may eat whatever he wants. . . .

Seventh, Paul further writes to Timothy: *The Spirit clearly says that in later times some will abandon the faith and follow deceiving spirits and things taught by demons.* [These false teachers will] *forbid people to marry and order them to abstain from certain foods, which God created to be received with thanksgiving by those who believe and who know the truth. For everything God created is good, and nothing is to be rejected if it is received with thanksgiving, because it is consecrated by the word of God and prayer.*[9] These are Paul's words. And what could be more plainly said? . . . Hear this then: there is no harm in eating whatever you wish to eat, so long as you eat it thankfully. . . .

Eighth, as Paul writes in his epistle to Titus: *To the pure, all things are pure, but to those who are corrupted and do not believe, nothing is pure. In fact, both*

---

4. Acts 10:13–15.
5. 1 Corinthians 6:12.
6. 1 Corinthians 8:8.
7. 1 Corinthians 10:25.
8. Colossians 2:16.
9. 1 Timothy 4:1–3.

their minds and consciences are corrupted.[10] ... They are unbelievers, who do not accept that the salvation, mercy, and freedom of Christ are not so broad and deep as indeed they are. ...

Ninth, as Paul says in the epistle to the Hebrews: *Do not be carried away by all kinds of strange teachings. It is good for our hearts to be strengthened by grace, not by eating ceremonial foods, which is of no benefit to those who do so.*[11] In these words we hear ... that without doubt or qualm we may depend absolutely on the certainty of the holy Gospel. ... For that Gospel is nothing else but this: the good news of the grace of God, on which we may rest our hearts. And so, we know and trust that Gospel grace to be so certain and available, that we place our faith in no other doctrine and put no trust in food, either by eating or refusing this or that kind of food ... for that these food prohibitions and proscriptions have done no good for those who have followed them is plain to see.

These scriptural passages, it seems to me, are sufficient to show that all foods may be eaten by Christian believers. ... And if any Christian wants to dispute these arguments, he must dispute Scripture itself: but then he is no Christian, as he does not accept Christ's teaching. ...

No woman ever sold Jesus or betrayed him, but a man named Judas

from Marie Dentière, *A Very Useful Letter to Marguerite de Navarre* (1539)

Dentière's letter to Marguerite de Navarre has three distinct parts, extracts from the first two of which are given here. In the first, the dedicatory address, Dentière alludes to the quarrels within the Genevan church about which Marguerite had sought information. She calls on Marguerite to defend the church, and to implore her brother, Francis I, to do so as well. Further, she advances the cause of women as participants in religious discussion, and laments the scorn heaped upon them by both Roman and Reformed clerics.

The second part of Dentière's letter, with the heading "Defense of Women," is a unique document of women's participation in the Reformation. It is a powerful affirmation of women's role in the Bible and in the church, celebrating the Old Testament matriarchs and the female companions of

---

10. Titus 1:15.
11. Hebrews 13:9.

Jesus, and defending women's right to study Scripture and even—for this was prohibited by Catholics and reformers alike—to preach. The third and longest part delineates the Reformed position on several key doctrines, including justification by faith, the Lord's Supper, and repentance, and concludes with an attack on the corruption of the Roman clerical hierarchy.

Most honored Lady, just as those who truly love the truth want to know and discern how they are to live in this age so fraught with danger, so too must we women know how to avert and evade all errors, heresies, and false doctrines, whether these come from false Christians, Turks, infidels, or others whose beliefs are suspect, as you have yourself fully demonstrated in your writings. And given that, in the past, many good and faithful servants of God who were called to write, preach, and declare the law of God, and the coming of his Son Jesus Christ, and Christ's deeds, death, and resurrection, were rejected and rebuked, especially by the experts to whom the people looked for guidance; and not only were those advocates rejected, but even God's own Son, Jesus Christ, who is himself the Law; it should not then surprise us if in our day we see the same repudiation of those whom God has inspired to write, speak, preach, and declare the very message that Jesus and his apostles declared and preached.

The whole earth resounds with maledictions, and its inhabitants are distressed by confusion, disturbance, dissension, and division between this faction and that, greater than has ever been seen on this earth: bitter rivalry, malice, rancor, spite, greed, lewdness, larceny, looting, assault, murder, riot, rape, arson, poison, wars of kingdom against kingdom, and nation against nation. It is the reign, in sum, of all abominations: father against son and son against father, mother against daughter, daughter against mother, to such an extent that one betrays the other, the mother abandoning her own daughter to utter iniquity. The state of things is such that scarcely any of those who inhabit the earth know what they are to do, when these things are done by those who call themselves Christians. And of all this, no one dares to say a word: for one sees things this way, the other that; this one thinks he does right, while the other does wrong; this one is wise, the other foolish; this one knows everything, the other nothing. . . . In sum, there is nothing but discord. But one or the other must be wrong: for there is only one God, one faith, one law, and one baptism.[12]

---

12. Ephesians 4:4–6: "There is one body and one Spirit, . . . ; one Lord, one faith, one baptism; one God and Father of all, who is over all and through all and in all." Dentière adds to Paul's "one faith, one baptism," also "one law," alluding to the existence of a politically unified nation, and to the contemporary motto "*une foi, une loi, un roi,*" for which see Mary B. McKinley, Introduction to her edition and translation of Dentière, *Epistle to Marguerite de Navarre and Preface to a Sermon by John Calvin* (Chicago: University of Chicago Press, 2004), 52n4.

But I wanted particularly to write to you, most honored Lady, not to instruct you, but to urge you to intercede with the king, your brother, to put an end to these divisions that reign over the places and the people that God appointed him to command and govern; and in your possessions as well, given to you by God to oversee and manage. For what God has given to you, and revealed to us women as much as to men, should not be stashed away and buried in a hole. And although we are barred from preaching in public and from the pulpit,[13] we are nonetheless permitted to write and counsel each other in all charity.

This letter is written not only for you, my lady, but also to embolden all other women held in captivity, who fear that, like me, they will be cast out of their country, and torn away from their friends and family, for the word of God. It is written especially for those desperate women yearning to know and discern the truth, who know not what road, what pathway to take, who until now have been tormented and afflicted within, but now may be healed, consoled, and inspired to follow the truth, which is the Gospel of Jesus Christ. Until now, this truth has been so suppressed so that no one dared utter a word about it, for women, it seemed, were to be barred from reading or thinking about holy Scripture. This is the main reason, my Lady, that I have written you this letter, hoping to God that in the future women will not be so deprecated as they have been in the past. . . . Amen.

Defense of women

Not only will some carpers and enemies of the truth charge us with too much brashness and boldness, but so too will some believers, saying that women go too far in writing to each other about holy Scripture. To these one can rightly respond that all the women named and noted in holy Scripture should not be deemed too bold, but rather, should be . . . praised for their character, deeds, demeanor, and good example as well as for their faith and teaching. . . . In the Old Testament, look first before all others to the mother of Moses, who, disregarding the king's command, contrived to save her son from death and have him reared in Pharaoh's household.[14] . . . Should Ruth be despised for being a woman, when her story is chronicled in a book that bears her name?[15] I should think not, given that she holds her place in the genealogy of Jesus Christ.[16] . . . As for the grace that has been shown to women, what

---

13. Cf. 1 Timothy 2:12, the often-cited prohibition against women's speaking in public: "I do not permit a woman to teach or to assume authority over a man; she must be quiet."
14. Exodus 2:1–10.
15. Book of Ruth.
16. Matthew 1:5.

greater grace has been shown to any creature on earth than that bestowed on the virgin Mary, the mother of Jesus, who was chosen to give birth to the Son of God?[17] . . . What preacher was ever greater than the Samaritan woman, who did not hesitate to preach Jesus and his word, announcing boldly to the entire world what she had heard from Jesus, that God must be worshiped in spirit and in truth?[18] And who but Mary Magdalene can boast of having been shown the first manifestation of the great mystery of the resurrection of Jesus?[19] . . .

Granted that there has been imperfection in all women, yet men have not been exempt from it. Why must women bear the blame, seeing that no woman ever sold Jesus or betrayed him, but a man named Judas?[20] Who but men, I ask you, have discovered and concocted so many ceremonies, heresies, and false doctrines on this earth, by which poor women have been seduced? . . . If God, therefore, has shed his grace on decent women, revealing to them through his holy Scripture something good and pure, should the enemies of truth prevent them from writing, speaking, and declaring it to each other? Ah, they will not be able to stop us, and we would be fools to hide the gift that God has given us. May he give us grace to persevere to the end. Amen.

The intolerable blasphemy of the Mass, and a welcome conversion

from John Calvin, *Letters*, to Renée de France, duchess of Ferrara, and Jeanne d'Albret, queen of Navarre (1541, 1561)

The duchess Renée hosted a number of evangelicals in her court at Ferrara—over her husband's objections, which eventually prevailed—including some disdained by Calvin for their laxity. In Calvin's letter of October 1541, after encouraging Renée, in her position of prominence, to employ her power to advance the kingdom of Christ, he disparages a clerical adviser who claimed that she might prevaricate, rejecting neither Catholic nor evangelical practices, by both hearing Mass and participating in the Lord's Supper. Calvin

---

17. Matthew 1:20–21.
18. John 4:4–30.
19. John 20:1–2.
20. Matthew 26:14–16.

then instructs Renée on the errors of the Mass in much the same terms that Karlstadt and Zwingli had also employed. The celebration of the sacrifice of the Mass, he argues, is tantamount to a repudiation of Christ's suffering and death, since Christ died once and for all time, performing the perfect sacrifice by which we are cleansed of our sins and reconciled to God. In the Lord's Supper, in contrast, that unique sacrifice is commemorated, but not repeated—for to do so is an abomination.

Twenty years later, on January 16, 1561, Calvin writes Jeanne d'Albret, queen of Navarre, to rejoice at the news of her recent and sudden conversion—"in the space of just a few hours." He had learned of it from his associate Theodore Beza, who had been dispatched to her court in July 1560 and since returned to Geneva. Jeanne's conversion was of the greatest consequence. Defying her husband, who remained Catholic despite Beza's best efforts, she reared her son in the Reformed faith, protected evangelical refugees in her court, and supported the Huguenot (French Reformed) party in the French Wars of Religion.

To Renée de France, duchess of Ferrara: Geneva, [October] 1541

Now, Madame, putting this personage aside, I come to the present matter. He suggests to you that the Mass is not so wicked or hateful, but that it is permissible for him to say, and for the faithful to hear, that those who oppose it disrupt the Church and undermine the weak whom we are especially charged to sustain. As to the first point, I doubt that I should bother to argue it, seeing that you are fully convinced that the Mass is a sacrilege, the most detestable that can be imagined, and fearing to make myself ridiculous by pressing a point about which you yourself have no doubt. Nor is the short space of a letter sufficient to contain what could fill a large book. Nonetheless, I shall touch on it briefly, as though in passing, so as to resolve all uncertainty.

In that the Mass is a sacrifice, established by mortals for the redemption and salvation of both living and dead, as they claim, it is an intolerable blasphemy by which the suffering of Jesus Christ is nullified, as though it had no efficacy whatsoever. But we say instead: believers have been redeemed by the blood of Jesus, having obtained through him the remission of their sins, their justification, and the hope of eternal life; which means that this perfect Savior, in delivering himself to the Father, and surrendering himself to immolation, has offered himself as an eternal sacrifice by which our sins have been cleansed and purged, and we ourselves received into the grace of the Father, and adopted as heirs to a celestial inheritance. . . . If, however, the death of Jesus is not recognized as the ultimate sacrifice, performed once and for all time, and powerful for all eternity, what then is left of it, as it will have been erased and robbed of all effect?

I realize that these liars say, to cover up their abomination, that they make the same sacrifice that Jesus made, a notion that entails several blasphemies.

For that sacrifice can be made by no one except himself. And if he is sacrificed again, as the apostle Paul says, then he suffers still.[21] So you can see that one of these two alternatives presents itself: either to recognize the awful blasphemy of the Mass, and detest it; or in accepting it, to trample underfoot the cross of Jesus. . . .

And so, Madame, since it has pleased the Lord God in his goodness and infinite mercy to instill in you the knowledge of his name, and to enlighten you with the truth of his holy Gospel, accept as your own the vocation to which he calls you. For he has rescued us from the depths of darkness where we had been kept captive, so that we may directly follow the light of his truth without deviating to the left or the right, seeking more and more to be instructed by him and profiting more abundantly from that holy wisdom of which he has given us a first taste. . . . Certainly, if we proceed with zeal and passion, he will so guide us that we will not stray from the right path. And though there remains within us some residue of ignorance, he will give us a more profound revelation when we are ready to receive it, at a time that he knows best. Our goal must be to understand how his holy doctrine bears fruit in us, for it is that which transforms our heart and spirit so that his glory, in its innocence, integrity, and holiness, shines forth within us. If that transformation does not occur, we take the name of God in vain, vaunting ourselves for our knowledge of his Gospel. I do not say this to admonish you for doing what you do not presently do, but so that the work that God has begun in you advances each and every day. . . .

*****

To Jeanne d'Albret, queen of Navarre: Geneva, [January 16, 1561]

Madame, I cannot sufficiently tell how greatly I rejoiced at the letter that you were pleased to write to my brother, Monsieur de Chalonné,[22] conveying how God has powerfully acted in you in the space of just a few hours. For though he had long since planted in you some good seed, as you now understand, it was nearly choked by the thorns of this world. For if we do not daily exercise ourselves in the study of holy Scripture, the truth we once knew will dwindle bit by bit until it vanishes altogether, unless the merciful God supplies a remedy. And so he has now in his infinite goodness intervened to protect you from that outcome. . . .

I speak with some familiarity, Madame, thinking that you will willingly give me permission to do so, as I have also received this benefit from your letter, that it has given me an opening and opportunity to write to you. And so,

---

21. Hebrews 9:25–26.
22. An alias for Calvin's lieutenant and eventual successor, Theodore Beza.

Madame, I urge you to prize the mercy of God as it deserves, not only because he has rescued you in a flash from the shadows of death and opened your eyes to the light of life in his Son, . . . but also because he has implanted faith in his Gospel deep in your heart, like a living tree that will duly yield its fruit. . . .

Eternal election: The inscrutable profundity of God's judgment

from John Calvin, *Institutes of the Christian Religion* (1559)

A God who is omniscient and omnipotent, as the God of the Bible is, sees everything and every creature in the cosmos he has created entirely and once for all time. In creating all things and all living beings, he has done so for certain ends. To a believer, these truths would seem to be inescapable, and yet people seek endlessly to escape them. Yet this "inscrutable profundity of God's judgment" must be confronted—cautiously. It is dangerous to probe too boldly into the mysteries of God's intentions, but at the same time, it is cowardly not to explore them, guided always by the word of God found in Scripture. The free and bounteous grace that God bestows on some, it must be accepted in the end, he denies to others. His predestination of some to salvation and others to perdition is necessarily just and proper, however much it appears baffling and absurd. These arguments Calvin presents forcefully and systematically in his *Institutes of the Christian Religion*, laying out fundamental principles of Reformed Protestantism that, nonetheless, many Christians, both lay and clerical, denied and defied.

Book 3, chapter 21: On eternal election, by which God has predestined some to salvation, and others to destruction

1. *The necessity and benefits of eternal election.* Now it is the case that the life-giving covenant is not preached equally to all humankind, and among those to whom it is preached, it does not have the same effect. . . . In this diversity is observed the inscrutable profundity of God's judgment; nor can it be doubted that this variety also supports God's decision about eternal election. For if it is clear that by God's choice salvation is offered on the one hand to some, while to the contrary others are denied it, great and difficult questions quickly arise which cannot be resolved unless godly minds have grasped fully the concepts of election and predestination.

Many find this topic perplexing, for they think it rather arbitrary that of the common pool of humanity, some are predestined to salvation, and others to destruction. How foolishly they entangle themselves will soon become clear. For in that very fog that engulfs them is found not only the utility of this doctrine, but also its sweetness. We shall never be as fully persuaded as we should be that our salvation flows from the fountain of God's freely given mercy until we have comprehended his eternal election, which reveals the grace of God in this antithesis: that he does not promiscuously extend to all the hope for salvation, but gives to some what he denies to others. . . .

The perils of curiosity. Human curiosity makes the discussion of predestination, which is already rather complicated, truly perplexing and even dangerous. For it can be contained by no limits, as it wanders down forbidden paths and dares to storm the heavens: leaving to God no secrets, if that were possible, unexplored and undisclosed. Yet these many whom we see thrashing about in this effrontery and shamelessness—some of them otherwise by no means bad—should be asked at some point what limit is to be placed on their behavior.

First let them be aware, when they inquire into predestination, that they intrude upon the mysteries of divine wisdom, where they may lunge boldly and rashly yet not satisfy their curiosity, and stumble into a labyrinth from which there may be no exit. Nor is it right that mortals pry with impunity into those things which the Lord has chosen to hold hidden within himself, and rip from the eternal realm the sublimity of wisdom that God intends for us to adore, not understand, so that it may fill us with awe of him. Those secrets of his will that he has chosen to disclose he has revealed to us in his Word—to the extent, that is, that they are in our interest and for our benefit to know. . . .

2. *Predestination is to be understood only through Scripture.* . . . If we keep this thought in mind, that the Word of the Lord is the one and only way that can guide us in investigating whatever we may properly hold concerning him, and the only light that can illumine whatever it is fitting for us to see, it will easily deter and restrain us from too great presumption. For we shall know that as soon as we transgress the boundaries of the Word, we have lost our way and fallen into a wilderness where we must constantly wander, falter, and fail. Let this, then, above all, be before our eyes: to seek any understanding of predestination other than that expressed by the word of God is no less insane than to walk where there is no path or to seek where there is no light. . . .

3. *Evading discussion of the doctrine of predestination.* There are others . . . who want to suppress any mention of predestination: indeed, they advise us to avoid any discussion of it as one would steer clear of a reef. Although surely their moderation is praiseworthy, by which they so cautiously refrain from exploring these mysteries, yet they withdraw so far from the matter that they disparage the human mind, which does not allow itself to be coerced. Therefore, to restore the balance, we shall need to return to the Word of the Lord,

which offers us a sure rule for the understanding. For Scripture is the school of the Holy Spirit, in which just as nothing is lacking that is necessary and useful to know, so also nothing is taught unless it is important to know. . . .

4. *This doctrine is not harmful to believers.* . . . I desire only this . . . , that we not query what the Lord has kept secret, nor neglect what he has revealed; for the former should be condemned as brazen curiosity, and the latter, ingratitude. . . . But those who are so cautious or so cowardly that they want to bury the doctrine of predestination lest it trouble the faint of heart, how, may I ask, will they disguise their arrogance in charging God, as they do implicitly, with crass ignorance? As though he had not foreseen this problem that they have cleverly whisked away? Whoever despises the doctrine of predestination, clearly, is blaming God for having so inconsiderately let something slip that discomfits the church.

5. *Predestination and foreknowledge.* . . . When we say that God has foreknowledge, we mean that all things always were and forever will be before his eyes. Thus he has no knowledge of things future or past, but all things are in the present, and present in such a way that they are not envisioned like ideas in his mind (as happens with us when our minds retain a memory of things seen), but rather appear before him so that he actually perceives and discerns them. And this foreknowledge extends to the furthest limit of the cosmos and to all creatures. By predestination we mean God's eternal decree, by which he has determined within himself what destiny he chooses for each and every human being. For all are not created equal, but some are preordained to eternal life, and others to eternal damnation. Accordingly, as each person has been assigned to one or the other of these ends, we say that he has been predestined to life or to death. . . .

7. *The election of individuals.* Although it is now quite clear that God by his secret counsel freely chooses those whom he wishes, while rejecting others, his free election is only fully explained when we consider those individuals to whom God not only offers salvation, but so assigns it that there is no hesitancy or doubt about the certainty of the gift. . . . So God's free gift is displayed in the adoption of Abraham and his descendants, though it was denied to others. But the power of his grace is still more splendidly expressed in the members of Christ, for they are joined to him as their head, and will never be separated from their salvation. . . .

A summary. As Scripture clearly shows, then, we say that God by his eternal and immutable counsel determined once for all time those whom he would one day receive into salvation, and those he would instead consign to destruction. This determination with regard to the Elect, we maintain, is founded on his freely given mercy, without regard to human merit; while to those assigned instead to damnation, by his just and unassailable yet also incomprehensible judgment, he bars the door to life eternal.

Resisting tyranny—by force of arms if necessary

from Theodore Beza, *On the Right of Magistrates*[23] *over Their Subjects* (1574)

"On the right [*droit*] of magistrates over their subjects" is the literal translation of Beza's treatise from which the following passage is extracted; but what do those words mean? They do not, in fact, describe what the work is about. The title might better be rendered "The just rule [*droit*] of magistrates over their subjects," implying that magistrates have a responsibility to rule justly, not merely a right to rule. But best would be "The extent to which magistrates have power"—that is, a right to rule, or authority [*droit*]—"over their subjects." This title exceeds the license of the printed word, almost reversing its apparent meaning, for it suggests that subjects have a right to resist as much as magistrates have a right to rule; but it is fully in accord with Beza's message.

For the author's meaning in the text, if not the title, is exquisitely clear. Only God is just, he patiently explains, and embodies justice. A subject is not bound to obey the magistrate's commands if they are contrary to God's will. If the magistrate has become a tyrant—a notorious tyrant, Beza specifies, one whose iniquity is self-evident—his subjects may defy him. For the people were not created by and for the sake of the magistrates; rather, the magistrates, and even the sovereign magistrate, was created and empowered by the people. Here expounded in brief, in the service of religious freedom, is the theory of the constitutional right of resistance to abusive power.

1. One God, and only he, must be obeyed without exception.

There is no will other than that of the one God, and him alone that is perpetual and unchangeable, the measure of all righteousness. Consequently, it is to him alone that we owe unfailing obedience. As for the obedience owed to princes, if they always gave voice to God's commandments, they too, it would have to be said, as much as God himself, must be obeyed without exception. But since the contrary is too often true, this condition must be observed: they are to be obeyed provided that they command nothing that is impious or iniquitous. Those commands are impious that command us to do what is prohibited by the First Table of God's

---

23. Beza uses the term "magistrate" to mean any public official invested with power, and "sovereign magistrate" to mean the supreme secular ruler, such as a king or prince.

Commandments,[24] or forbid us to do what they command. Those commands are iniquitous that cannot be obeyed without violating, or failing to perform, the duty that each person, whether acting in a public or private capacity, owes to his neighbor. . . .

3. How far does the principle extend that the impious or iniquitous commands of magistrates are not to be obeyed?

How far then, it is asked, does this principle extend that the impious or iniquitous commands of magistrates are not to be obeyed? I respond that each person must act according to his vocation: whether it is general and public, or it is private. Now if, in the former case, your magistrate commands you to do something that God forbids, as when Pharaoh instructed the Egyptian midwives to kill the first-born sons of the Hebrews, or when Herod commanded his agents to kill the Innocents of Bethlehem,[25] then you will have done your duty by refusing to execute such an act. . . . But if the tyrant forbids you, as a private individual, to do what God has commanded, then you will not have done your duty by merely resisting his order unless you also obey the will of God. . . .

4. How can a subject defend himself if he has been injured by a magistrate?

At this point one can further ask what a man of good conscience must do, if the magistrate, rather than ordering him to do something evil, instead intends evil toward him? . . . And what if the source of this evil intent is the sovereign magistrate himself? Certainly, Jesus Christ, and all the martyrs who came after him, teach us to suffer patiently the harms done us; and it is the glory of Christians that they suffer injustice from all, but are unjust to none. Can it be, then, one may ask, that there is no remedy against a sovereign who abuses his power in violation of all divine and human law? Yes, certainly there is, and it can be exercised by human means—and when I speak thus, I beg that no one suspect that I support in any way those mad Anabaptists or other seditious and mutinous sectarians, whom I believe, on the contrary, are worthy of universal hatred and due punishment for their crimes.[26]

---

24. The "First Table" generally refers to the first four commandments prescribed in Exodus 20:1–11, concerned with the duty of human beings to God, the remaining commandments pertaining to civil society. It was a distinction made by the Reformed church, and embraced by some Puritans and later Protestant groups.

25. Beza cites from Scripture two cases where a ruler commands mass murder: Exodus 1:15–19, where Pharaoh plans to control the Hebrew population by enlisting the midwives to kill all their male newborns; and Matthew 2:16, when Herod aims to destroy preemptively any rival "king of the Jews," whom it had been prophesied would be born in Bethlehem, by ordering the slaughter of all male infants under two years of age—an event later referred to as "the massacre of the Innocents."

26. Beza emphatically distinguishes his views from those of radical sectarians, principally Anabaptists, for whom see Chapter Six, who were viewed as rebels against established political authority, and in some cases were indeed such.

To speak the truth as the situation requires, those who teach that one may in good conscience resist a notorious tyranny do not thereby deprive good and legitimate magistrates of the authority God has given them, nor do they encourage rebellion. To the contrary, the authority of magistrates cannot be established, nor the public tranquility conserved, which is the true goal of all states, unless tyrannies are prevented from taking root, or are abolished if they do. The issue then is to identify by what just means, in accord with the will of God, subjects may use to resist the notorious tyranny of a sovereign magistrate—even, if necessary, by force of arms. To address this matter, I suggest first of all the arguments that follow.

5. Do subjects have some just and godly means of resistance against the notorious tyranny of a sovereign magistrate, even, if necessary, by force of arms?

First, let me explain that the people in no way issued forth from magistrates, but that, choosing to be governed either by a prince or some designated rulers, the people themselves preexisted their magistrates. In consequence, the people were not created for the magistrates, but on the contrary, the magistrates were created for the people—in the same way that a tutor exists for his pupil, and not the pupil for the tutor; and the shepherd for his flock, and not the flock for the shepherd. This point being made, it is also proven by the evidence of the histories of all the nations, as when God himself, having himself chosen Saul to replace Samuel at the request of the people, nonetheless wished, in addition, that the people themselves choose and accept Saul as king. [Other examples follow]. . . .

Whenever, then, the issue arises of the duty of magistrates, everyone must agree that it is proper to remind them of their duty, and even at times to admonish them frankly when they seem not to measure up to their office. But when the issue is to resist notorious tyrants, or even punish them for their crimes, behold, there are those who recommend such remedies as patience and prayers to God, and who call seditious, and condemn as false Christians, all those who do not bend their neck to the boot.

This is dangerous terrain; accordingly, I beg the reader once again to recall what I said earlier, so as not to draw false inferences from what I shall argue here. I praise Christian patience, then, as a virtue supreme among the virtues, and understand that it is to be vigorously encouraged as leading to the prize of eternal bliss. I detest rebellions and riots of all kinds as monstrous; I agree that, especially in affliction, we must depend on God alone; I acknowledge that prayers joined by repentance are the necessary and proper remedies for the suppression of tyranny, recognizing that it is most often an evil or scourge sent by God to chastise a sinful people. But for all that I deny that it is not permissible for people oppressed by a notorious tyranny to make use of just remedies alongside of repentance and prayers. . . .

Chapter Six: The Radical Reformation

The "radical Reformation," as it was named by the premier historian of the phenomenon, George H. Williams,[1] could be considered the "fourth" Reformation, as Williams does, following after Luther's, Zwingli's, and Calvin's. Or it could be seen as the "second" Reformation, as it is deemed by Lionel Zuck: "second" because it is the dialectical response or logical antithesis to the "magisterial" Reformation of Luther and his successors, wrought in cooperation with "magistrates," whether princes or city councils.

Whether it is the second or the fourth Reformation, the radical Reformation is contemporaneous with the original Reformation movements of the sixteenth century. From the beginning, those who were liberated by Luther's challenge to ecclesiastical authority, and who drew on earlier fonts of counter-establishment feeling—recently those spearheaded by Wyclif and Hus (see Chapter One), and even earlier, those of the Waldensians and other heretical and mystical streams—raised their voices in counterpoint to his. Like their predecessors, the sixteenth-century radicals envisioned their movement as the vanguard of a new society, superseding the failed contemporary one. In seeking to create the kingdom of God on earth, in the present moment, the radical Reformation repudiated longstanding and fundamental Christian doctrines.

This chapter presents a sampling of the three streams of the radical Reformation, as Williams classified them: one exemplifying Spiritualism, Anabaptism (Dutch and Moravian), and Evangelical Rationalism. It culminates with a defense of toleration, which would be the eventual outcome of radicalism—realized nowhere more fully than in Anglo-America, a completely new society, and a laboratory for religious freedom (see Chapter Ten). Because the excerpts in this chapter are presented according to these thematic divisions—the first an exemplar of Spiritualism, followed by representatives of Anabaptism, concluding with advocates of Rationalism—while they all cluster in the middle fifty years of the sixteenth century, they do not appear in strict chronological order.

Impressed by the *Ninety-Five Theses* (1517), the young cleric Thomas Müntzer (1489–1525) journeyed to Wittenberg to meet Luther, and may have later attended, in 1519, the Leipzig debates between the Catholic spokesman Johann Eck and, in turn, Karlstadt and Luther. By 1520, Müntzer became a church pastor in Zwickau, where he developed theological views

---

1. For works of Williams, Zuck, and others cited in this introduction, see Texts and Studies: Chapter Six.

that Luther would roundly reject. For although Müntzer agreed with Luther's critique of the contemporary church, he would abandon two of Luther's central principles: that justification is by faith alone, and that truth proceeds only from Scripture. Instead, Müntzer believed that the godly can freely seek to achieve the kingdom of God on earth, in the pattern of the Old Testament prophets and New Testament apostles; and that they will be guided in that course by the direct inspiration of the Holy Spirit, quite apart from the written text of the Bible.

In 1521, having angered the Zwickau authorities, Müntzer fled to Prague, where he again caused controversy, and in 1523, settled as a pastor in Allstedt, where he came to the attention of the brothers Frederick the Wise, Elector of Saxony (Luther's patron), and Duke John. Invited to speak at the ducal castle in Allstedt, on July 13, 1524, Müntzer delivered his *Sermon to the Princes*, based on the apocalyptic vision in the second chapter of the biblical book of Daniel. On reading it, Luther dispatched an infuriated "Letter to the princes," denouncing Müntzer. Müntzer fled to Mühlhausen, to become one of the leaders of the doomed Great Peasants' War that engulfed the southern and central German lands from late 1524 until its bloody suppression in June 1525.

Both economic and religious grievances energized the peasants' revolt, and the latter, especially, called to Müntzer. He became the unofficial leader of the movement in which he recognized the stirrings of the apocalyptic nation of the Elect. The princely armies that suppressed the revolt, applauded by Luther, slew more than 100,000 peasants. Müntzer himself was captured—extracted, some have said, from underneath a bed where he was cowering—tortured, and, on May 27, 1525, beheaded.

Along with many radical reformers, Müntzer opposed infant baptism, an issue that became central to the Anabaptist movement that arose in the 1520s. Zwingli acted swiftly to contain the Anabaptist sect of Swiss Brethren, one of the first to appear, that emerged in the midst of his following in Zurich. From Switzerland and neighboring southern Germany, the movement spread throughout Europe. It was highly diverse, ranging from the radical Münsterites at one pole, whose attempt to create a New Jerusalem in that city ended in turmoil and slaughter, to the pacifist Hutterites and Mennonites at the other.

Central for the Anabaptist[2] movement was the imitation of Christ as depicted in the Gospel: his itinerant mission, his suffering, his martyrdom. Those who followed him lived in communities psychologically or actually set apart from the corrupt world, as contemporary society was characterized.

---

2. The term "anabaptist," used by the opponents of the movement, was pejorative: it means one who "baptizes again." Practitioners did not use the term of themselves, and since they saw infant baptism as invalid, did not believe that the "believer" baptism they advocated was a second baptism but the only one.

Some of these communities followed such practices as the common ownership of property, and the refusal to take oaths, or participate in civil government, or bear arms. Common to most Anabaptist groups was the principle of adult, or "believer" baptism, undertaken as a conscious commitment following instruction and conversion. Since European Christians, at this time, were all baptized as infants, those joining the Anabaptist community were baptized for a second time—a practice deemed heretical by mainstream Protestants and Catholics. The unorthodox custom of adult baptism, and the resistance of Anabaptists to official churches and secular government, prompted the persecutions that began almost immediately and continued into the latter half of the seventeenth century.

The excerpts that follow reflect the experience of two Anabaptist communities: that in the Netherlands, a site of particularly ferocious persecution, and the Hutterites of Moravia (Czech Republic). Theleman Janszoon van Braght colorfully documented the Dutch persecutions of the 1530s through the mid-1600s in his 1660 compilation *Het Bloedigh Tooneel der Doops-Gesinde, en Wereloose Christenen* (The Bloody Theater, or Martyrs Mirror of the Defenseless Christians). Given here are passages from the testaments of two mothers to their children, written in prison by Maeyken van Deventer and Janneken Munstdorp, both executed in 1573. Their messages reflect the Anabaptist principles of separation from the world and conscientious imitation of Christ's journey, and in their pleas for their children to understand and embrace their commitment, that of adult baptism as well.

Peter Riedemann (1506–1556), an ethnic German born in Silesia (modern Poland) and a shoemaker by trade, presents in his *Account of Our Religion, Teaching, and Belief* a different variety of Anabaptism than that seen in "bloody Antwerp" and other centers of Dutch persecution. It is a more comprehensive statement of the beliefs of an Anabaptist community than the better-known Schleitheim Articles (1527) of the Swiss Brethren. The Hutterite community for which Riedemann speaks arose in the 1520s on the intersecting borders of modern Austria, the Czech Republic, and eastern Germany, and coalesced in Moravia, where it was episodically persecuted before being finally dispersed in 1622.

Riedemann became the leader of the Hutterites following the martyrdom in 1536 of its founder, Jakob Hutter ("hatmaker"). By that time, Riedemann had already suffered a first imprisonment; and before his peaceful death in 1556, he spent a total of nine years in prison for his faith. It was while a captive in 1540–1541 that he wrote in German his *Rechenschaft*, or *Account of Our Religion*, a summation of Hutterite belief. It was printed in a small edition in 1543 and 1545 intended for presentation to the Landgrave (count) Philip of Hesse, and then by the Hutterite community in 1565; it was reissued in editions of 1902 and 1938.

Riedemann's *Account of Our Religion* can be compared to the nearly contemporary compilations of Melanchthon's *Loci communes* (Commonplaces, or Fundamental Principles, 1521) and Calvin's *Institutes of the Christian Religion* (1536–1559), which, similarly, have the goal of presenting the essential principles of those religious groups. But these latter works are more formal and technical than Riedemann's, and written for a learned audience—in effect, for a specialized sacred priesthood of the sort the Hutterite leader despised.

Riedemann's compact and straightforward *Account*, in contrast, was written for the small circle of Hutterite believers, called the "brethren," or brothers. It begins by presenting the main tenets of Hutterite belief, following the order of the Apostles' Creed, in these matters not greatly differing from the general line of Christian doctrinal thought. Discussion then turns to the manner of living practiced by the Brethren—and here the divergence from the practices of most mainline Protestants or Catholics is striking. For the Hutterite community separated itself sharply from the surrounding contemporary society, its members not serving in civil government, or performing military service, or taking oaths, or holding private property. Riedemann's discussion of this last practice, the common ownership of goods, is excerpted here.

The scattered remnants of the Moravian Hutterites eventually emigrated, mainly to the United States and Canada, where other of Europe's persecuted religious groups had also taken refuge—among them the Amish and Mennonite communities with roots, like the Hutterites, in Anabaptist movements of the radical Reformation. They brought to the Western Hemisphere a religious radicalism that informed American commitments to the freedom of worship and separation of church and state, and American tolerance for ideologies of pacifism and nonresistance.

As much a Protestant, arguably, as his Protestant opponents, based on his close study of Scripture and personal encounter with Jesus Christ, the theologian, physician, lawyer, and astrologer Michael Servetus (c. 1509) died at the stake in Calvin's Geneva, with the most prominent living reformer consenting to his execution. As a young man, a religious experience had aroused his awareness of the humanity of Jesus Christ—a humanity neither Catholics nor Protestants disputed, as it was consonant with the doctrine of the Incarnation. For Servetus, however, as he argues in his *On the Errors of the Trinity* (1531), Christ's human nature as displayed in the New Testament requires a reconsideration of the doctrine of the Trinity as formulated in the early centuries of the church and enshrined in the Athanasian Creed.

The Athanasian formulation, long accepted by Catholics and not disputed by most Protestant churches, viewed God as consisting of three distinct persons—the Father, the Son, and the Holy Spirit—each eternal and coexistent. Instead, echoing the Arian position repudiated by the early church, Servetus saw Jesus, the Son, as created by the Father in the womb of his mother Mary.

As for the Holy Spirit, it was a divine impulse within the human heart, or perhaps an angel-borne communication of the divine will, but certainly not a coeternal member of a Trinity. For Servetus, indeed, a three-fold God was a three-headed monster, to worship whom was tritheism (the worship of three gods), not monotheism (the worship of one). Jews and Muslims, he suggested, who were strict monotheists, would find Christianity a more palatable option without its triune deity.

Servetus advocated other unorthodox ideas unacceptable to religious leaders of all stripes. His astrological predictions raised eyebrows, and few embraced his prophecy that the world would end in 1585, dealt its deathblow by the Archangel Michael. Embedded, ironically, in his huge theological summa *The Restitution of Christianity* (1553), the work that provoked his prosecution for heresy in the very year of its publication by both Catholic and Protestant tribunals, was his astute and largely accurate hypothesis of the pulmonary circulation of the blood—unknown to the Englishman William Harvey, who was credited with his own discovery of the circulatory system that followed decades later.

In April, 1553, Servetus escaped the Catholic inquisitors of Vienne (France), who in his absence were left to burn his effigy atop a pile of his books. Fleeing to Italy by way of Geneva, he was spotted at a church service—he had gone to hear Calvin preach—and arrested, prosecuted, and condemned to death for his heresies. Calvin did not object, but recommended beheading as a humane alternative to burning. Servetus burned nonetheless, on October 27, 1553. One of many Reformation martyrs, Servetus was the first modern martyr for the cause of religious liberty. His death shocked the European public as the killings of Anabaptist bakers and shoemakers and other such pedestrian slaughters had not, and launched the drive realized centuries later to end the prosecution of crimes of conscience and the capital punishment of unbelief.

The key figure in this cultural shift is Sebastian Castellio (1515–1563), a Savoyard[3] professor of Greek who had been fired by Calvin and settled in Basel, only a hundred or so miles from Geneva. A city where Erasmus had often sought shelter, Basel was now, in his wake, home to a lively circle of dissidents who cheered Castellio on. Here in March 1554, a few months after Servetus' death in October 1553, Castellio published *On Heretics: Whether They Should Be Punished, and How They Should Be Treated*, simultaneously in Latin and French versions.[4]

In September 1554, Calvin's lieutenant Theodore Beza (see Chapter Five) responded to Castellio in his treatise *On the Punishment of Heretics by the Civil*

---

3. Formerly an independent duchy, Savoy is now a region of southeastern France.

4. Castellio was unaware that Calvin had, the month before, published his self-justificatory *Defense of the Orthodox Faith in the Sacred Trinity*, to which Castellio would write a response in 1562, not published until 1612.

Magistrate, to which Castellio responded in turn in March 1555. Meanwhile, Castellio's book had been circulating widely, especially in France, to the horror of Calvin and Beza, but also in Germany, where it was immediately translated, and in the Netherlands, where it was translated into Dutch in 1620 and 1663, in tandem with religious controversies occurring in that region. In Amsterdam, it was read by the Frenchman Pierre Bayle, the early Enlightenment critic of what he saw as religious fanaticism. From Europe, the work reached Roger Williams (see Chapter 10) in Rhode Island, and informed his arguments for unlimited freedom of religion.

Castellio's book is, in large part, a collection of passages from the works of theologians, as the extended title informs us: *On Heretics: Whether They Should Be Punished, and How They Should Be Treated, According to the Opinions of Luther and Brenz, and of Many Other Authors Both Ancient and Modern*. The authors include, among others, the Church Fathers John Chrysostom, Jerome, and Augustine; the early Reformation era giants Luther and Erasmus; and Castellio's contemporaries from the Basel circle and beyond, among them Johann Brenz, Coelius Secundus Curio, and Sebastian Franck. These ample statements of a spectrum of anti-persecutory positions are preceded by a preface and followed by an epilogue, both by Castellio under different pseudonyms. The excerpts given here from the preface present briefly and lucidly Castellio's case against the persecution of heretics—inviting, indeed, the nobleman to whom the work is addressed to conclude that the real heretics are not the innocents drowned, dismembered, and burned for their determination to lead godly lives, but the intolerant theologians who hound and destroy them.

Once Servetus was burned in Calvin's Geneva in 1553, and Castellio responded from Erasmian Basel in 1554, the notion that persons should be prosecuted for their thoughts or beliefs became increasingly absurd and indefensible.

The godless have no right to live, unless the Elect permit them to

from Thomas Müntzer, *Sermon to the Princes: An Exposition of the Second Chapter of Daniel* (Allstedt, July 13, 1524)

At the castle of Allstedt on July 13, 1524, Thomas Müntzer delivered his *Sermon to the Princes* to Duke John of Saxony[5] and his son John Frederick. It draws on the second chapter of the biblical book of Daniel, an apocalyptic

---

5. Brother of Luther's protector Frederick, and, in 1525, his successor as Elector.

passage valued by spiritualist and heretical Christians across the centuries, which would have considerable resonance throughout the Reformation era.

The Israelite captive Daniel had been summoned to interpret the vision experienced by the Babylonian king Nebuchadnezzar of *an enormous, dazzling statue, awesome in appearance*,[6] with a head of gold, chest and arms of silver, a belly and thighs of bronze, legs of iron, and feet of iron mixed with clay. Daniel explained that the different elements of the statue signified the succession of empires that ruled the ancient Mediterranean world: the Babylonian, Persian, Greek, and Roman, and a fifth kingdom of mixed peoples and regimes. Meanwhile, *the God of heaven will set up a kingdom that will never be destroyed*, but will *endure forever*.[7]

Müntzer identifies the Fifth Monarchy as the mixed rule of the church of Rome and the feudal lords of Europe, a corrupt and hypocritical regime now in its last days. It would be succeeded by the kingdom of the godly Elect, or "chosen," that Daniel had prophesied. He exhorts Duke John and his son to "seek wholeheartedly the righteousness of God and boldly uphold the cause of the Gospel!" They must draw their swords, killing the enemies of Christ, and usher in that new eternal kingdom.

Müntzer argues that Christ is mocked by the clergy, and turned into a heathen idol.

Surely, there is neither hope nor help for Christendom in its misery, wretchedness, and ruin, if it is not roused by eager and earnest servants of God with daily Bible reading, psalm singing, and sermons. But for that to happen, many a preening parson will need to step aside, or be battered soundly about the head. How else should he be dealt with when Christendom is under vicious attack by savage wolves? . . .

This is certain: Christ the Son of God, with his apostles, and before them, his holy prophets, established a perfectly pure Christendom, sowing its fine grains of wheat in the fields[8]—that is to say, planting the pure seeds of the word of God in the hearts of the Elect.[9] But the corrupt and careless clergy have not troubled themselves to preserve and maintain that church, but have rather looked to their own interests, and not Jesus Christ's.[10] As a result, the

---

6. Daniel 2:31.
7. Daniel 2:44.
8. Cf. Matthew 12:24–30, Mark 4:26–29, Luke 8:5–15, Ezekiel 36:29.
9. The Elect, or "chosen," are those chosen by God and predestined for salvation. Müntzer here affirms a concept that had been embraced by Jan Hus and would be central for John Calvin.
10. See Philippians 2:4, 2:21.

weeds—that is, the sins of the godless—have overgrown and overpowered the fields of wheat. . . .

For the scribes spurned Christ,[11] and still do so today, crucifying him over and over again, in fact, since the first years of the church. They made a laughingstock of the Spirit of Christ and do so still. . . . They have robbed Christ's sheep of the voice of their shepherd,[12] and transformed his crucified body into a grotesque and ludicrous idol . . . a little gilded tinsel god for poor peasants to embrace . . . , and yet there is nothing there but a counterfeit of wood.

There now: a wooden heathen idol and a coarse, boorish, and brutish people, who cannot grasp even the least notion of God, is that not a shame, a sin, and a scandal? I hold fast to this, that . . . Jesus Christ has been trampled and stomped on as hard as could be, and made the floormat on which all the feet of the world deposit their filth. . . .

Müntzer now speaks of the direct illumination of the human soul by the Holy Spirit, apart from the written word of the Bible.

Now, anyone who understands how powerful is the knowledge to be gotten from the natural light of the mind would surely try no more to make sense of extracted passages of Scripture, as the learned do with one or two little scraps,[13] but he would quickly experience the operation of God's Word welling up from the depths of his heart.[14] . . . You will perhaps inquire, "How then does it come into his heart"? Answer: It comes from God above to us below in a celestial flash. . . .

Any man who has not been illumined by or opened to the living word of God cannot speak deeply of God,[15] even if he has wolfed down a hundred thousand Bibles! . . . He who wishes to become illumined by and opened to the Word must first have God remove from him his fleshly lusts. . . . For a bestial man cannot hear what God says to him in his soul,[16] but he must be led by the Holy Spirit to a genuine understanding of the clear and pure meaning of the Law.[17] Otherwise his heart is blind, and he crafts for himself a Christ made of wood, and deceives himself. . . .

Müntzer turns finally to the prophesy in Daniel 2, and the coming reign of the Elect.

---

11. See Psalm 118:22; Matthew 21:44–46; Mark 12:10–12; Luke 20:17–19.
12. Cf. John 10:16.
13. Cf. Isaiah 28:10; Jeremiah 8:8.
14. John 4:14.
15. Romans 8:9.
16. 1 Corinthians 2:14.
17. Psalm 19:7–8.

For if Christendom is not to become what it was in the age of the apostles,[18] . . . why should we preach at all? What use then is the Bible and the visions of which it tells? But the truth is, and I know it to be certain, that the spirit of God is at this time revealing to many of the godly Elect that a compelling, irresistible, and imminent Reformation is absolutely necessary and must be fully accomplished. Like it or not, the prophesy of Daniel remains in force, even if no one heeds it. . . . The Daniel prophesy is as clear as the sun, and the Fifth Monarchy[19] of the world is at this moment coming to an end. . . .

Müntzer exhorts the princes to take up the cause of Christ's Elect.

Therefore, revered and beloved princes, be informed directly by the word of God, and do not permit yourselves to be deceived by hypocritical priests, but stand strong with dignity and purpose. . . . Seek the true steadfastness bestowed by the will of God. . . . Your deeds will be just, so long as you seek wholeheartedly the righteousness of God and boldly uphold the cause of the Gospel! . . .

Now to be effective governors, you must begin to govern from the ground up, as Christ has commanded. Drive his enemies from the company of the Elect, as you have been tasked to do. My friends, don't pretend that the power of God will do this without your having to lift your swords—you might as well let them rust away in their scabbards! . . .

Now some simpletons will surely be outraged by this book,[20] in which I say . . . that the godless who hold power over us should be killed, especially the priests and monks who accuse the Holy Gospel of heresy, and consider themselves to be the real Christians. . . . For the godless have no right to live, unless the Elect permit them to. . . .

Hear, children, the instruction of your mother

from the martyr testaments of Maeyken van Deventer (Rotterdam, 1573) and Janneken Munstdorp (Antwerp, August 10, 1573)

Shortly before their executions, these two Anabaptist martyrs wrote letters, or testaments, to their young children, explaining the reasons for their

---

18. See Acts 2:16–47.

19. The reign of the Roman church in alliance with secular European powers, from the era of the apostolic church down to Müntzer's day.

20. Müntzer's sermon was in due course published and circulated as a small book or pamphlet.

death and summoning their offspring to the true faith, as they saw it, and, implicitly, to the same sacrifice. Composed by literate women with considerable powers of self-expression, they lack the scattering of biblical references and the doctrinal subtleties of many of the products of Reformation thought. They share with other maternal martyr testaments some key themes. The authors convey their acceptance of imminent death, as it is the will of God, and an opportunity to follow in the path taken by prophets, apostles, and Jesus Christ himself. They speak with warmth of husbands from whom they have been separated or who have already suffered martyrdom. They comfort their children—Maeyken's four youngsters, and Janneken's one-month-old daughter, born in prison—with great warmth, offering their testaments as a means of remembrance of departed parents, while summoning the young to reject a corrupt world and to pledge themselves to Christ. They testify to the determination of these mothers not only to impress on their children the memory of their parents, and the dignity and necessity of their cause, but to transmit to them a cultural heritage, a religious commitment which, if the children embrace it, will triumph over the horrors that surround them.

From the testament of Maeyken van Deventer, to her four children

My children according to the flesh, but not, sadly, according to the spirit, this is my testament that I, your mother, leave behind for you, my beloved children Albert, Johann, Egbert, and Truyken. . . .

My children, I must leave you young in your earthly existence; the Almighty wishes us to be reunited in the world to come, a reunion that God the Father . . . will cause to happen soon. Each day I await my death, whereby, if it pleases the Lord, I may offer up my life and my body for the sake of his holy name. I hope that this will happen soon, and that the good Lord will not neglect me much longer.

When you hear this, do not be saddened as those in the world might be who have no hope of heaven and no thought of the life to come. Instead, give thanks to the Almighty that you have a mother who was found worthy to shed her blood for his name's sake, and who, by his great grace and mercy, may be counted as a witness or martyr.

And so, my children, hold in reverence this testament I bequeath to you. I cannot leave you gold or silver, or any of the fine treasures that the worldly prize and give their children. I have nothing of that sort with me, but left all with your father in the flesh; nor have I ever sought such things, but have sought that which is eternal, and does not pass away. Follow that same path, and you will live forever. And follow the instruction that I write down for you here in this testament, just as Jesus Christ, our guide, left his to us as an everlasting testament, sealed in his blood. Just such a testament do I now in turn leave to you, which I too will seal with my blood, as did our savior.

My children, do not take this testament lightly, do not regard it as trifling, do not disregard it: it is better than gold, for it will save your souls. If you do all this that I write to you, you shall see me again in great splendor, and you will be like kings and queens. But you must set yourselves apart from the corruptions of this world, for it will pass away along with all its temptations.

Hear, my children, the instruction of your mother,[21] incline your hearts to understanding, and open your ears to hear the words of my mouth, for I seek the salvation of your souls. Believe me, and otherwise no one at all, so that you may join me and have eternal life. See, my children, I am showing you the path of my Bridegroom and our guide, Jesus Christ, who went before me, the path that leads to truth, as the Lord has commanded me. And see, I take up my cross and follow the savior of all the world. Do the same, my little children. I shall go before you, and not look back, for this is the path of the prophets and martyrs, and see, I shall now drink from that cup from which they drank. . . .

My children, I, your mother, I am the instrument by which you have been brought into this wretched world, I long for your salvation. Believe what I have written and left to you, and otherwise believe no one, unless they agree with holy Scripture. If you do this, you will come to me, and I to you. . . .

From the testament of Janneken Munstdorp, to her one-month-old daughter

. . . I commend you, my small, beloved child, to the great, almighty, and fearsome God, . . . that he may preserve you . . . who are still so young, and whom I must leave here in this corrupt, perverse, and vicious world. Since then the Lord has so directed and ordained that I must now leave you here, here bereft of father and mother, so do I here commend you to the Lord. . . .

So it has come to be, my dear lamb, that I who am by the will of God kept here bound and captive can help you in no other way, since by the will of God I had to leave your father, whom I had had for only a little while. We had only half a year to live together before we were taken into custody, because we sought the salvation of our souls. They took him from me, not knowing if I was pregnant; and so I had to remain in prison and see him taken away; and that I had to remain behind grieved him sorely. So I have remained here since, and carried you in great sadness for nine months under my heart, and then in captivity gave birth to you in great pain, after which they took you from me. I lie here still, each morning expecting to die, and so soon follow your beloved father.

---

21. An echo of (among other similar passages) Proverbs 1:8: "Listen, my son, to your father's instruction and do not forsake your mother's teaching."

Therefore I, your loving mother, write you now, my beloved child, something to think about, so that you may remember your dear father and mother.

Now that I am delivered up to death and must leave you here alone, I commemorate myself to you in this brief testament so that, when you have reached an age of understanding, you may exert yourself to fear God. May you then seek to know and reflect on why, and for whose name's sake, we both died. And do not be ashamed to recognize us before the world, for you shall know that it happened for no unjust cause. You need suffer no shame on our account: it is the path taken by the prophets and the apostles, the narrow path that leads to eternal life, for no other path will ever be found that leads to salvation. . . .

And now, Janneken, my dear lamb, who are still so small and young, I bequeath to you this letter along with a gold coin that I had with me in my prison, which I leave here for you as an eternal farewell and testament, by which you may remember me, as also by this letter. Read it, when you have come to an age of understanding, and guard it so long as you live as a memento of me and of your father. . . .

All created things belong to all in common

from Peter Riedemann, *An Account of Our Religion, Teaching, and Belief* (1540–1541)

The community of goods was a central feature of sixteenth-century Hutterite communities whose descendants, relocated to North America, even today support themselves with collective agricultural and manufacturing enterprises. The principle of community property distinguishes the Hutterites from the mainstream Reformation churches of Luther, Zwingli, and Calvin, which honored the acquisition of property through work and thrift, just as they largely respected civil society, which was also resisted by many Anabaptists.

As expounded in one chapter, excerpted here, of Peter Riedemann's *Account of our Religion*, the principle of commonly-held property is grounded both in the natural order and in Scripture. The personal ownership of property, Riedemann explains, is inherently evil, corrupting the soul of the owner who first takes or seizes some part of God's creation, and then clings to it, setting his heart upon it—and so is alienated from God, with whom his heart should rest. From the Old Testament, Riedemann notes God's bounteous creation of all things for human benefit; the Original Sin of Adam and Eve who seized and appropriated one part of that creation; and the Tenth

Commandment against coveting the goods of others. From the Gospels, he cites several passages extolling spiritual over earthly riches, and repeats the admonition of Jesus Christ that to be his disciple, one must renounce all other goods. From the Acts of the Apostles, Riedemann describes the early church, where all property was shared, and from the letters of Paul, he cites several passages elevating the welfare of the whole over the ambitions of the few: "For as Paul says, no one should enjoy abundance while another suffers in want, but all should be equal. . . . "

Now all the saints[22] share in all that is holy, that is to say, in God,[23] who likewise has given them title to all things in his Son, Jesus Christ. This gift of God's is not to be held by anyone for himself, but each holds it for the sake of the others. Likewise, Christ has nothing for himself, but offers everything to us; and in the same way, the parts of his body do not exist for themselves, but for the whole body, and for all its members.[24] For his gifts are not given to one member alone, or for the sake of one member, but they are given to sanctify all the members, and the whole body.

Now all of God's gifts—not just the spiritual, but also the material—were given to his people in such a way that no one holds any one of them for himself or alone, but together with all of his fellows. So it follows that the fellowship of the saints consists not only in spiritual, but also in material goods.[25] For as Paul says, no one should enjoy abundance while another suffers in want, but all should be equal. . . . [26]

Furthermore, it is seen in all created things, in evidence still in our day, that from the beginning, God ordained that people not have things of their own, but to own all together. But by unjust takings, by which individuals took for themselves what they should not,[27] and abandoned that which they should take, they acquired things for themselves and joined themselves to them, and became more and more accustomed to doing so, and hardened. By such unjust takings and seizings of created things, they have been driven so far from God that they have quite forgotten the Creator, and have lifted up

---

22. The community of believers is the gathering of the Elect, those chosen by God, and are thereby the "saints," a term that has quite a different meaning among some Protestant groups, and certainly Anabaptists, than in the Catholic or more traditional Protestant churches.
23. 1 John 1:1–3.
24. Philippians 2:1–8; 1 Corinthians 12:1–27.
25. Acts 2:42–47; 4:32–37.
26. 2 Corinthians 8:13.
27. For the original unjust taking of the fruit of the Tree of Knowledge, see Genesis 3:2–6.

and revered as gods the creatures that God gave to his people to have dominion over them. . . .[28]

Now, however, . . . just as created things that are too high above the earth for people to seize hold of, such as the sun and the whole course of the heavens, and daylight and air and such, do not belong to any person alone but equally to all, so too were all other created things made to belong to all people in common.[29] That they remained in common, and were not seized, is the result of their having been too high above the earth for people to gain possession of them. Otherwise, having been corrupted by their unjust takings, people would have seized them and possessed them, along with all other created things, as their own property.[30]

That this is so, and that God's other creations are no more than these made for private possession, is evidenced by the fact that at their death people must surrender all created things, . . . and take nothing with them, nor possess anything as their own.[31] On this account Christ called all material things alien to matters of the spirit. . . . [32]

Now because material goods do not really belong to us but are alien, the Law commands that no one should covet them[33]—that is, no one should crave or value material things, because they are alien to us. Therefore whoever wishes to belong to Christ and follow him must give up taking and owning created things.[34] . . . For whoever wishes to be restored anew to the image of God must put aside what leads away from God, which is the seizing and holding of created things. . . .[35]

Whoever then is freed from created things may reach for what is just and godly, and when he has grasped it and made it his treasure, he anchors his heart upon it, and renounces all else,[36] and cares nothing for his possessions, and regards them as no longer his but as belonging to all God's children.[37] Therefore we say that just as all the saints have common ownership of spiritual

---

28. Romans 1:21–25.

29. Alluding generally to the creation of the heavens and all creatures as told in Genesis 1.

30. For the connection between taking and the coming of sin into the world, see Genesis 3:2–6; Romans 5:12–14.

31. 1 Timothy 6:7.

32. See Luke 16:19 for the opposition between love of God and love of things: "No one can serve two masters. Either you will hate the one and love the other, or you will be devoted to the one and despise the other. You cannot serve both God and money."

33. Exodus 20:17; Deuteronomy 5:21.

34. See Matthew 10:38–39; Mark 8:34–37; Luke 9:23–25, 14:33.

35. See Ephesians 4:22–24; Colossians 3:1–2.

36. Alluding to Luke 12:33–34.

37. Luke describes such sharing of possessions in Acts 2:44–45, 4:32–37.

gifts,[38] much more should they have common ownership of material things, and not claim these as their own and crave to possess them,[39] as such possession is an alien thing; but rather they should regard them as belonging to all of God's children, and so demonstrate that they are participants in the fellowship of Christ[40] and have been renewed in the image of God. . . . [41]

For this reason, too, the Holy Spirit in the early days of the church gloriously rebuilt this kind of fellowship, where none boasted of personal possessions but all was held in common.[42] The Spirit desires the same of us still: as Paul says, with no one *looking to your own interests but each of you to the interests of the others.*[43] . . . [The early churches established under Paul were ordered in this way,] and with joyful hearts gladly and readily lived in fellowship, holding in common not only all spiritual but also all material goods, seeking to follow Christ their master, and wishing to become like him and one with him,[44] who himself showed us the way and commanded us to follow him.[45]

Do you think they were discussing hypostases?

from Michael Servetus, *On the Errors of the Trinity* (1531)

In a great spiritual awakening, through his study of Scripture, Servetus as a young man encountered Jesus Christ as a living figure, who had existed in historical time and was incarnate in human flesh. It is by this man, he subsequently argued in his theological works, and not by one of the abstract categories of the Athanasian Trinity, that human beings attained salvation. This understanding of the historical and embodied Christ is the overarching theme of his investigation *On the Errors of the Trinity*, which extended to seven books and occupies some three hundred printed pages in a modern

---

38. 1 John 1:3.
39. See above, note 11.
40. See 1 Corinthians 10:16.
41. Colossians 3:10; see also Ephesians 4:22–24.
42. 1 Corinthians 2:14.
43. Philippians 2:4.
44. Philippians 2:5.
45. Matthew 10:24–25; Luke 14:33.

edition.⁴⁶ It is presented in miniature in the first section of the first book, of which excerpts are given here.

In the very first sentence, Servetus asserts that attention should be paid to the "man Jesus Christ," rather than the abstract entity, or *hypostasis* (the Greek term for substance), of the Word (*Logos* in Greek), which had existed through all time, and was identified with the Son in the trinitarian totality of Father, Son, and Holy Spirit, identified by the Church Fathers as the three persons of a single God. Both his name, Jesus, and the appellation Christ (Greek for "the anointed one," the Hebrew Messiah) referred to a human being, an assertion Servetus defends with ample scriptural citations, of which only a select few are repeated below. Their accumulation defends the author's argument that those who knew Jesus in the flesh, and especially his disciples and apostles, knew a living human person and not a confabulated hypostasis.

Book One, §1

In examining the holy mysteries of the divine Trinity, I have decided I must begin with the man Jesus Christ, seeing that most investigators begin with airy speculation about the Word,⁴⁷ ignoring Christ as the foundation, and giving little or no attention to the man, nearly consigning the real Christ to oblivion. But I shall lead them back to the question of who Christ is. . . .

Who will deny that from the beginning he was called Jesus? That is, as an infant, on the day of his circumcision, at the angel's command, he was assigned that name. . . . Now Jesus . . . is a man's personal name, and Christ is a surname. The Jews all willingly called him Jesus, but refused to call him Christ⁴⁸ . . . and on this question the apostles frequently debated with them, whether Jesus was or was not the Christ. But that he was Jesus there was never any doubt or question, nor did anyone deny it. You see where this discussion leads, and with what intent Paul testifies before the Jews that Jesus is the Christ.⁴⁹ . . . About what Jesus do you think he was speaking? Do you think they were discussing hypostases?⁵⁰ I must therefore affirm that he is both Christ and Jesus. . . .

---

46. That of Rolande-Michelle Bénin and Marie-Louise Gicquel; cited in Texts and Studies, Chapter Six, under Servetus.
47. The Word, or *Logos* in Greek, spoken by God at the beginning of Creation and incarnated as Jesus: John 1:1; 1 John 1:1.
48. That is, they refused to call him the Messiah (Hebrew for the Greek *Christos*), the one anointed by God to be the savior of Israel.
49. Acts 18:4–5, 24–28.
50. The term *hypostasis* (singular), meaning "substance" in Greek, is used of the three members of the Trinity, the three together constituting three *hypostases*, or distinct substances, in the one *ousia*, or being, of God.

Furthermore, as Tertullian states . . . the name Christ also denotes a being of human nature. . . . Who, he asks, is the Son of man, if he is not himself a man born of a man, a body born of a body?[51] . . . Again, on the authority of holy Scripture, it is perfectly clear that it is a man who is named Christ. . . . In Matthew we read of *Mary, of whom Jesus was born, who is called the Messiah*, or *Christ*.[52] Take note of the article, and take note of the surname, for the former and the latter plainly indicate that the being referred to is perceived by the senses. . . .

And if Christ were not a man, both Christ's question and Peter's response would be absurd in this exchange: Christ asked, *"But who do you say that I am?"* and Peter answered, *"You are the Messiah, the Son of the living God."*[53] . . . And again, Christ's testimony is very clear when he calls himself a man: *but now you are trying to kill me, a man who has told you the truth that I heard from God.*[54] And Timothy calls him: *one mediator between God and humankind, Christ Jesus, himself human.*[55] . . . And John the Baptist spoke of Christ as *a man who comes after me. . . .*[56]

Likewise, when they came to arrest Jesus and he asked, *Who is it you want?* and they answered *Jesus of Nazareth*, he replied *I am he.*[57] And Judas said, *The one I kiss is the man; arrest him.*[58] And elsewhere Jesus said to the disciples, *It is I myself! Touch me and see.*[59] . . . And Peter said, *this Jesus, whom you crucified, . . . God has raised this Jesus to life, and we are all witnesses of it. . . .*[60]

Likewise, of what man do you think the apostle Paul speaks when he says this: *just as through the disobedience of the one man the many were made sinners, so also through the obedience of the one man the many will be made righteous*;[61] and also this: *for since by man came death, by man came also the resurrection of the dead.*[62] For Scripture does not take the word "man" here in a connotative sense, as though it were an abstraction, but it calls that particular

---

51. Tertullian, *Adversus Praxeam* 28; *Adversus Marcionem* 4.10.
52. Matthew 1:16. (NRSV)
53. Matthew 16:15–16. (NRSV)
54. John 8:40. (NRSV)
55. 1 Timothy 2:5. (NRSV)
56. John 1:30.
57. John 18:4–8.
58. Matthew 26:48.
59. Luke 24:39.
60. Acts 2:36, 32.
61. Romans 5:19.
62. 1 Corinthians 15:21 (King James Version [KJV]).

man Adam.[63] We, however, wish that our foundation be a connotative man and a sophistic substance.[64] Put away these sophistical tricks, and you will see a great light! The words of Christ are themselves the foundation of the church, and they are plain and transparent. Let us imitate the apostles who preached Christ using no rhetorical artifices of human construction.[65] The words spoken by God are pure words and are to be heard with simplicity. As the apostle Paul attests: not with lofty eloquence is the testimony about God to be preached, but plainly, as though we had become children, as though knowing nothing else *except Jesus Christ and him crucified.*[66]

Then we will know for sure just who are the real heretics

from Sebastian Castellio, *On Heretics: Whether They Should Be Punished, and How They Should Be Treated* (1554)

After this I looked, and there before me was a great multitude that no one could count, . . . wearing white robes.[67] . . . So it is written in the Book of Revelation, the last of the New Testament. An elder then asks about those clad in white: *Who are they, and where did they come from?*[68] For Castellio, who adapts this vision of a white-robed multitude to drive home his point to Christoph, duke of Württemberg in the preface to his work *On Heretics*, they are the ordinary people who follow Christ in their daily lives, as he had commanded, having been sanctified by his death and resurrection. For their obedience to the Lord, they are condemned as heretics by the powerful—princes and magistrates, pastors and professors—who fault the followers of Christ for their disregard of such theological niceties as predestination, the Trinity, and free will. Nor is it found sufficient to condemn the simple followers of Christ: they must be drowned, whipped, chained, disemboweled, drawn and quartered, and burned at the stake. Innocent in heart and deed, guilty only of disregard for theoretical matters nonessential for salvation, they are a new generation of martyrs, like those who came, as is written in

---

63. In the next verse, 1 Corinthians 15:22: "For as in Adam all die, so in Christ all will be made alive."
64. Servetus appears to be mocking scholastic argumentation here.
65. 1 Corinthians 2:1; 2 Peter 1:16.
66. Based on 1 Corinthians 1:17 and 1 Corinthians 2:1–2, quoting at end.
67. Revelation 7:9.
68. Revelation 7:13.

Revelation, *out of the great tribulation,* having *washed their robes and made them white in the blood of the Lamb.*[69] Surely Christ does not approve this torture of his followers; for if he did, what horrors then would be left to be done by the devil?

Martinus Bellius, to Christoph, Duke of Württemberg.

If you, most splendid Prince, had told your subjects that you would return to them at some unstated future time, and had commanded them all to clothe themselves in white robes, and thus clad in sparkling white to present themselves to you at whatever time it was that you arrived—what would you do, if you had found when you came at last that they hadn't bothered with the white robes, but busied themselves with altercations? . . . Would you have been pleased?

And what if they quarreled not only with words, but also with blows and sword thrusts, and these over here wounded, or even killed, those over there with whom they disagreed? . . . Prince, would you commend these citizens?

What if some few of them had taken care to put on those white robes, as you had commanded, while others menaced them on that account, or killed them? Would you not destroy such evildoers?

And what if, still worse, they claimed that these murders were committed at your command and in your name, although you had expressly forbidden such things? Would you not consider such a claim to be outrageous, and deserving of harsh punishment?

I ask you now, my Prince, kindly to listen to my explanation of why I have said these things. Christ, the prince of the world, as he was departing from this earth, told his listeners that he would return at an uncertain day and time, and commanded them to prepare white robes for his coming[70]—that is to say, that they should live godly lives, in friendship and without quarreling, each loving one another.

Now let us consider, I ask you, how well we perform that task. How many exert themselves at all to ready that white robe? Who is there who strives to live a holy, just, and godly life in this world, in expectation of the coming of the Lord? For nothing is there less concern. . . . Instead, we dispute about . . . where exactly Christ is now, what he is doing, in what manner he sits at the right hand of God the Father, or in what way he is one with the Father; and we grapple over the Trinity, and predestination, and free will, . . . and other things of this sort, the knowledge of which has nothing to do with being

---

69. Revelation 7:14.
70. Cf. Matthew 25:13; Mark 8:38; Luke 9:26, 18:8; Acts 1:7; Revelation 3:3, 6:11, 16:15.

saved by faith, . . . nor can they be known before our hearts are purified, . . . nor if they were known, would they change us for the better. . . .

But meanwhile if there were anyone who wished to ready his white robe, that is, to live a godly life, then all the others, . . . in wholesale agreement, without any hesitation, accuse him of being a heretic for seeking to be justified by works. . . . They falsely accuse him of horrific crimes he never considered, and so denigrate and denounce him to the crowd . . . which arouses such a savage rage that some are infuriated . . . if the victim is first strangled before going to the stake, and not tormented by being burned alive. . . .

I ask you, most illustrious Prince, what will Christ do, do you think, when he comes? Will he praise these doings? Will he approve of them?

. . . . .

This frenzied rush to judgment, which advances daily and spills blood everywhere, impels me, most illustrious Prince, to seek to stop the bleeding—especially the blood that is shed wrongfully, that is, the blood of those who are called heretics. Today the label of heretic has become so hateful, so heinous, so ugly, that anyone who wants to destroy his enemy can do so most speedily by accusing him of heresy. For as soon as people hear that word, the word alone arouses their hatred, . . . and they viciously and violently hunt down not only him who has been accused, but all those who dare breathe a word in his defense. . . .

Now truly, I do not say these things because I love heretics; rather, I hate heretics. But I want to point out these two great dangers. The first is that a person may be deemed a heretic, who is not a heretic. This was no small thing when it happened long ago, for Christ himself, and his followers, were slain as heretics; while in our own age, which is certainly not more holy, but rather more corrupt, it is likely to happen again. . . . The other danger is that even if the accused really is a heretic, he may be more grievously and harshly punished than Christian teaching allows.

. . . . .

What then is to be done amid this turmoil? . . . Caught in this web of hatred and persecution, we go daily from bad to worse. . . . Who would wish to be a Christian when he sees that those who confess the name of Christ are mercilessly destroyed at the hands of other Christians by fire, water, and sword, and more cruelly treated than bandits or cutthroats? . . .

O Christ, Creator of the world and King, do you see all this? Have you been so made other than you were, so cruel, so contrary to yourself? For when you were on earth, there was no one gentler, no one more merciful, no one more meek. . . . Have you now changed so much? . . . I ask you in the name of your holy Father, do you now ordain that those who do not understand your doctrines and precepts as they are set forth by our teachers deserve to be drowned, gutted, . . . dismembered, roasted in the flames, and tormented for as long as can be managed with every kind of torture? Christ, do you command these things, and approve them? . . . Christ, if you do these things, or order them to be done, then what have you left to be done by the devil? . . .

But here I shall desist. And I believe that you now understand fully, my Prince, how distant are these deeds from the teachings and counsels of Christ. Let us, then, now listen to the opinions of others. When you hear them speak, you will know for sure just who are the real heretics.

Chapter Seven: The English Compromise

Unlike the Reformation that unfolded on the Continent, crafted under the aegis of city magistrates and petty princes, the English Reformation centers on the single giant figure of the king: King Henry VIII, who remade the ecclesiastical polity of England, primarily, so that he might dispense with an infertile wife and father a legitimate male heir; but secondarily, so that he might gain authority over an overweening clergy and appropriate the wealth of the church. The Reformation Henry launched was long and turbulent, winding through the reigns of, in turn, his youngest child, Edward VI; his eldest, Mary I; and her junior, Elizabeth I. Although the last word had not been said by the time Elizabeth died—there would be nearly a century more of turmoil—still by then, England had become decisively Protestant, although in a manner other than that desired by Luther, Zwingli, or Calvin. The excerpts in this chapter illumine a few moments in the noisy symphony of this first phase of the English Reformation.

In 1529, Henry had already shifted his attentions from his first wife, Queen Catherine, mother of Mary, to his second, Anne Boleyn, eventual mother of Elizabeth. To effect that second marriage, he needed to break with the Roman church, which would not sanction the necessary divorce. The arrival in his hands of a boisterous pamphlet by the Protestant Simon Fish (d. 1531), purporting to be a plea from the beggars of the realm complaining of competition from mendicant monks, focused his thoughts on the benefits to be gained from undoing the complex apparatus of ecclesiastical property and authority in his realm.

As a student at Gray's Inn,[1] Fish had acted in a play critical of Cardinal Thomas Wolsey, then the king's Lord Chancellor, and fled to Antwerp (modern Belgium), where his fourteen-page pamphlet, *A Supplication for the Beggars*, was published early in 1529 and smuggled into England. The work was addressed to King Henry, and delivered to him by one of his staff, or perhaps even by Anne Boleyn. The king read it with intense interest—understandably, for it pinpointed issues of immediate moment. Fish returned to England in late 1529, perhaps in time to witness, in October of that year, the fall of Wolsey and the elevation of Thomas More to Lord Chancellor. He was soon after arrested, charged with heresy, and imprisoned, dying in prison of the plague in 1531.

Fish was not a major figure of the English Reformation, but he wrote a major book, as pointed and timely as it was brief. Its main arguments were

---

1. One of the four Inns of Court providing training for future barristers, or litigators.

economic and political: even as church tithes, taxes, and fees were impoverishing the people, the clergy had acquired for their own use (by Fish's reckoning) one-third of the wealth of England, thereby so dominating the political process that the king was isolated and incapacitated. It is precisely these threats to his sovereignty that Henry acted upon beginning in 1534, when by the Act of Supremacy he became head of the church in England, and continuing through 1541, during which years he oversaw the dissolution of hundreds of religious houses and the appropriation of their stupendous wealth for the crown.

Fish's momentous pamphlet was phrased as a witticism: it posed as a plea from the beggars of England. It elicited that same year a much longer response by none less than Thomas More, also wittily construed: entitled *A Supplication of Poor Souls in Purgatory*, it purported to be a petition by the residents of that afterlife domain whose existence Fish had challenged. Ironically, Fish would die of natural causes before he could be burned at the stake; but More was beheaded in 1535, having refused to recognize the supremacy of the king over the church in England, the remedy Fish had implicitly proposed.

By 1529, then, the erection of two of the essential pillars of the new English church had been envisioned: the king's ecclesiastical sovereignty, and the appropriation of church wealth. What remained was to establish the fundamentals of the new faith. That task was accomplished by the publication of two books: an official English Bible—vernacular translations of the Bible had previously been strictly forbidden in England—and the complementary *Book of Common Prayer*, supplying the proper words for every liturgical purpose in the reinvented service of Protestant worship. The force behind these pivotal books was Thomas Cranmer (1489–1556), Archbishop of Canterbury, the once-Catholic prelate who helped elevate the king over the old church, dismantle its age-old customs and institutions, and guide England to a Protestant future.

Cranmer was not himself the translator of the *Great Bible* that King Henry VIII ordered to be used in every parish church in England. Most of it was the work of William Tyndale (1494–1536), who, as an exile in Germany and the Netherlands in the 1520s, translated the New Testament and part of the Old, a labor cut short by his execution for heresy in 1536. At Cranmer's direction, Myles Coverdale completed the translation, but in some haste, working from Latin translations and Luther's German version. Scholarly method by this time, after the work of Desiderius Erasmus and humanist predecessors, required translation from the original Greek and Hebrew texts (which Luther had utilized). Subsequent English Bibles, including the Bishops' Bible of 1559, and the epochal Authorized Version of 1611, compiled at the direction of King James I by a team of fifty-four scholars, would meet this standard. But in the meantime, the *Great Bible* was first published in 1539 and immediately reissued in 1540 with the preface by Cranmer (repeated in subsequent editions) that is excerpted below. It was a monumental and pathbreaking achievement.

So, too, was the *Book of Common Prayer*, its first two editions appearing in 1549 and 1552 under Cranmer's direction. Subsequent editions largely reproducing the original text are still in use and remain the basis of Anglican and Episcopalian worship worldwide. Seeking compromise between conservative and reformist theological views, it firmly establishes Protestant understandings of such matters as the Lord's Supper, baptism and burial, and saints and images.

By 1553, when Mary Tudor ascended the throne, Cranmer had spent twenty-six years in the service of her two predecessors: Henry VIII, her father, and Edward VI, her brother. Now he was imprisoned for treason and heresy, and, notoriously, wavered in his defense of the faith and of all he had previously accomplished. Brought to the stake in 1556, he repudiated his six recantations, and plunged the hand by which he had signed them deep into the flames, before his whole body was consumed.

Cranmer's death in 1556 at age sixty-seven followed that of Jane Grey, at age seventeen, in 1554: the former after a long career as reformer, priest, and administrator; the latter after a nine-day reign as queen (July 10–19, 1553) and six months of subsequent imprisonment. The daughter of a niece of Henry VIII, Grey (1537–1554) had been raised as a possible successor to the throne, and the councilors of Edward VI preferred her, a Protestant, to her Catholic cousin Mary. She had received a fine humanist education, appropriate to her rank, and was profoundly imbued with Protestant principles.

Grey expected to be pardoned by Queen Mary, who had always been cordial to her. But a series of uprisings in early February 1554 impelled the queen to order her execution. Four days before that event,[2] Mary sent her personal confessor Dr. John Feckenham, a learned Benedictine, to meet with Grey and reconcile her to the Catholic church. He challenged her beliefs, and she defended them masterfully—an impressive performance by a young woman held in captivity. As impressive, arguably, was its aftermath: Feckenham offered to accompany Grey to the scaffold, and she agreed; there, moments before her death, they recited alternately, in English and Latin, the fifty-first psalm, offering to God "a broken and contrite heart."[3]

Soon after they had spoken in her cell, Grey recorded the conversation as a dialogue entitled *A Certain Communication*, of which the greater part is given here. At its conclusion, she signed her name, authenticating it. The manuscript of this brief work, along with other letters and poems, was published immediately

---

2. As noted in the first pamphlet publication described below; in the second, the time is given as two days.
3. Psalm 51:17.

after her death in 1554 as a pamphlet entitled *An Epistle of the Ladye Jane*. Another pamphlet containing these works was published in 1554 or 1555, and they were incorporated in the first (1563) edition of John Foxe's *Acts and Monuments*, the massive compilation of English Protestant martyr narratives.

Unlike the debate held between Feckenham and Grey, that between the native Londoner Edmund Campion (1540–1581) and his Protestant persecutors was no polite sparring, but a violent and desperate confrontation. That was not Campion's intention: he had proposed a duel of wit, a reasoned debate between him and the powerful and learned of the realm, where he confidently expected to persuade his opponents of the greater truth of the Catholic faith.

A brilliant scholar at Oxford en route to a major career in the Anglican church, Campion tacitly held Catholic views that necessitated, in 1569, his flight to Rome by way of Ireland and Douai in France.[4] In Rome in 1573, he joined the Jesuit order,[5] and eventually their English Mission: a group of English Jesuits pledged to serve English Catholics and reclaim that nation for the Catholic faith.

It was an inherently perilous project. The English authorities saw Catholic priests as not merely heretics, but worse, traitors. Capture meant torture, the coerced betrayal of associates, and a hideous death at Tyburn, where stood a scaffold that Campion thought, passing by on one of his adventures, resembled the cross on which Christ died.

In 1580, anticipating capture, Campion wrote in English the statement given in large part here to then-reigning Queen Elizabeth's Privy Council.[6] It has acquired the title "Campion's Challenge" or "Brag," from words he had supplied: he did not wish, he demurred, "to say anything that might sound in any way like an insolent brag or challenge." He stated openly that he was a Catholic priest whose ambition was to restore England to the ancient faith. He would do so through persuasion, and suggested three venues—the Privy Council itself, the assembled scholars of the universities, and a panel of legal experts—in which he might lay out compelling arguments for conversion. The "Challenge" was quickly printed by Campion's co-religionists, and circulated widely: it was to serve as prophylaxis, preventing his being completely silenced by his persecutors. In 1581, at much greater length but in the same spirit, Campion published in Latin his *Ten Reasons* arguing the superiority of the Catholic to the Protestant faith, and challenging the scholars of Oxford and Cambridge to meet in disputation and respond.

---

4. Site of the English College, a seminary for Catholic exiles.

5. Founded in 1534 to defend the papacy and the Catholic church against the Protestant Reformation and to missionize around the world.

6. Privy Council: body of advisors to the English sovereign, wielding great power.

That same year, Campion was captured, tortured, and executed, as he had expected, at Tyburn. But death was not enough for his executioners: they demanded humiliation. Ravaged by torture, dispirited, and incoherent, Campion was at last summoned to debate, alone, against the assembled finest minds of the English universities. The transcript of his questioners' inquisition with his inadequate response was then published, a memorial of the triumph of Protestant over Catholic in the age of Elizabeth.

In 1581, when Campion met his destined end at Tyburn, Margaret Dakins Hoby (c. 1571–1633) was a privileged girl of ten, pampered and courted, who would later be married three times to members of England's leading families. Yet she was fully immersed in the Anglican culture that prevailed in Elizabethan England under the watchful eyes of that queen's ministers, to which was added a thorough training in Puritan disciplinary practices. Regardless of her considerable fortune, she led an earnest and conscientious life, as her diary attests, guided by unyielding religious principles.

Hoby's diary, the first written by a woman in English, reflects her privileged position, but the evidences of wealth and power glimpsed in the background are overshadowed by the religious commitments of its author. The diary begins in 1599, when Hoby was twenty-eight years old and three years into her third marriage. It portrays a young woman vigorously in charge of her household, supervising—and working alongside of—her servants, assisting neighbors, and managing properties. Her busy days also featured multiple sessions of private prayer, self-examination, meditation, Bible study, and devotional reading, as well as consultations with the resident chaplain. The diary ends in 1605, well before the death of its author in 1633. It survives in its original, autograph manuscript format, now digitized and available through library networks, and in two twentieth-century editions. Included here are a few excerpts from the earlier period, 1599–1602, chosen as representative of the range of Hoby's activity.

This chapter opens with the epochal struggle between the king of England and pope of Rome, mirrored in the covert plea to Henry VIII by Simon Fish that he nationalize the Catholic church. It ends less than a century later in another timbre: with a sober gentlewoman, a second-generation Protestant, who when she was not dyeing wool with her servants or tending to this neighbor's childbirth or that one's newborn calf, was occupied in prayer and self-examination, or discussions with her learned chaplain on the finer points of the doctrine of infant baptism. The entries in her diary allow the reader to explore the mental world of Christian believers in the last years of Elizabeth's reign, embodying the English compromise between the old church and the new that that would hold, though challenged mightily in the next decades, into modern times.

All five texts appearing in this chapter were originally written in the English of the sixteenth century, at times distant from our own. Language, punctuation, and spelling have been modernized so as to make them more accessible to contemporary readers.

They have gotten into their hands the third part of your realm

from Simon Fish, *A Supplication for the Beggars* (1529)

The protagonists of Fish's pamphlet, the beggars of England, complain to their king of "their woeful misery"; no longer receiving sufficient alms,[7] they have become "needy, impotent, blind, lame, and sick," and "are left to die of hunger." The problem is a parasitical clergy, who monopolize a disproportionate share—Fish says one-third—of the nation's wealth. Although the beggars really compete, to follow Fish's narrative, only with the mendicant friars, all the other categories of clergy, including bishops and archbishops, abbots and priests, and many lesser officials, collectively drain the wealth of the people with their fees and taxes. And they dominate in the political arena as well: "Are they not stronger in our own parliament house," he asks the king, "than yourself?" Beyond these major depredations in the realm of economic and politics, they wage a sexual war against the men of England, corrupting "every man's wife, every man's daughter, and every man's maid," while foisting their illegitimate progeny on deceived householders, whose estates then fall into the hands not of their own legitimate heirs, but the offspring of debauched clerics. The solution: strip them of their property, and send them out to live by the labor of their hands.

To the king our sovereign lord.

Most lamentably do your poor lowly beadsmen[8] complain to your highness of their woeful misery. They are the wretched and hideous wretches on whom, for horror, scarcely any of you dare look, . . . needy, impotent, blind, lame, and sick, who live only by alms, whose number so greatly increases each day that all the alms of all the well-disposed people of your realm are not

---

7. Alms: gifts to the poor.
8. Beadsman or bedesman: archaic term meaning "one who prays for the soul of another"; roughly, "your loyal servant."

half enough to sustain them, but they are left to die of hunger. And this most pestilent mischief has come upon your said poor beadsmen for this reason, that during the reigns of your royal predecessors, there has craftily crept into your realm another group of idle beggars and vagabonds, not impotent but strong and powerful, who counterfeit holiness, who since they arrived . . . have increased before your eyes not only into a great multitude, but even into a kingdom. These are not shepherds, but ravenous wolves in shepherds' clothing who devour their flocks: the Bishops, Abbots, Priors, Deacons, Archdeans, Suffragans, Priests, Monks, Canons, Friars, Pardoners, and Summoners.[9]

And who is able to count this idle, ravenous lot who, doing no labor, have begged so importunately that they have gotten into their hands more than the third part of all your realm. The best lordships, manors, lands, and territories are theirs. Besides this, they have the tenth part of all the grain, meadow, pasture, grass, wool, colts, calves, lambs, pigs, geese, and chickens, plus . . . the tenth part of the wool, milk, honey, wax, cheese, and butter. More, they so closely watch their profits that the poor housewife must hand over every tenth egg, lest she . . . be taken as a heretic. . . .

How much money do they take in for probates of testaments, privy tithes, pilgrimage offerings, and for first Masses?[10] Every man and child who is buried must pay something for Masses and dirges to be sung for him, or else they will accuse the friends and executors of the deceased of heresy. How much money do they get for funerals, for the hearing of confessions, . . . for cursings and then absolutions? What a pile of money do the pardoners gather in a year? . . . Finally, the infinite number of begging friars, what do they get in a year? Here, if it please your Grace[11] to take note, you shall see a thing far out of joint. . . .

Oh grievous and painful exactions thus yearly to be paid . . . ! And this will they have or else arrange for him who will not give it to them to be taken as a heretic. What tyrant ever oppressed the people like this cruel and vengeful pack? . . . What good Christian people will be able to succor us poor lepers, blind, sore, and lame, that be thus yearly oppressed? Is it any marvel that your people so complain of poverty? . . .

And what do they do, all this greedy sort of brawny, idle, holy thieves, with these yearly exactions that they take from the people? Truly nothing, but exempt themselves from obedience to your Grace! Nothing but transfer all sovereignty, power, lordship, authority, obedience, and dignity from your Grace to themselves! Nothing but that all your subjects should fall into disobedience and rebellion against your Grace, and be under them. . . .

---

9. A list of clerical positions, suggesting their burdensome proliferation.
10. An assortment of fees demanded by the clergy of the common people.
11. The king, here and below, to whom the work is addressed.

And then, and what do they more? Truly nothing but apply themselves, using all the tricks they have, to do with every man's wife, every man's daughter, and every man's maid, that cuckoldry and debauchery should reign over all among your subjects, that no man should be certain of his own child, but that their bastards might inherit each man's possessions, depriving their legitimate children of their inheritance in subversion of all right and godly order in the administration of estates. More, by their abstaining from marriage,[12] they do slow the rate of population increase, whereby the whole realm eventually, if this situation continues, shall be made an uninhabited desert. . . .

What is the remedy? To make laws against them? I am in doubt whether you will be able to do so. Are they not stronger in our own parliament house than yourself? What a number of Bishops, Abbots, and Priors are lords of your parliament? Are not all the learned men in your realm paid by them to speak in your parliament house for them against your crown and dignity and the commonwealth of your realm, only a few of your own learned councilors excepted? . . . Who is he, however sorely aggrieved for the murder of his ancestor, or ravishment of his wife or daughter, or robbery, trespass, mayhem, debt, or any other offence, who dares lay it to their charge in any kind of action?—and if he do then is he thereupon accused by their wiliness of heresy. . . . So are your laws made captive by them that no man that they choose to excommunicate may be admitted to pursue any action in any of your courts. If any man in your sessions dare be so bold as to indict a priest of any such crime, he will have . . . such a yoke of heresy laid on his neck that it will make him wish he had not done it. . . .

Set these brawny bullies abroad in the world to get them wives of their own, to get their living with their labor by the sweat of their brow according to the commandment of God.[13] . . . Tie these holy idle thieves to carts to be whipped naked about every market town till they will fall to labor, so that they not take away by their importunate begging the alms that the good Christian people would give to us sore, impotent, miserable people, your beadsmen. . . . Then shall these great yearly exactions cease. Then shall your sword, power, crown, dignity, and the obedience of your people not be stolen from you. . . . Then shall the population increase. Then shall your commons[14] grow in wealth. Then shall the Gospel be preached. Then shall none beg our alms from us. . . . Then shall we daily pray to God for your most noble estate long to endure.

---

12. These clerics, despite their alleged debaucheries, which resulted in illegitimate and thus less desirable births, were all nominally celibate.

13. Genesis 3:19.

14. Commons: the common people.

Who would refuse light in darkness? In hunger, food? In cold, fire?

from Thomas Cranmer, *Preface to the Great Bible* (1540)

Astonishingly, given the vast scope and high importance of the *Great Bible*, Cranmer's preface is simple in plan and utterly lucid. He describes two groups of potential readers: first, those who have not read the Bible before, and are encouraged to do so; and second, those who when they read, may be tempted to engage in controversies, manipulating the text to an end for which it was not intended. In the first group, Cranmer envisions nearly the whole population of England. In the second, he gently warns those who might be tempted to do so against disrupting the unity of the faith: so that "every man who comes to the reading of this holy book, ought to bring with him first and foremost the fear of almighty God . . . showing himself to be a sober and fruitful hearer and learner."

For two different sorts of people, something should be said at the outset of this book by way of a preface or prologue. . . . For truly there are some who are too slow and need the spur, some others who seem too quick, and need more of the bridle. . . . In the former sort are those who refuse to read or to hear read the scripture in the vulgar[15] tongue. . . . In the latter sort are those who by their inordinate reading, indiscreet speaking, contentious disputing, . . . slander and hinder the word of God. . . .

And as touching the former, I would marvel much that any man should be so foolish, as to refuse in darkness, light; in hunger, food; in cold, fire. For the word of God is light: *Your word is a lamp for my feet.*[16] It is food: *Man shall not live on bread alone.*[17] It is fire: *I have come to bring fire on the earth.*[18] . . . I would marvel . . . at this, save that I consider how much custom and usage may do. . . ; for it is not much above one hundred years ago, since Scripture has not been accustomed to be read in the vulgar tongue within this realm. . . .

---

15. Vulgar tongue: English, the language of the people (Latin *vulgus*), the vernacular.
16. Psalm 119:105.
17. Matthew 4:4.
18. Luke 12:49.

But now to leave custom aside, and to weigh . . . what benefit there is that scripture be had and read by the lay and common people. . . . Let no man make excuse. . . . Is it not for you to study and to read the scripture, because you are encumbered and distracted with cares and business? . . . Your wife provokes you to anger; your child gives you occasion to take sorrow and pensiveness; your enemies lie in wait for you; your friend (as you take him to be) sometimes envies you; your neighbor . . . picks quarrels against you; . . . poverty is painful to you; the loss of someone dear and well-beloved causes you to mourn; prosperity raises you up, adversity brings you low. Briefly, such diverse and such manifold occasions of cares, tribulations, and temptations, beset you and besiege you round about. Where can you have armor or fortress against these assaults? Where can you have salves for your sores but of holy Scripture? . . .

Do you not note and consider how the smith, mason, or carpenter, or any other handy craftsman, whatever need he be in, whatsoever other shift he make, he will not sell nor pawn the tools of his occupation. For then how should he do his job, or get his living without them? Of like mind and affection ought we to be towards holy Scripture. For just as mallets, hammers, saws, chisels, axes, and hatchets, are the tools of their occupation, so the books of the prophets, and apostles, and all holy writers inspired by the Holy Spirit, are the instruments of our salvation. Wherefore let us not hesitate to buy and provide ourselves with the Bible . . . ; and let us think that to be a better jewel in our house than either gold or silver. . . .

Perhaps they will ask me: What if we do not understand what we read, that is contained in the books? . . . Yet . . . the Holy Spirit has so ordered and arranged the scriptures, that in them tavern-keepers, fishermen, and shepherds may find their edification in the same way that great scholars do their erudition. For those books were not made for vainglory, as were the writings of the ancient philosophers and rhetoricians, so that the makers win admiration for their high styles and obscure manner of writing, of which nothing can be understood without a teacher or interpreter. But the apostles and prophets wrote their books so that their special intent and purpose might be understood and perceived by every reader. . . .

Here . . . all manner of persons, men, women, young, old, learned, unlearned, rich, poor, . . . lords, ladies, officers, . . . virgins, wives, widows, lawyers, merchants, . . . of whatever estate or condition they be, may in this book learn all things that they ought to believe . . . both concerning almighty God, and concerning themselves and all others.

Briefly, to the reading of the Scripture none can be enemy. . . . Therefore, as touching this first part of my preface, I will here conclude, and take it as a conclusion sufficiently determined and established, that it is convenient and good that the Scriptures be read by all sorts and kinds of people, and in the vulgar tongue, . . . especially now that the king's Highness, being supreme head, next after Christ, of this Church of England, has approved with his royal assent their setting forth, which should be for all true and obedient subjects sufficient reason for their doing so, without further delay, argument, or resistance. . . .

Then, now, to come to the second and latter part of my preface. There is nothing so good in this world, but it may be abused, and turned from unhurtful and wholesome to hurtful and noisome purpose. . . . Wherefore I would advise you all who come to the reading or hearing of this book, which is the word of God, the most precious jewel and most holy relic that remains upon earth; that you bring with you the fear of God, and that you do it with all due reverence, and not use your knowledge of it for the vainglory of frivolous disputation. . . .

I say this not to dissuade men from the knowledge of God, and reading or studying of the Scripture; for I say that it is as necessary for the life of man's soul, as for the body to breathe. . . . I do not forbid you to read, but I forbid you to argue. Neither do I forbid you to use your reason so far as is good and godly: but I do not allow such reasoning to be done out of season, and out of measure and good order. . . . Therefore . . . , the fear of God must be the first beginning, and as it were an . . . introduction to all those who shall enter into the very true and most fruitful knowledge of the holy Scriptures. . . .

Therefore to conclude this latter part of my preface: every man who comes to the reading of this holy book, ought to bring with him first and foremost the fear of almighty God, and then next, a firm and stable purpose to reform his own self in accord with its instruction, . . . showing himself to be a sober and fruitful hearer and learner. . . .

What did he take, and break, and give, but bread?

from Lady Jane Grey, *A Certain Communication* (1554)

In this dialogue recorded by Lady Jane Grey just four days before her execution, John Feckenham, an expert contender in theological debates, engages Grey on a series of doctrinal issues that divided Catholics and Protestants. First, he elicits from her a statement of trinitarian belief, which he would have found satisfactory: she affirms her belief in God the Father, God the Son, and God the Holy Spirit as the three persons of one God. He then probes into her views on the efficacy of good works for salvation and is rebuffed: she holds that justification is by faith alone, a signal Protestant position. He asks whether there are seven sacraments, the Catholic view, to which she replies there are only two, baptism and the Lord's Supper (or Eucharist, the sacrament of Holy Communion), both scripturally attested. Crucially, he inquires into her understanding of the substance of the bread and wine consumed at the Eucharist, to which her firm and extended response is that the meal commemorates, but does not reenact, Christ's one sacrifice on the cross for the redemption of sinners. Further, she advocates communion in both kinds (both bread and wine), while generally only the consecrated bread was distributed to the Catholic laity. Feckenham chides Grey, finally, for relying on Scripture rather than on the church. "Shall I believe that church?" she responds; "God forbid. . . . "

A certain communication, between the Lady Jane, and Master Feckenham, four days before her death, even word for word, her own hand being put thereto.

FECKENHAM speaks first: What thing is required in a Christian?

JANE: To believe in God the Father, in God the Son, in God the Holy Ghost, three persons and one God.

FECKENHAM: Is there nothing else required in a Christian but to believe in God?

JANE: Yes, we must believe in him, we must love him with all our heart, with all our soul, and all our mind, and our neighbor as our self.

FECKENHAM: Why then faith justifies not, nor saves not.

JANE: Yes, in truth, faith (as Saint Paul says) alone justifies.

FECKENHAM: Why then does Saint Paul say: If I have all faith without love, it is nothing.[19]

JANE: True it is, for how can I love him in whom I trust not? Or how can I trust in him whom I love not? Faith and love agree both together, and yet love is comprehended in faith.

FECKENHAM: How shall we love our neighbor?

JANE: To love our neighbor is to feed the hungry, clothe the naked and give drink to the thirsty,[20] and to do to him as we would do to ourselves.[21]

---

19. Cf. 1 Corinthians 13:2: "if I have a faith that can move mountains, but do not have love, I am nothing."
20. Cf. Matthew 25:36–37; Romans 12:20.
21. Cf. Matthew 7:12; Luke 6:31.

FECKENHAM: Why then is it necessary to salvation to do good works and it is not sufficient to believe?

JANE: I deny that and I affirm that faith only alone saves. But it is meet for Christians, in token that they follow their master Christ, to do good works, yet may we not say that they profit to salvation. For, although we have all done all that we can, yet we be unprofitable servants, and the faith only in Christ's blood saves.

FECKENHAM: How many sacraments are there?

JANE: Two; the one the sacrament of baptism, and the other the sacrament of our Lord's Supper.

FECKENHAM: No, there are seven.

JANE: By what Scripture do you find that?

FECKENHAM: Well, we will talk of that hereafter. But what is signified by your two sacraments?

JANE: By the sacrament of baptism, I am washed with water and regenerated by the Spirit; and that washing is a token to me that I am the child of God. The sacrament of the Lord's Supper is offered unto me as a sure seal and testimony that by the blood of Christ, which he shed for me on the cross, I am made partaker of the everlasting kingdom.

FECKENHAM: Why, what do you receive in that bread? Do you not receive the very body and blood of Christ?

JANE: No surely, I do not believe so. I think that at the supper I receive neither flesh nor blood, but only bread and wine. When that bread is broken, and that wine drunk, I am reminded that the body of Christ was broken for my sins, and his blood shed on the cross; and with that bread and wine, I receive the benefits that came by the breaking of his body and the shedding of his blood on the cross for my sins.

FECKENHAM: Why, does Christ not speak these words: *Take, eat, this is my body?*[22] Could we ask for any plainer words? Does he not say that it is his body?

JANE: I grant he says so . . . [but] God forbid that I should say that I eat the actual natural body and blood of Christ, for then either I would consume my redemption,[23] or else there would need be two bodies, or two Christs. . . . If one body was tormented on the cross, and they did eat another

---

22. Matthew 26:26; Mark 14:22; Luke 22:19; 1 Corinthians 11:24.
23. That is, she would then eat, and thereby destroy, the body that had redeemed her.

body, then he must have had two bodies. Otherwise, if his body were eaten, it was not broken upon the cross; or else, if it were broken upon the cross, it was not eaten by his disciples.

FECKENHAM: Why is it not as possible that Christ by his power could make his body both to be eaten and broken, in the same way that he was born of a woman without the seed of man, and he walked on the sea although he had a body, and other such like miracles as he wrought by his power alone?

JANE: Yes, in truth, if God had wished to perform a miracle at his Supper, he might have done so; . . . But I ask you to answer this one question: Where was Christ when he said: *Take, eat, this is my body?* Was he not at the table when he said these words? He was at that time alive, and did not suffer until the next day. Well, what did he take, but bread? And what did he break, but bread? And what did he give, but bread? Look, what he took, he broke; and look, what he broke, he gave; and look, what he gave, they did eat. And all this he did while he himself was at supper with his disciples, or else they were deceived.

FECKENHAM: You ground your faith upon authors who say in one breath one thing and its opposite, and not upon the church, on which you should rely.

JANE: No, I ground my faith upon God's Word and not upon the church. For . . . the faith of the church must be tried by God's Word, and not God's Word by the church, nor my faith by the church. Shall I believe . . . the church that takes away from me that half part of the Lord's Supper, and will let no layman receive it in both kinds, but only the priest? . . . Shall I believe that church? God forbid. . . .

With these and such like persuasions, Feckenham would have had me . . . incline to the church, but it would not be. There were many other things about which we reasoned, but these were the chief.

By me,

Jane Dudley[24]

---

24. Dudley was Grey's married name. Her husband was Guildford Dudley, the son of the nobleman who managed Grey's accession.

We shall either win you heaven, or die upon your pikes[25]

from Edmund Campion, *Challenge to the Privy Council* (1580)

In a communication phrased in tones of utter politeness, Campion informs Queen Elizabeth's Privy Council, sparing those honorable gentlemen the labor of investigating his case, that he preemptively confesses to his Catholic faith and his ambition to restore England to the Catholic fold. He has come to England commissioned by the Jesuit order "to preach the Gospel, to minister the Sacraments, to instruct the simple, to reform sinners, [and] to confute errors." He will not meddle in political matters, but wishes to put forth his case in three venues: the Privy Council itself, the assembled scholars of the universities, and a panel of legal experts. Bold "in declaring the majesty of Jesus [his] King," he believes his evidence is "impregnable," and that his Protestant opponents will be unable to "maintain their doctrine in disputation." He and his colleagues are determined "to carry the cross you shall lay upon us," and not to despair in the face of torture and execution. If that is to be the outcome, then he will meet his persecutors in the afterlife, where they may be reconciled at last. He does not wish to "brag" or to "challenge" the Councilors, he assures them, but his firm convictions fearlessly stated constitute a challenge nonetheless.

To the Right Honorable, the Lords of Her Majesty's Privy Council:

Since I have come from Germany and Bohemia . . . and transported myself into this noble realm, my dear country, for the glory of God and benefit of souls, I thought it like enough that, in this busy, watchful, and suspicious world, I should either sooner or later be intercepted and stopped on my journey.

Wherefore, providing for all events, and uncertain what may become of me, when God shall perhaps deliver my body into captivity, I supposed it necessary to put this in writing in preparation, desiring your good lordships to give it your reading, so that you may know my purpose. By doing so, I trust I shall relieve you of some labor. For that which otherwise you would have had to seek out and investigate, I do now lay into your hands by plain confession. And so that the whole matter may be presented in order, . . . I structure it as nine points, or articles, directly, truly and resolutely opening my full enterprise and purpose.

1. I confess that I am (although unworthy) a priest of the Catholic church, and through the great mercy of God vowed now these eight years into the order of the Society of Jesus. In doing so, I have pledged myself to a special kind

---

25. Pikes: the kind of spear commonly used by foot soldiers of that time.

of warfare under the banner of obedience, and also resigned all my interest or possibility of wealth, honor, pleasure, and other worldly felicity.

2. As instructed by our General Provost, which is to me a warrant from heaven and oracle of Christ, I journeyed from Prague to Rome (where our General Father is always resident) and from Rome to England, as I might and would have done joyously into any part of Christendom or Heathendom,[26] had that been my assignment.

3. My charge is . . . to preach the Gospel, to minister the sacraments, to instruct the simple, to reform sinners, to confute errors—in brief, to cry alarm spiritual against foul vice and proud ignorance, with which many of my dear countrymen are abused.

4. I never intended, and am strictly forbidden by our Father that sent me, to deal in any respect with matters of state or policy of this realm, as these are things unrelated to my vocation, and from which I gladly restrain and sequester my thoughts.

5. I do ask, to the glory of God, with all humility, and under your supervision, three sorts of impartial and quiet audiences: the first, before your Honors, at which I will discourse of religion, so far as it touches the general welfare and your nobilities; the second, at which I will expand on my case, before the Doctors and Masters and chosen men of both universities, at which I will endeavor to defend the faith of our Catholic church by proofs innumerable . . . ; the third, before the lawyers . . . at which I will defend the said faith by the common wisdom of the laws standing yet in force and practice.

6. I would be loath to say anything that might sound in any way like an insolent brag or challenge. . . . Yet I am so bold in declaring the majesty of Jesus my King, and such confidence in his gracious favor, and such assurance in my cause, and my evidence so impregnable, and because I know perfectly that no one Protestant, nor all the Protestants living, nor any sect of our adversaries . . . can maintain their doctrine in disputation. I shall sue most humbly and instantly for combat with all and every of them, and the most prominent that may be found: protesting that in this trial the better prepared they are, the more welcome they shall be.

7. And because it has pleased God to enrich the Queen my Sovereign Lady with notable gifts of nature, learning, and princely education, I do profoundly trust that if her Highness would deign to attend such a conference as . . . I have suggested, or to hear a few sermons . . . that I will deliver, such manifest and fair light . . . may be cast upon these controversies, that possibly her zeal of truth and love of her people shall incline her noble Grace to

---

26. Heathendom or Heathenness: Campion viewed the world as divided between Christian and non-Christian, or heathen lands.

discourage some proceedings hurtful to the realm, and deal more equitably with those of us who are oppressed.

8. Moreover I doubt not but you, her Highness' Council, . . . when you shall have heard these questions of religion explained faithfully, which many times by our adversaries are huddled up and confounded, will see upon what substantial grounds our Catholic faith is built, how feeble that side is which circumstances have allowed to prevail against us, and so at last for your own souls, and for many thousand souls that depend upon your government, will condemn error when it is revealed, and pay attention to those who would spend the best blood in their bodies for your salvation. Many innocent hands are lifted up to heaven for you daily by those English students, whose posterity shall never die, who . . . are determined never to give up on you, but either to win you heaven, or to die upon your pikes. And touching our Society, be it known to you that we, all the Jesuits in the world, have made a league . . . cheerfully to carry the cross you shall lay upon us, and never to despair of your recovery, while we have a man left to enjoy your Tyburn,[27] or to be racked[28] with your torments, or consumed with your prisons. The expense is reckoned, the enterprise is begun; it is of God, it cannot be withstood. So the faith was planted: so it must be restored.

9. If my offers are refused, and my endeavors cannot succeed, and I . . . shall be rewarded with punishment, I have no more to say but to recommend your case and mine to almighty God, the searcher of hearts; may he send us his grace, and see us at accord before the day of judgment, to the end we may at last be friends in heaven, when all injuries shall be forgotten.

And I later returned to private examination and prayer

from Lady Margaret Hoby, *Diary* (1599–1605)

The few selections given here from the *Diary* of Lady Margaret Hoby for the period 1599 to 1602 are representative of her various activities and concerns. She assists a neighbor woman in labor, checks out a deformed newborn calf for another, dyes wool with her women servants, manages the household and, in her husband's absence, the landed property—all while,

---

27. Tyburn: then a village outside London (in modern times part of the metropolis), which was the principal place of execution of convicted traitors and heretics.
28. Rack: the instrument of torture most commonly used on England's political prisoners.

intermittently and uncomplainingly, she tends to her own ill health and bouts of sleeplessness. Without diminishing these responsibilities, of paramount importance to her are religious duties: church attendance, of course, and not only on Sunday, and not only once; and a host of other, private practices, such as frequent prayer, the recording of sermons heard, the review of lectionary passages read and annotation of her Bible accordingly, periods of self-examination and meditation, and frequent talks with "faithful divines," of whom one was kept ready at hand, on her paid staff.

1. August 13, 1599

In the morning, after private prayers and order taken for dinner, I wrote some notes in my testament until 10 o'clock. Then I went to walk, and, after I returned home, I prayed privately, read a chapter of the Bible, and wrought[29] until dinner time. Afterwards I . . . did some things about the house until 4, then I wrote out the sermon into my book preached the day before, and, when I had again gone about in the house and given order for supper and other things, I returned to examination and prayer: then I walked until supper time, and, after catechizing, meditated a while on what I had heard, with lament to God for pardon both of my [sins of] omission and commission of which I found myself guilty, I went to bed.

2. August 15, 1599

In the morning at 6 o'clock, I prayed privately. That done, I went to a woman in travail of child, with whom I was busy . . . until 1 o'clock, about which time, she being delivered and I having praised God, returned home and betook myself to private prayer. . . . Then I went to work until after 5, and then to examination and prayer; the Lord make me thankful, who has heard my prayers and has not turned his face from me. Then I talked with Mrs. Brutnell until supper time, and after walked a little into the fields, and so to prayers, and then to bed.

3. May 6, 1600

After private prayers I ate some food with Mr. Hoby, and then took horse and rode to Hurwoodall, to see our farm that we bought from Thomas Calsone. Then I came home and went to dinner. Afterward, I was busy in the house and talking with Mr. Daunie, who invited me to be a witness at his child's baptizing, which I refused, in regard that my conscience was not persuaded of the charge I was to undertake, nor thoroughly taught touching the responsibility of witnesses . . . ; but I will inquire more of this matter, God

---

29. Wrought: did textile tasks, such as sewing or embroidery.

willing, with the next faithful divine,[30] being loath to deny, if I may, any friend such a courtesy. Afterward, I went about the house and took order for supper, and later returned to private examination and prayer. Afterward, I went to supper, then I read, and lastly went to bed.

4. May 9, 1600

After private prayers I ate a little and then walked abroad with Mr. Hoby. Afterward, I did diverse things in the house and then went to dinner. Afterward, I was busy until towards night, at which time I walked with Mr. Hoby and Mr. Rhodes,[31] and talked touching baptism. Then I went to private examination and prayer, having had a long rest now, I thank God, who, of his mercy, I pray to strengthen me so in this release that I may be prepared for new assaults.[32] After that I went to supper, then to the reading, and so to bed.

5. May 3, 1601

[The Lord's day.] After I had been to church, I prayed, and, after dinner, talked of good things to some of my neighbors, and, when they were at catechizing,[33] I wrote notes in my Bible on the chapter.[34] Afterward, I dressed the sores I had in hand, and, when I had written a letter to my mother, I went to private examination and prayer.

6. May 5, 1601

After prayers I went to the church, where I heard a sermon. Afterward, I came home and heard Mr. Rhodes read.[35] After dinner, I went abroad, and when I had come home I dressed some sores. Afterward, I heard Mr. Rhodes read, and wrought within a while. Afterward, I went to see a calf at Munckmans, which had two great heads, [and] four ears. . . . The heads had long hairs like bristles about the mouths, such as no other cow has. The hind legs had no parting from the rump, but grew backward, and were no longer but from the first joint; also, the back bone was parted about the middle, and a there was a round hole in the midst of the calf's body. One would have to think all this came from some kind of stroke it had in the cow's belly. After this, I came in to private meditation and prayer.

7. May 9, 1601

This day I kept to my chamber and took medicine, being all the night before pained in my teeth so that I neither slept nor rested.

---

30. Faithful divine: spiritual adviser.
31. Richard Rhodes, her chaplain.
32. That is, of pains that had temporarily abated.
33. An additional, perhaps informal religious service.
34. That is, the reading in that day's lectionary.
35. That is, from the lectionary.

8. April 6, 1602

In the morning, having slept well, I promised to my self health and quiet, according to the nature of man who thinks the present condition will never alter; but God, who sees their thoughts long before, does usually show his children the vanity of their cogitation by sending some gentle cross that may pull them from dreaming of earthly quiet, which I found, I praise God. . . .

9. May 2, 1602

[The Lord's day.] This day, I praise God, having my health, I heard all the services with good profit; yet I had some conflict with one of my kinsmen, for a friend I cannot call him. And God's mercy and truth is ever with me, God make me thankful, amen.

10. May 6, 1602

I praise God I had health of body. However so justly God has suffered Satan to afflict my mind, yet my hope is that my Redeemer will bring my soul out of troubles, that it may praise his name; and so I will wait with patience for deliverance.

Chapter Eight: Catholic Reform and Renewal

The reform of the Catholic church was already centuries in progress when Luther broke with Rome and the papacy to launch the Protestant Reformation. As seen in Chapter One, such dissidents as John Wyclif and Jan Hus had raised fundamental questions about the ecclesiastical system and church doctrine more than a century before, summing up long-brewing discontents, and pointing to critiques still more dogged and profound. So in a sense, the Catholic Reformation of the sixteenth century was not so much a response to the Protestant challenge as the culmination of deep streams of discontent.

Among many others, three forms of discontent may be noted. First, resentment of the clergy, viewed as indifferent, incompetent, immoral, and self-indulgent, was widespread. Second, both individuals and states chafed against the taxes and tithes extracted to support the ecclesiastical establishment. Third, laypersons hungered for spiritual sustenance, turning to the cult of saints, or to alternate institutions, including confraternities and other such sodalities, and to varieties of mysticism and heresy.

Yet the Catholic Reformation was also a Counter-Reformation, a process by which the church of Rome responded to Protestant defection. Early attempts to seek a compromise on doctrine and practice, culminating in the Colloquy of Regensburg in 1541, gave way to the massive effort of the Council of Trent. That body of elite churchmen, meeting intermittently over eighteen years (1545–1563), generated a host of decrees buttressing the papacy, the ecclesiastical order, the sacramental system, and the cult of saints. At the same time, they repudiated the doctrines of *sola fide* (justification by faith alone) and *sola scriptura* (by Scripture alone), and imposed new discipline on the clergy, the cloistered religious (especially women), and the private life of the laity.

Not only councils and delegations, but also many individuals engaged in the struggle to restore the authority of the church and to chart the course of post-Reformation Catholic spirituality. Among them are the authors of works of which excerpts appear in this chapter, illustrating diverse aspects of Catholic Reform and Counter-Reformation.

The Venetian nobleman Gasparo Contarini (1483–1542)—intellectual, politician, and finally, cardinal of the church—wrote *The Duties of a Bishop* in 1517, only months before Luther initiated the indulgence controversy that precipitated the break with Rome (see Chapter Three). Writing as a conscientious layman who had himself undergone a profound spiritual experience, Contarini argues implicitly that the church will be reformed when its bishops are. Bishops played (and still play) a critical role in the ecclesiastical order: they presided over a diocese, a territorial unit encompassing a principal church, the bishop's cathedral, and several other churches administered by priests obedient to the bishop. Bishops ensured that worship services were properly conducted, supervised the behavior and performance of priests, and presided over networks of assistance to the poor and sick.

Contarini's concern with the spiritual condition and administrative effectiveness of the bishop reflects the prevailing discontent with clerical performance. He voices the same concern again twenty years later, in an official report composed in 1537 by a committee of which Contarini was chair: the *Consilium de emendanda ecclesia* (Report on the Reform of the Church), which identifies a series of abuses committed by bishops, often absentees, regarding the proper selection of candidates, the management of finances, and the care of the flock. The deficiencies he had identified as a young man, before the Protestant threat had materialized, persisted still when, as cardinal, he urged the pope to advance the interests of a beleaguered church by insisting on its reformation. Many of these recommendations resurfaced in the decrees of the Council of Trent, effectuating the reforms that Contarini had envisioned years earlier.

Where Contarini called for clerical reform, Reginald Pole (1500–1558) forcefully defended the church and papacy in his treatise *On the Unity of the Church* (1536). The son of a Plantagenet mother and a Tudor father, thereby heir to both the present and previous English royal dynasties, Pole directed the treatise to King Henry VIII, who had declared himself supreme head of the church in England.

In 1530, Pole had refused to support Henry, his kinsman and patron, in the latter's quest to divorce his wife—the "great matter," as it was called, that set the English Reformation in motion. In 1532, Pole decamped to Italy, where he had previously studied, supported by Henry's largesse; and there he remained for more than twenty years, becoming a cardinal and entering papal service. Meanwhile, Henry notoriously divorced Catherine of Aragon and married Anne Boleyn, defying the pope. In 1534, Parliament approved the Act of Supremacy that recognized Henry as the only head of the church in England.

Pole was outraged, and then further horrified by the execution for treason in 1535, with Henry's assent, of two Catholic luminaries who had refused to approve the king's actions: the bishop John Fisher and the former royal chancellor, Thomas More.[1] When Henry's advocates approached Pole to urge his acceptance of the new order, Pole responded in May 1536 by sending to Henry the manuscript of his mammoth treatise attacking the king for his usurpation of papal authority.

---

1. Both were canonized as martyr saints in 1935.

Infuriated, Henry dispatched spies and assassins to pursue Pole in Italy. Worse, he had Pole's brothers and their associates, and even his mother, arrested for treason. In 1539, all but one of the men was executed; in 1541, Pole's sixty-eight-year-old mother, too, was beheaded.[2] Pole was proud, he remarked, to be the son of a martyr. Made a cardinal in 1537 (though he was not yet a priest), he served the pope in various missions until, in 1554, he returned to England, following the ascension to the throne of Henry's daughter, Mary, a Catholic. As papal legate to England, charged to oversee its recovery for the Catholic church, Pole served as Mary's adviser, and was awarded with the dignity of Archbishop of Canterbury. It was the position previously held by Thomas Cranmer (see Chapter Seven), who in 1556 had been sent to the stake at Mary's command, one of the nearly three hundred victims of her regime whom Pole made no attempt to save.

Even as Pole confronted the king of England, and Contarini and his colleagues urged their reform program on the pope, Ignatius of Loyola (1491–1556) formed a new religious order, the Society of Jesus, to advance the restitution and renewal of the church. A Spanish nobleman from the Basque region, while recovering from a wound received in battle, Ignatius underwent a religious experience that changed his life. Leaving his military career behind, he studied theology at Alcalá (Spain) and Paris, where he led a group of companions to pledge themselves to the principles that would animate the Society of Jesus. Reuniting in Italy in 1537, Ignatius and his companions presented their project to the pope, who recognized the new order in 1540. The following year, Ignatius became its Superior General.

Thereupon, the Jesuits, as members of the Society were called, undertook their mission to support the papacy, recover European lands lost to the Protestants, and, in the wake of the adventurers and explorers who had opened the pathways to the East and the West, to missionize the peoples of the globe. In pursuit of these goals, they constructed an immensely successful network of schools that combined humanist intellectual principles with Christian instruction, thereby educating not only future Jesuits, but virtually the whole of Europe's Catholic elite.

While actively directing the far-flung Jesuit enterprise, Ignatius was also a prolific author, most notably of the *Spiritual Exercises* (published in 1548), a series of prayers and meditations meant to guide the reader to Christian commitment. But the twelve volumes of his letters more fully document the range of the Jesuit project in Europe and abroad. Of that multitude, a 1554 letter to the priest Peter Canisius, then stationed in the German lands, is given here nearly in its entirety. It conveys the challenges the Jesuits faced as they tried

---

2. Margaret Plantagenet Pole, beatified as a martyr in 1886.

to recover ground lost to the Protestants by launching a cultural campaign to counter the message of their adversaries.

Like Ignatius of Loyola, Teresa of Ávila (1515–1582) founded a religious order: that of the Discalced Carmelites.[3] The first foundation, the convent of Saint Joseph (San José) in Teresa's native Ávila, a town of central Castile (modern Spain), embodied the cardinal principles of the new order: those of poverty (neither the entity itself nor its individual members would derive income from private property) and enclosure (the residents would be strictly separated from the world). These strict regulations enacted ideals posed for conventual life by the decrees of the Council of Trent, countering the latitudinarianism that had sometimes disgraced the nunneries of the pre-Reformation era. While Ignatius enacted the spirit of Catholic reform, therefore, by engaging actively in the world to regain apostates and win new converts, Teresa did so by striving for perfection in the conduct of the religious life.

Teresa is better known as a mystic than as the founder of monasteries, and as one of the inventors of mental prayer: deeply meditative silent prayer, that is, as opposed to spoken or chanted vocal prayer, often in chorus, as was common in Catholic practice. Her mystical raptures are famously displayed in the sculpture by Gian Lorenzo Bernini, *The Ecstasy of Santa Teresa*, representing her experience in 1559 or 1560 of "transverberation," when her heart was pierced by the flaming arrow of divine love. She records these aspects of her career in the earlier chapters of her autobiography, *The Book of Her Life*. Its culminating chapters, however, from which excerpts are given here, narrate her persistent and ingenious efforts to found a Carmelite convent guided by strict principles of poverty and enclosure. She realized that goal on August 24, 1562. During the remaining twenty years of her life, she founded fourteen more Discalced convents and two monasteries, partnering with her former pupil, Saint John of the Cross, also a mystic, who adopted the same cause.

Divine love, like a flaming arrow, famously pierced the heart of Teresa of Ávila. So, too, did it strike the heart and conscience of Francis de Sales (1567–1622), a Savoyard[4] nobleman who renounced his inheritance in order to become a priest. By 1602, he had climbed in the hierarchy to the position of Bishop of Geneva, an episcopal see over which he presided from neighboring Annecy,[5] on the Savoyard side of the Swiss border, an exile required because of Geneva's domination by a Calvinist regime. Unlike Teresa, Francis remained active in the world, assuming the mission to win

---

3. "Discalced" means "barefoot," signifying poverty, which members observed by wearing only sandals, not shoes. This new order was a branch of the older Carmelites.

4. Savoy was at this time an independent duchy on the Italian peninsula, closely related to France.

5. Annecy: in modern France.

laymen and laywomen to a life of devotion—the devout life. The devout lived in the world, but inspirited by the love of God, were committed to serve the sick, the poor, and the desolate. He sets forth this vision in his *Introduction to the Devout Life* (1609), a classic of Catholic devotional writing.

In 1610, like Ignatius and Teresa, Francis also founded a new religious order, in partnership with Jeanne de Chantal: the Order of the Visitation, whose members were cloistered nuns dedicated to charitable service. In 1633, the younger contemporaries of Francis and Chantal, Saint Vincent de Paul and Saint Louise de Marillac, founded an order of laywomen taking annual vows, whose purpose was likewise the service of those in need: the Daughters of Charity. These institutions incorporate the ideal of the devout life that Francis initially introduced to laypersons of every rank and vocation.

Just as Francis poses a notable contrast to Teresa of Ávila, he does so as well to other figures earlier encountered in this volume. One is the English Puritan Margaret Hoby (see Chapter Seven), his contemporary, who as a layperson engaged in strenuous spiritual exercises more focused on self-examination and discipline than on active service to the needy. Another is the Italian Cardinal Gasparo Contarini, for whom the dutiful and diligent work of the bishop, rather than the spontaneous and spirit-driven charitable activity of the laity, was central to the Catholic mission. A third, strikingly, is the German reformer Martin Luther, for whom salvation could come only by faith, and not by acts of will. He would have repudiated forthwith the confidence in free will implied by the ideal of the devout life advocated by Francis de Sales.

By the seventeenth century, the Catholic church had been remade—not merely reformed. Essential institutions and rites were reaffirmed, and a new discipline was imposed on clergy and laypeople alike, now summoned to adhere to standards that were often inoperative during an earlier era marked by disorder and turbulence—as well as inventiveness and creativity. But in addition, the church had now aroused a new warmth of commitment among clergy and laity alike, lit by that divine flame of which Teresa and Francis spoke, that would enable it to prosper into modern times.

A good bishop will not fail to perform this office

from Gasparo Contarini, *The Duties of a Bishop* (1517)

Calling up the Greek philosophers Plato and Aristotle alongside the medieval theologian Thomas Aquinas, Contarini sketches an ideal of the bishop as a good man, and something of a philosopher. This exemplary cleric will engage in daily worship, guide his flock in their understanding of Christian doctrine, and encourage the schooling of boys (girls in this era were rarely schooled); and while leaving the supervision of cloistered women to their religious orders, and of laywomen to their husbands and fathers, he should regulate excessive finery in dress—an incitement, it was generally believed, to sin. Throughout, as a leitmotif, he exhorts the bishop to reside in his diocese and perform all duties himself, not delegating them to vicars.

The seven selections here focus on moments where Contarini seems to speak most powerfully in his own voice, or where he anticipates themes that will be central in the yet-impending Reformation. In the first, he describes the intense religious feeling that he himself had experienced as a young man, as we know from other sources. In the second and third, he underscores the bishop's responsibility to choose worthy priests and to preach the word of God. In the fourth, he advises the bishop to discourage an excessive devotion to the cult of saints. In the fifth and sixth, he calls for close attention to the expressed needs and to the sustenance of the poor. In the last, he counsels wise management of episcopal funds, and denounces excessive expenditure.

The sometimes anodyne recommendations of Contarini's book are serious, for the abuses tolerated in episcopal performance undermined the authority and credibility of a church that would soon need to confront relentless critics.

The bishop's daily routine begins with morning prayer and meditation.

To worship God properly . . . it is first necessary that the bishop . . . say each day the holy prayers of praise[6] . . . with a great spiritual intensity directed to God. . . . Nothing else should distract him when he sings praise to God, but he should expend every effort to understand what the words mean, and with a certain impulse of the spirit . . . to embrace them. This intensity possesses such a wondrous force . . . that no one who has not experienced it would believe it. . . .

After morning prayer, as the dawn unfolds, there is an hour poised between night and day, at a time when the body has fully shrugged off sleep and the mind has been stirred by offering praise to God, when I would recommend that kind of prayer be said to God that is uttered without sound, but solely by the elevation and agitation of the mind. No rational operation can set the mind on fire more briskly than this arousal of the soul . . . which ignites within the soul such a flame of divine love, that the mind so affected can

---

6. The morning office of Lauds, the first of the seven (formerly eight) of the Liturgy of the Hours, or Divine Office.

think of nothing other than God, nor does it know itself, nor any other thing, when it knows God. . . .

The bishop should be diligent in the ordination of priests.

The bishop appoints clergy to holy orders,[7] and supervises them in office. From the outset, therefore, he must make thorough inquiries, and exercise sound judgment in promoting clergy to these ranks. In our day, I find, nearly all err badly, failing to exercise any judgment, admitting corrupt and grossly ignorant men to the priesthood, and the access to divine power that it affords—who then handle each day with their filthy hands and vicious minds the holy sacrament of Christ's body.[8] . . . Great care must be taken lest the bishop to whom we here offer guidance permit such a monster to be admitted to the priesthood.

The bishop should preach the word of God.

Let me urge our bishops not to abandon utterly the ancient custom observed by our fathers in the faith: during the rites of the Mass . . . , these illustrious men used to deliver a sermon to the entire populace by which they both instructed those ignorant of Christian truths, and vigorously persuaded them to lead worthy lives. . . . Today, the monks and friars[9] have usurped this function because of the laziness and indifference of the bishops; yet this task, or rather this honor of instructing the people, should really belong to him. . . . Let the bishop deliver a sermon that expounds the Gospel, or discusses another part of holy Scripture or moral philosophy. . . . A good bishop will by no means fail to perform this office, as I see it, unless he believes himself to be wholly incompetent to do so. . . .

The bishop should discourage superstitious practices, and urge restraint in the cult of saints.

All such superstition should be assiduously expunged: so that with regard to the saints, when they are invoked in heaven, or their relics are venerated, or . . . their images are displayed in churches, these things must be done in a decent and orderly way, so as to take the people by the hand and lead them step by step to the proper worship of the one God. The prudent bishop or priest will need tactfully to discourage any abuse in these matters, lest mindlessly and foolishly we destroy, as the heretics have done, the very worship of God, faith in the sacraments, and the hierarchical order of the church. Let

---

7. In this case, to the priesthood.
8. That is, the Mass.
9. Mainly Franciscan and Dominican friars, as well as some members of other religious orders.

the people be taught constantly, rather, that God is to be loved and adored in all things and above all things, while all else is loved because of God, without whom nothing was made; and without whom the saints themselves would be nothing. . . .

The bishop should hear the petitions of his parishioners with empathy and attention.

The bishop should receive, and hear, those who seek him out as judge, or counselor, or defender. Let him show them kindness and cordiality, . . . and immediately resolve what matters he can, judging rightly and fairly, giving sound advice to those seeking counsel, and extending whatever aid he can. Nor should he cease in his efforts until everyone has been heard . . , so that, if possible, all are sent away happy, and none are sad. . . . Many bishops, I realize, delegate these tasks to a vicar, demonstrating, I believe, a certain lassitude of spirit. . . . I shall never approve this dereliction of responsibility to a vicar, except when the bishop is ill, or committed to some other matter that cannot be set aside, or is not capable of performing his office. . . .

The bishop must care for the poor, not indulge in luxuries.

For if the holy Scriptures, and especially the Gospel, require laymen who are bound by no religious vows, whose wealth is acquired by labor, to provide charitable assistance to the poor, how much more should it be required of bishops, . . . whose wealth has not been won by their own exertions, but by testamentary bequests supporting divine worship and poor relief? Rather, they should be considered the executors and guardians of goods bequeathed to the poor. . . . The bishop should . . . not be constrained by any narrow rules, but spend everything that remains, beyond what supports a modest table and frugal existence, on the cost of divine worship and, even more, the needs of the poor. For it is shameful, to my mind, and a great sin, for a bishop to take anything from the little the poor possess, or to expend the funds intended for them on magnificent furnishings or an army of servants or other such superfluities. . . .

The bishop should manage responsibly the revenues and expenditures of his diocese.

Among the duties related to expenses and expenditures are those having to do with increasing the revenues of the bishopric. For if the bishop neglects this responsibility, he will not be able either generously to support the poor, or satisfy the requirements of divine worship. He must therefore work diligently and energetically to ensure that the episcopal revenues not diminish, and that neither the city supervisor and country steward invade the funds set aside for the poor. . . . This is especially to be avoided: that the country steward . . . cruelly extort sums from debtors, since so many poor peasants fall into debt, and cannot pay what the steward demands without seizing it from the mouths of their children and their entire household. This must be judged utterly foreign to Christian piety, and would be wholly reprehensible in a layman, let alone in a bishop, the shepherd of a Christian flock. . . .

You have usurped this new and unprecedented honor

from Reginald Pole, *On the Unity of the Church* (1536)

In 1534, while Pole pursued his studies in Italy, Henry VIII was recognized as supreme head of the church in England, and in 1535, sanctioned the execution for treason of two Catholic leaders who had refused to acknowledge that supremacy. Shocked by these events, Pole composed his immense treatise *On the Unity of the Church*, brief excerpts of which are given here. Written in a frenzied, at times hysterical tone unusual for the genre, it touches on three main points.

First, it discusses Pole's relationship with Henry: a tormented one. Henry had bankrolled Pole's education and intellectual leisure in Italy, yet now, the protégé must in conscience turn on his benefactor. Pole's struggle with himself is reflected in the many short questions that pepper the treatise: What is he to do? How can he change Henry's mind? Will he suffer for his disloyalty?

Second, and centrally, it challenges Henry's claim to be supreme head of the church in England and repudiates the arguments constructed to support it. The church is one, and can have only one head. In all its history, no king, no matter how ambitious or avaricious, had usurped the leadership of the church. In all of Scripture, no support can be found for the claim of a king to be head of the church.

Third, with great anguish, it reflects on the executions of John Fisher and Thomas More, innocent men consumed by vengeful royal power, framing their deaths not as futile but as triumphant, indeed, as martyrdoms: "For that same axe that seemed to take their life instead, in truth, brought them immortality . . . and consigned you [the king] to eternal death."

What I should write to you, my Prince, at this time, or what I should not write, on my life I do not know; nor have I quite decided whether I should write to you at all. . . . But if, to begin, I should write to you, what better cause could there be than that you not only desire, but even command that I do so? And you even propose an argument to be addressed that closely relates to those studies in which I have been engaged now for several years—studies supported by you as my benefactor. This could indeed be seen as a compelling reason to write. . . . And so it is done: if it was initially a sense of duty that moved me to write, since you, to whom I owe so much, asked this of me, now surely must be added that of gratitude that inclines and impels me to do so. . . .

Yet, on the other hand, many are the impediments, many doubts deter me. This above all: it is not your zeal to learn the truth that prompts you to present me with this task of debating the power of the Roman pontiff, since you have usurped this new and unprecedented honor, appropriating for yourself the power and title of the supreme head of the church in England. Nor do you seek to know my opinion concerning the matter you have posed for discussion, as though I were permitted to express my views freely and expound them in writing. Rather, you announce your position as though it were some kind of official decree or decision, and so defend it—though it is quite contrary to the truth—that anyone who disagrees you deem an enemy and traitor, and condemn to the same punishment as the most vicious malefactor.[10]

What then? Since I cannot agree with you, shall I then oppose this action of yours, laying bare what is in my soul, and even commit it to writing? And by so doing, shall I by my own hand and testimony accuse myself of the crime of *laesa maiestas*?[11] Shall I thereby ignite against me the anger and detestation, without hope of any good outcome, of him by whose generosity to me, above all others, I have benefited? . . .

But that I would needlessly exhaust myself if I tried to change your mind, nothing declares more clearly than this: the spilled blood of those[12] whose only crime was to hold the same views as mine. At first, they bore only your displeasure and discontent when they refused to desert the cause of truth. But in the end, though wholly innocent, they suffered the punishment assigned to vile traitors. This was their reward, this the prize they won for their labors: the effort they expended on your behalf was of no benefit to you, but procured their deaths. . . .

But what am I doing? How can I speak in this way about these men, of whose virtue, learning, and love of God, so many and such glowing testimonies abound, not only at home but also abroad, and throughout the length

---

10. The terrible penalty assigned for treason in England at this time was to be hanged, drawn, and quartered, the penalty Edmund Campion suffered in 1581 (see Chapter Seven). Pole raises that specter here.

11. *Laesa maiestas* (French lèse-majesté, English *lese-majesty*): the ancient Roman crime, revived in the European kingdoms, of "injured majesty," the insult of royal dignity, often equated to treason.

12. Bishop John Fisher and Sir Thomas More, executed in 1535.

and breadth of Christendom; than whose deeds, across the ages to come, nothing greater nor more illustrious will be recalled? Can I somehow withdraw those words of mine that said that they labored in vain in the service of the church, that they met their death for no purpose? . . . Can I possibly feel in my soul, or pronounce with my tongue, that in the end, after all the trouble and toil they had sustained for the cause of Christ, their blood was shed without meaning or purpose?

I cannot, my Prince, I cannot. May I utterly forswear such godlessness. I would be mired in impious fraud and deceit if I did this, for I would be an ingrate to God. For what could be more lacking in gratitude than this: that with God and my conscience as witnesses, I could deny having gained as much fruit from their death as I have gained from these many years of study, engaged in the reading of the best authors, pursuing only the enrichment of my mind? Could I really pretend to deny that their death was fruitful? . . .

So now, I repeat, may I not be so godless as to say that they died in vain, since I know their death has borne me great fruit. With that impiety set aside, then all timidity of spirit vanishes, revealing for what cause those men did not hesitate to offer themselves up to torment: for they preferred that their own heads be severed from their bodies, than that they accede to the king's proposition that the head be severed from the body of the church.

Concerning that cause I myself, who by God's providence has been kept far from danger, shall compose a written statement of my own position. Never, indeed, with the help of God, shall I fail to publish it, openly to all, as circumstances demand, and so bear witness. . . .

But now I am uncertain how I am to write to you, how to speak to you, how to address you. . . . What shall I do then? How shall I begin? . . . Now everyone who knows me is aware that I have been studying for many years how to understand and heal illnesses of the soul; and thereby I come to recognize in you certain signs of a serious and pernicious disease, for which remedies exist, if you are only willing to be cured. . . . Should I then be silent concerning your deeds, which I know to be the whole cause of your condition? Should I then knowingly dissimulate concerning this sickness of your soul, not even daring to speak its name?

Especially since everyone else, distressed by the savagery of your actions, believes and reports that you are not merely ill, but that you have wholly lost your mind—having breathed out your last breath of life at the same moment that those holy men, at your command, lost theirs. For that same axe that seemed to take their life instead, in truth, brought them immortality; and while it struck their necks, it penetrated the very vitals of your soul, and consigned you to eternal death, I note with great sorrow, from which no one but God alone can bring you back to life. . . .

The heretics have spread their false theology to the masses

from Ignatius of Loyola, *Letter* to Father Peter Canisius (Rome, August 13, 1554)

Writing to the priest Peter Canisius, a Jesuit agent stationed in the German lands who has since been credited with the great success of the Counter-Reformation in that region, Ignatius lays out a program of cultural response to the Protestant threat. The Protestants, whom Ignatius calls "heretics," have found a way to reach the hearts and minds of the common people: by effective preaching and teaching, and by publishing a flood of small books and pamphlets, easily understood and cheaply purchased.

To these threats, Ignatius recommends two main countermeasures. First, to quickly equip an army of preachers and teachers, a "summary theology" must be constructed, an abbreviated statement of core Catholic doctrines assimilable by those unable to pursue a university course in theology. These recruits, once properly trained, could reach the common people in their schools and villages, while the summary theology could, as well, be utilized in a number of additional forms: as catechisms, for instance, and textbooks.

As a second countermeasure, Ignatius urges a response to the pile of Protestant booklets and pamphlets with publications equally brief, accessible, and cheap. Well-educated Jesuits could easily produce suitable works, composed in good prose and conveying sound Catholic doctrine. Canisius did indeed follow this path, and such works as his *German Catechism* helped recover much of southern Germany for the Roman church.

Given the progress that the heretics have made in so short a time, spewing the poison of their evil doctrine across so many peoples and regions, . . . our Society,[13] appointed by divine providence as . . . a force by which this great evil may be countered, must diligently prepare appropriate remedies, and do so promptly. Such remedies, moreover, must be applicable in many situations, and employed as soon as possible, so as to preserve that which remains sound, and cure that which has already been infected by the plague of heresy that especially affects the northern lands.

The heretics have spread their false theology to the masses, adapting it to their capacity. They preach it to them in the schools, and publish it in pamphlets that can be bought and understood by the common people, thus

---

13. The Society of Jesus, whose members are Jesuits.

broadcasting their message in print even where their ministers cannot do so in person. . . . So it behooves our Society to employ the following means to oppose and overcome these evils that they have inflicted upon the church.

First of all, since what is taught in the universities is an advanced theology . . . appropriate only for sharp and disciplined minds, while weaker and untutored ones founder and fail, another summary theology must be devised. This abridged theology shall deal very briefly with matters of substance that are not controversial. Controversial matters might be treated at greater length as the capacity of the people allows, demonstrating the truth of dogma with the sound testimony of Scripture, tradition, conciliar decrees, and learned authorities, while refuting contrary doctrines.

Such a summary theology could be taught quickly, since it would not delve deeply into peripheral matters. In but a little time, many theologians could be trained, ready to preach and teach in many places. The more able students would continue to pursue the advanced course in theology, while those who could not profit from it would be removed and trained in this abridged course.

The major points of this summary theology, presented as a brief catechism, could be taught to little children, just as they are now taught Christian doctrine. It could also be taught to adults who are not too infected with alien ideas and capable of reasoning. Likewise, it can be taught to younger students in elementary schools, who may learn it by heart.

Those in higher grades, and those at the university studying philosophy and theology, when they are not attending lectures, should study the summary theology described above. In this way, all those who have the aptitude to do so will be instructed in the fundamental principles of theology, and could teach and preach Catholic doctrine, and refute contrary arguments, sufficiently well to address a popular audience. It is especially important to do this in the colleges[14] of northern and southern Germany, in France, and other places where the same need exists. Those who are not capable of advanced study, or who are not of sufficient age, . . . should be taught this summary theology and some cases of conscience[15] so as to be equipped to be good workers and contributors to the common good.

Local priests and day students[16] in the upper schools, or indeed whoever wished to do so, having acquired this theological instruction, could then swiftly deliver in many regions this antidote to the poison of heresy. Thus instructed, and holding the book in their hand, they will be able to preach to the people and teach the essentials of Catholic doctrine in the schools.

---

14. The Jesuit colleges were a network of high-quality secondary schools.
15. Cases of conscience: exercises in moral decision-making.
16. The Jesuit colleges were generally boarding schools, but they accepted some local day students, often of lesser social rank.

Expanding the number of the colleges and schools of the Society in many regions, especially where there is reason to expect a good number of students, would be an excellent way to assist in this mission of the church. It might be necessary to permit colleges to be formed with a smaller number of students than our Society usually requires. . . .

Not only in those places where we have a residence, but in neighboring places as well, our most capable students could be sent to teach Christian doctrine on Sundays and feast days. Even day students, if they were qualified, could be sent out by the rector for the same purpose. In this way, they will set examples of good learning and sound morals—not being driven by avarice—and so refute the worst charges, those of immorality and ignorance, that the heretics make against the Catholic clergy.

And since the heretics write many pamphlets and booklets, by which they attempt to supplant Catholic authors, and especially the Jesuits, and so establish their false dogmas, it would be useful if our authors respond to these with brief and well-written defenses and treatises, which could be quickly produced and cheaply purchased. In this way, we could combat the harm done by the books of the heretics, and spread sound doctrine abroad in works that are simple, but lively, exposing the wicked stratagems and tricks of our adversaries. . . . But these should be put together by learned men well-grounded in theology, and adapted to the capacity of the masses.

By these means, we can perform an important service for the church, and quickly respond to outbreaks of heresy wherever they occur before the poison has grabbed hold, when it becomes much more difficult to uproot it from the heart. We must be as diligent in healing the people as the heretics have been in infecting them. We have this advantage over them: our doctrine is well-grounded, and therefore enduring. The most gifted of those we have trained may pursue their studies at the Roman College,[17] and the others in Germany north and south as well as in France. Later, sent to the many regions where we have established residence, they will be the directors and instructors of others.

I took great care not to do anything against obedience

from Teresa of Ávila, *The Book of Her Life* (1565)

The tale of the founding by Teresa of Ávila of the convent of Saint Joseph in the Discalced Carmelite order, though here much condensed, tells itself in

---

17. The first and principal Jesuit university.

Teresa's words. During the two years from the first formation of the thought to its realization, she met with many reversals and obstacles, but with the support of female colleagues, family members, and a few friendly clerical figures (among others quite unfriendly), including confessors, advisers, and learned theologians, she achieved her goal. Given that clerical opposition, and the hostility of the townspeople who feared so daring an experiment, she operated in secrecy. Yet conscious of the audacity of her mission, especially for a woman, she was scrupulous about conforming to church norms, taking "great care not to do anything against obedience." A principal aim was to preserve the requirement of poverty, to which the townsfolk at first objected, but in the end accepted—and indeed, contributed the alms that supported the nuns who had forsworn the ownership of property.

I began to discuss the matter with . . . the widow I mentioned, who had the same desires. She began to draw up plans to provide the new house with income. Now I see that there was little chance these plans would succeed, but our desire made us think they would. Yet since, on the other hand, I was so perfectly content in the house in which I was because it was very much to my liking and the cell in which I lived was just what I wanted, I was still delaying. . . .

One day after Communion, His Majesty[18] earnestly commanded me to strive for this new monastery with all my powers, and He made great promises that it would be founded and that He would be highly served in it. He said it should be called St. Joseph and that this saint would keep watch over us at one door, and our Lady at the other, that Christ would remain with us, and that it would be a star shining with great splendor. . . .

Hardly had the knowledge of it begun to spread throughout the city when the great persecution that cannot be briefly described came upon us: gossip, derision, saying that it was foolishness. . . . Indeed, among people of prayer and, in fact, throughout the whole city there was hardly a person who was not then against us; the project seemed to almost everyone to be a lot of nonsense. . . .

I was very much disliked throughout my monastery[19] because I had wanted to found a more enclosed monastery. They said I was insulting them; that in my own monastery I could also serve God . . . ; that I had no love for the house; that it would be better to procure income for this place than for some other. . . . I saw clearly that in many matters my opponents were right, and sometimes I gave them explanations. Yet since I couldn't mention the main

---

18. As Teresa regularly denotes God.
19. That is, her convent.

factor, which was that the Lord had commanded me to do this, I didn't know how to act; so I remained silent. . . .

My confessor gave me permission again to dedicate myself entirely to this foundation. . . . We agreed to carry on in total secrecy, and so I got one of my sisters who lived outside this city to buy the house and fix it up, as though it were for herself, with money the Lord provided, in certain ways, for its purchase. It would take long to recount how the Lord was looking after it, for I took great care not to do anything against obedience. But I knew that if I said anything to my superiors, everything would be lost. . . . In procuring the money, acquiring the house, signing the contract for it, and fixing it up, I went through so many trials of so many kinds that now I'm amazed I was able to suffer them. . . .

. . . [T]he Lord . . . told me I should petition Rome in a certain way, which He also indicated to me, and that He would take care that we get our request. And so it came about, for the petition was made the way the Lord told me and it was granted easily. . . .

Since I consulted in all things with so many, I nonetheless found almost no one with this opinion,[20] neither my confessor nor the learned men with whom I dealt. They brought out so many reasons against poverty that I didn't know what to do. Since I knew it was in the rule and saw that observing poverty would be more perfect, I couldn't persuade myself that the monastery should have an income. . . .

I found so many disadvantages in having an income . . . that I did not else but dispute with learned men. I wrote about it to the Dominican religious who was helping us. He sent me two pages with objections and theology written on both sides on why I shouldn't do it. . . . I answered him that I didn't want to benefit from theology if it wasn't conducive to my following my vocation, my vow of poverty, and the counsels of Christ with total perfection, and that in this case he did me no favor with his learning. . . .

One day while praying intensely to God about this matter, the Lord told me I shouldn't in any way fail to found the monastery in poverty, that this was both the will of His Father and His own, and that He would help me. This took place during a deep rapture with so many remarkable effects that I couldn't have any doubt the desire was from God.

. . . The very night I reached this city our patent and our brief for the monastery arrived from Rome. I was amazed, and, when they learned of the great need there was for my being here and of the coincidence the Lord had prepared for me, so too were those who knew how He made me come quickly. . . .

---

20. That a convent dedicated to poverty—having no income-producing assets—was to be preferred.

Everything was done in deep secrecy; if it hadn't been, nothing could have been accomplished.... The Lord ordained that my brother-in-law become ill, [so] my superiors gave me permission to stay with him. With this excuse nothing became known....

When everything was ready the Lord was pleased that on St. Bartholomew's day[21] ... with all due authority and power our monastery of our most glorious father St. Joseph was founded, in 1562.... Since this house that was converted into a monastery was the one in which my brother-in-law lived..., I was there with permission; and I hadn't done anything without getting advice from learned men so as not to go one iota against obedience. Since these learned men observed that for many reasons the monastery would be very beneficial for the whole order, they told me I could go ahead even though I did so secretly and was careful that my superiors not find out about it. If these learned men had told me an imperfection lay in what I was doing, no matter how small, I would have given up founding a thousand monasteries, how much more one....

Once the liturgical Offices[22] were initiated the people began to grow very devoted to this house. More nuns were accepted, and the Lord started to inspire our most vigorous persecutors to show us much favor; and they gave us alms. So they approved of what they had so greatly disapproved.... And there isn't anyone at present who doesn't think it was right to let the house be founded. Thus they are so careful about providing us with alms that, without our asking or begging from anyone, the Lord stirs them to send alms to us.... Since the nuns are few in number, if they do what they are obliged to, ... I am sure they won't lack anything or have need to be anxious or to importune anyone. The Lord will take care of them as He has up to now.

Devotion is to charity as the flame is to the fire

from Francis de Sales, *Introduction to the Devout Life* (1609)

In the opening chapters of his classic work of Catholic spirituality, Francis de Sales explains what is meant by "devotion." "Devotion" is the commitment of the soul to God, inspired by divine love. The "devout" are those who are so devoted. The "devout life," available to believers of all ranks and

---

21. August 24, 1562.
22. The performance of regular daily prayers, a prime obligation of the cloistered religious.

vocations, is a life of vigorous and cheerful service to the poor, the hungry, the lonely, and the lost.

These explanations are written in a lyrical French redolent more of parlors and pastries than bare monastic cells or the horrors of the stake, and by a narrator, a bishop, whose humility is compelling. This guidance is offered to a young girl, an abstraction, to whom is given the name Philothea, meaning "lover of God." Its truth seems to be self-evident. It is as though the formula at last had been found, 1,600 years after Jesus walked the earth, for following in his footsteps.

And yet this Salesian vision is new and radical. It banishes the anguish of penitence or the terrors of purgatory that had long afflicted believers, much as Luther had banished them with the triumphant victory of faith; but for Francis, and for Catholics, it is by good works, freely performed, driven by love, that the devout soul achieves its goal and wins its reward.

Chapter One: A description of true devotion

You aspire to a life of devotion, my dear Philothea, because being Christian, you know that it is very pleasing to almighty God. But since, as it happens, the little faults one commits at the beginning of an enterprise are greatly magnified as one advances, and become in the end nearly irreparable, it is necessary first of all to have a clear understanding of what true devotion is; for there is only one that is true, but many that are false and useless. . . .

The real and true devotion, Philothea, presupposes the love of God; or rather it is nothing else than a true love of God. I say the true love, and not just any kind of love. The kind of love that beautifies our soul is called "grace," which makes us worthy in the eyes of God. The kind that gives us strength to do what is good is called "charity." But the love that has reached that degree of perfection that it not only enables us to do what it is good, but more, it empowers us to do it diligently, swiftly, and often, that love is called "devotion." . . .

In a word, devotion is nothing other than a certain spiritual energy and vivacity, by which charity works within us, or we through it, swiftly and warmly. And since charity impels us to practice every one of God's commandments, devotion impels us to observe them with the greatest possible diligence and fervor. . . . And since devotion consists in the perfection of charity, it makes us quick, active, and diligent, not only in observing all of God's commandments, but, pushing us further, in doing all the good works that we can. . . .

Charity and devotion, finally, differ from each other as the flame does from the fire: for charity, which is the spiritual fire of the soul, becomes devotion when it flares into a brisk flame. In this way, devotion adds nothing to charity but the flame that renders it quick, active, and diligent, not only in observing God's commandments, but also in responding to divine instruction and inspiration. . . .

Chapter Two: The nature and excellence of devotion

. . . The world sees the devout fast, pray, endure abuse, heal the sick, sustain the poor, keep vigils, control their anger, suppress their passions, deny themselves the pleasures of the flesh, and do a thousand other hard and painful things. But the world does not see the inward devotion that renders all these things pleasant, easy, and sweet. . . . Devotion is in truth like a spiritual sweetener that overcomes the bitterness of every humiliation, and the peril of every consolation; it relieves the misery of the poor and the heedlessness of the rich; the desolation of the oppressed and the pretension of the privileged; the sadness of loneliness and the dissipation of worldliness; it is warmth in winter, and refreshment in summer; it is not vaunted by honor nor diminished by disdain; it is unmoved by pleasure or pain; and it fills us with a delectable sweetness. . . .

Chapter Three: That devotion is suited to all sorts of vocations and professions

When God created the world, he commanded the plants to bring forth their fruits, each one according to its kind. Likewise he commands Christians, who are the living plants of his church, to bring forth fruits of devotion, each one according to his station and condition. Devotion will be practiced differently by the nobleman, the artisan, the servant, the prince, the widow, the young girl, the married woman; and beyond these differences, the practice of devotion is also to be adapted to the strength, the enterprise, and the duties of each person. I ask you, Philothea, would it be proper if the bishop wished to live the solitary life of a Carthusian?[23] And if householders chose not to build their wealth any more than a Capuchin?[24] If an artisan spent all day in church like a member of a religious order, and if that religious professional engaged in all sorts of worldly business in the service of his neighbor, as does a bishop? Would these forms of devotion not be ridiculous, inappropriate, and intolerable? . . .

---

23. Carthusian: a monk belonging to an order with strict rules of enclosure, here contrasted to the life of a bishop who goes out and about among the people of his diocese.
24. Capuchin: a friar belonging to a branch of the Franciscan order strictly observing its principle of poverty.

True devotion not only does not interfere with the vocations and obligations pertaining to any person's station, but on the contrary, it adorns and beautifies them all. If a variety of jewels of all sorts of colors are thrown into honey, each one shines more brightly according to its type. In the same way, each person better performs his own vocation when its performance is enhanced by devotion. The family is more peaceful, love between spouses more sincere, service to the prince more loyal, and every kind of occupation less burdensome and more pleasant.

It is an error, and indeed a heresy, to wish to banish the life of devotion from the soldier's regiment, the artisan's shop, the prince's court, or the wedded couple's household. It is true, Philothea, that a purely contemplative devotion, such as that of the monastery or convent, is impracticable in these sorts of vocations. But other forms of devotion . . . are available for the perfecting of those who live in the world. . . .

Chapter Nine: The Expanding Reformation

After the tumultuous launch of Protestant reform in the sixteenth century, it might seem that new growth ceased. Yet even before the 1648 Peace of Westphalia concluded the disastrous Thirty Years War and shut the door on the age of religious violence, new green shoots had appeared. The Reformation, indeed, continued to expand into the eighteenth century. Within the European homeland, the expansion was not geographical, for Catholicism recovered territory from the Protestant domain, but rather intellectual, cultural, and spiritual, featuring an ebullience of religious feeling, and an enthusiasm for relatedness to God. The expansion was demographic as well: it reached out to workers, to women, to Christians of other persuasions, and even to Jews and to those called "infidels," inhabitants of lands and civilizations that did not know the name of Christ. Inclusionary where its predecessor had been exclusionary, this later phase of expanding Protestantism looked to the Enlightenment and to the modern world. That inclusionary impulse begins with Jacobus Arminius[1] (1560–1609), a professional theologian of the ilk of Luther and Calvin, who yet spoke with a different voice.

Born more than a decade after Luther's death and not quite four years before Calvin's, the Dutch-born Arminius abandons the sharp distinctions and absolute pronouncements of the age his predecessors had shaped, characterized by verbal animosities, armed conflict, and fearsome persecutions. While remaining throughout his life within the Calvinist fold—his followers, called Remonstrants, were later ejected from it in 1619—Arminius called for a gentler notion of predestination and grace than Calvin's, while looking beyond differences in matters of belief to a more universal and collaborative Protestant regime. His hopeful voice and tolerant outlook later traveled easily to England, where they flowered in John Wesley's Methodist movement, and eventually to Anglo-America. The excerpts presented here from his 1606 oration delivered on the occasion of his assumption of the office of rector at the University of Leiden showcase his invitation to all Christians to find the way to reconciliation and, if not agreement on all doctrinal issues, at least a cessation of hostilities.

Just as Arminius opened a new path while embedded within Dutch Calvinism, Jacob Boehme[2] (1575–1624) did so embedded within German

---

1. His self-styled Latin name, alluding to the German warrior who had defied the Romans; by birth, he was Jakob Hermanszoon.
2. As his name most often appears; properly Jakob Böhme, the original German form; anglicized as Behmen.

Lutheranism. A skilled shoemaker without formal education but with immense verbal capacity, Boehme experienced in his native Görlitz in 1600 a religious transformation that prompted him to write his first book, *Aurora* (The Dawning)—the first of many volumes reflecting his manifold spiritual experiences and offering guidance to Christian seekers. Boehme's message challenged the prevailing Lutheran orthodoxy whose sterility would have no doubt dismayed Luther himself, and summoned his readers to experience the joy and freedom of regeneration in Christ. The excerpt given here is from the brief work *Of True Repentance*, one of the several components of Boehme's 1622 volume, *The Way to Christ*.

As much as Boehme would influence religious developments of the later seventeenth and eighteenth centuries, his influence on secular intellectual movements should also be noted. Just as the vision of Arminius looked ahead to later European political developments, Boehme's foreshadowed, in Germany, the movements of romanticism and idealism, and would impact major philosophers of the coming age: among them, Hegel, Schopenhauer, Nietzsche, and Heidegger. In England, too, his works had great influence, and were translated into several seventeenth- and eighteenth-century versions that continued to be studied into the late twentieth century, when modern translations began to appear. They nourished the religious movements of Quakerism and Methodism, and prepared the way, more than any native English tradition, for the unique vision of William Blake.

Boehme died two years after the publication of *The Way to Christ*, at the outset of the Pietist movement, a surge of related religious impulses arising in Germany, the Netherlands, and England. Pietists shared an impatience with the ossified denominational churches—Lutheran, Calvinist, Anglican, the former two in their German, Danish, Swedish, and Dutch varieties—that emerged in the wake of the sixteenth-century religious revolution. As well, they elevated the importance of deep feeling and enthusiasm in Christian experience and stressed an inner-worldly Christianity, implicitly supporting the possibility of good works achieved by acts of free will. Departing from rigid constructions of the doctrine of predestination, they broadened the expectation of salvation, entertaining the possibility that all of humankind could achieve that end, toward which the way had formerly been seen as dauntingly strait and narrow. The remaining three authors included in this chapter are representatives of German Pietism and two closely related English movements: Quakerism and Methodism. All three terms, interestingly, were derogatory in origin, but later came to be adopted by their practitioners.

Johanna Eleonora Petersen (1644–1724), the first woman to write in the German language an autobiography published in her lifetime, also published fourteen religious works that are keystones of late-seventeenth-century Pietism. She wrote as a married woman and mother, whose intellectual collaboration with her husband was as remarkable as her independent vision. Her works include statements on the power of faith, the meaning of the apocalypse, and the nature of Jesus as twofold God-man. Her autobiography, moreover, is a model of what would become a standard genre in Pietist literature: the record of the author's spiritual evolution, itself the forerunner of modern autobiographical writing. Petersen offered, finally, a female, if not a feminist vision, in which the wisdom of God, personified as the biblical Sophia, and the Holy Spirit, the third person of the Trinity, are both figured as female, and fertile. Her vision recalls that of the twelfth-century mystic Hildegard of Bingen, also German, who had written of the viridity—the "greenness," or abundant fruitfulness—of God's cosmic creation. The excerpts given here from Petersen's autobiography, however, focus on another of her strikingly original insights: that of the "return of all things" to God at the end of time.

In contrast to Petersen's pro-female religious outlook, one that may fairly be termed feminist is encountered in the work of her older contemporary, the Englishwoman Margaret Fell (1614–1702), widow of Quaker founder George Fox. In Fell's vision, though God is not figured as female, females, as much as males, are empowered by God to communicate to others the insight that he has poured forth upon them. Emerging around the middle of the seventeenth century as the English Revolution reached its climax, Quakerism held that within each individual there dwelled the light of God. That belief meant that all persons were spiritual equals, both male and female, and those of any station or condition; and further implied that the doctrinal systems and clerical hierarchies that characterized most branches of Christianity were not only unnecessary but, indeed, superseded by the wisdom that might emanate from the humblest worshiper.

Within this conceptual scaffolding, the well-educated, well-born, and wealthy Margaret Fell took the stage, publishing some twenty-three religious tracts and pamphlets. These include *Women's Speaking Justified, Proved, and Allowed of by the Scriptures*, her best known work, of which excerpts are given here. In it, she marshals biblical testimony to demonstrate that God the Father and Jesus Christ his Son identified women, sometimes even ahead of men, as worthy recipients and exponents of divine truth.

John Wesley (1703–1791), the inheritor of several strains of radical Pietist thought from Boehme forward, was the inheritor also of the inwardness of their fifteenth-century forebear Thomas à Kempis (see Chapter One), whose message, even in the era of Enlightenment, still resonated. Wesley was the beneficiary, as well, of the faith and wisdom of his first and most important teacher: his mother Susanna, born a Puritan, married to an Anglican priest, but in outlook a Pietist. With a burning faith grounded in these traditions, Wesley crisscrossed England, addressing the poor and outcast, and awakening souls to Christ. Wesley's Methodism (he adopted the insulting label that his critics had hurled at his followers) became an impulse within Anglicanism as German Pietism was within Lutheranism, only later breaking away as a separate denomination. Wesley's pamphlet-length *Character of a Methodist*, excerpts of which are given here, encapsulates in brief not only the nature of Methodism, but more broadly of the expansive Protestantism of the later Reformation: it is not a creed, but a condition of spiritual exaltation.

The effect of religious discord is the destruction of religion itself

from Jacobus Arminius, *Oration 5: How to Settle Religious Differences among Christians* (February 8, 1606)

In this oration delivered on his assumption of the office of rector of the University of Leiden, Arminius takes on a large issue—the largest, arguably, of the age: how to settle the religious conflicts that had roiled Europe over the previous century, with their product of schism, persecution, and martyrdom. In the plain and systematic rhetoric of an academic lecture, he addresses three matters: the nature of religious discord; its causes; and its remedy.

In the first section, Arminius celebrates the value of unity in all things, and especially in religious matters; and as a corollary, the particular destructiveness of religious disunion. Normally optimistic, here he sadly casts an eye back on the previous century's record of sectarian conflict: a vista of "religious discord, which like gangrene has infected and wretchedly consumes all of Christianity."[3] His litany of the horrors committed in the name of religious belief recalls Sebastian Castellio's plea for an end to the persecution of heresy (see Chapter Six).

In the second section, Arminius pursues the causes of religious dissension. With a brief nod to power-hungry rulers, both princely and ecclesiastic, as inciters of conflict, he dwells mostly on psychological conditions: sins, traditionally conceived, but in his rather modern analysis, anxieties and desires that obstruct the individual's ability to act rationally.

In the third section, Arminius presents his remedy: a convocation of clerical and lay leaders of the various parties who, having sworn to avoid all bitterness and strife, will with due order discuss and resolve all areas of disagreement—even agreeing, where no reconciliation can be reached, to disagree peacefully. Hopeful and idealistic, Arminius offers a remarkable

---

3. Arminius, *Opera theologica*, 72. Full citation in Texts and Studies.

prescription for political as much as religious deliberation, forecasting the historic assemblies, parliaments, congresses, and conventions of the next two centuries.

Excerpts from the first and third sections are given here.

Arminius details how dissension spreads and endangers Christianity itself.

Hatred and rivalries give rise to schisms, sects, and factional divisions . . . such that competing places of worship are founded, consecrated, and frequented: synagogues vie with synagogues, churches with churches, altars with altars, that want to have nothing to do with each other. . . .

Now if one party believes it is more powerful than the other, it will launch persecutions against its adversary, seeking the enemy's utter annihilation. . . . It will attack the reputation, property, and bodies of the living; the tombs, ashes, and memory of the dead; and the souls of both the living and the dead. Every possible weapon is employed in this struggle: calumny, mockery, and curses; denunciations, excommunications, anathematization; . . . imprisonment and torture, deportation to desert islands, or consignment to hard labor; interdiction on land and at sea, or debarment from heaven and earth; water, fire, iron, crosses, stakes, racks, wheels, the teeth and claws of savage beasts, without respite, limit, or terminus. . . .

But if the two opposing parties are roughly equal in strength, or if one of them has long suffered oppression, or has wearied of persecution, or has been inflamed with a passion for liberty, . . . it will then summon up its courage and gather its strength. Then fierce wars will rage, . . . with opposing armies clashing savagely on the field of battle. Both sides maintain total silence about seeking peace, lest either say one word before the other about that possibility. . . . So unyielding is this reluctance, that anyone who mentions peace . . . would be seen as having deserted the common cause, as virtually a heretic, or a promoter of heresy, an apostate and a traitor. . . .

And so we see that religion itself, because of the sins of humankind, has been made the cause of discord and the scene of endless and cruel conflict. . . . The summit and conclusion of all the evils that arise from religious discord is the destruction of that which gave rise to all the controversy: religion itself.

*****

Having considered the nature and causes of religious discord, Arminius now prescribes a remedy.

This is the remedy: an open and orderly council of the contending factions, . . . in which calmly, carefully, and in fear of the Lord, the various opinions having been weighed and analyzed, and what is the word of God concerning these controversies discussed, debated, and discerned, it will then by common consent be declared to the churches. The chief church leaders will call and convene this council. . . . Not only will members of the clergy be called and admitted, however, but also laymen, whether officeholders of some rank or private citizens . . . and not just the representatives of one or of some of the contending factions, but of all them. . . .

In this council, the discussion will not turn to the rights and dignities of princes, nor the wealth, power, and privileges of bishops, nor a war against the Turks, but will concern only matters pertaining to religion. . . . The purpose of this congress will be to elucidate, preserve, and communicate the truth; to defeat error and secure the peace of the church; from all of which redound the glory of God and the eternal salvation of humankind.

The presidency of this council is filled by him who alone is the head and bridegroom of the church: to Christ, by the power of the Holy Spirit. . . . But for the sake of good and proper order, and to avoid confusion, it is necessary that authority be delegated to subordinates . . . whose task will be to convene the council, set the agenda, put matters to the vote, designate secretaries to count the ballots, and in general to govern the proceedings.

What must take place in this council is a thorough analysis of the controversies at hand, mature deliberation, and a free enunciation of views. . . . The discussion will not proceed by rhetorical presentation, but precise and systematic argument, with all disorderly and imprudent comment avoided. An equal length of time, sufficient for due consideration of the matter under discussion, will be allotted to each of the parties. To prevent wasting time on trivialities, all speeches to be delivered will first be composed in writing, from which they are to be recited. No one may cut off discussion, except by the decision of the whole gathering that the matter had received sufficient consideration. When each item has been presented, mature and serious deliberation will follow about the issues themselves, and the arguments presented by both sides. . . .

But if it happens that consensus cannot be reached on some articles, then there are two possible courses. First, it must be seriously explored whether it is not possible for there to be a fraternal agreement in Christ. . . . And if that reconciliation cannot be obtained, the second possibility is that . . . the parties nonetheless extend their right hands in friendship, and enter upon a solemn agreement, binding themselves as though by an oath, to refrain in the future from bitterness, reproach, and calumny; but rather, in a peaceful manner, to communicate to their followers what they think necessary, and to refute, with a zeal controlled by wisdom and tempered with kindness, those beliefs that they find harmful to salvation and to the glory of God. . . .

May the God of truth and of peace inspire in the hearts of magistrates, people, and clergy, a burning desire for truth and for peace. May he open their eyes to see in its nakedness the execrable foulness of religious discord, and awaken their minds to a clear understanding of the evils that flow copiously from it. Thereby they may exert all their thoughts, efforts, and prayers to this end, that all the causes of such an evil having been removed, mild and gentle remedies may be gathered and employed to heal this dissension....

Horrible chains bind the soul during this earthly life

from Jacob Boehme, *Of True Repentance,* in *The Way to Christ* (1622)

In this first of the component works of *The Way to Christ*, Boehme reaches out to ordinary people longing to come closer to God. To do so, the seeker must follow the way of repentance, and recognize how his soul "is wholly and altogether turned away from God" and "become faithless to him, . . . seeking itself only, in the temporal and transitory lusts of the flesh." Here Boehme's theology is pure Lutheranism: the individual must confront his sinfulness and accept from God salvation through faith. But though it had been revolutionary for Luther, the doctrine of justification by faith had become, in the late-Reformation climate of rigid dogmatisms, dry and sterile, while Boehme's portrayal of the sin-ridden soul and its regeneration, in contrast, is moving and vivid. His promise of the soul's liberation by union with Christ looks back before Luther to *The Imitation of Christ* of Thomas à Kempis (see Chapter One). But there is a difference. The Kempisian message is one of renunciation: it requires the seeker to give up this world, and live as though in another. Boehme asks, instead, not for renunciation so much as for self-examination and self-knowledge, calling on the individual to confess his depravity and depend on God's grace.

An eighteenth-century English translation from the German original, the text given here has been modernized to make it more accessible to contemporary readers.

THE AUTHOR'S PREFACE TO THE READER

Dear Reader,

If you will use these words properly, and are serious in intent, you shall certainly profit from them. But I desire that you be warned, if you are not serious, not to meddle with the cherished names of God, . . . lest they kindle the anger of God in your soul. This little book is only for those who wish to repent, and desire to begin. . . . May you be thereby commended to the eternal goodness and mercy of God.

OF TRUE REPENTANCE

When Man[4] will enter upon repentance, and with his prayers turn to God, he should, before he begins to pray, seriously consider the state of his own soul: how it is wholly and altogether turned away from God, become faithless to him, and only bent upon this temporary, frail, and earthly life; bearing no sincere love towards God and its neighbor, but wholly lusting and walking contrary to the commandments of God, and seeking itself only, in the temporal and transitory lusts of the flesh. . . .

He should consider the three horrible chains by which our souls are bound fast during the time of this earthly life. The first is the severe anger of God, the abyss, and dark world, which is the center, root, or constituent principle of the soul's life.[5] The second is the desire of the devil against the soul, whereby he continually tries and tempts it, and without intermission strives to divert it from the truth of God into his own evil nature and element. . . .

The third and most hurtful chain of all by which the poor soul is tied, is the corrupt and altogether vain, earthly, and mortal flesh and blood, full of evil desires and inclinations. . . . that has not kept the priceless covenant and atonement of the innocent death and passion of Jesus Christ; which covenant God by his grace alone has given or put into our humanity, and reconciled us to him. He must also consider that he has totally forgotten the covenant of holy baptism, in which he had promised to be faithful and true to his savior, and so wholly defiled and obscured his righteousness with sin (which righteousness, God had freely bestowed upon him in Christ), that he now stands before the face of God . . . and is not worthy to be called a son of the Father, and member of Christ.

He should earnestly consider that wrathful death awaits him every hour and moment, and will lay hold on him in his sins, . . . and throw him into the pit of hell as a forsworn person and breaker of faith, who ought to be reserved in the dark dungeon of death to the judgment of God.

He should consider the earnest and severe day of God's Last Judgment,[6] when he shall be presented living with his abominations before God's tribunal. . . . That there he shall stand in great shame and ignominy, and also

---

4. "Man": The proper noun is in the original and retained here, to signify a human being in the abstract, regardless of gender or personal identity.

5. God's anger causes the soul to live in an "abyss," or a "dark world"; that is, in hell.

6. Last Judgment: in Christian theology, God's eternal and final judgment at the end of time of all of humankind.

in great terror and desperation, and that it shall forever grieve him to reflect that he has trifled away so glorious and eternal a state of salvation and happiness, for the pleasure of so short a time. . . .

He must consider that the ungodly Man has lost his noble image—God having created him in and for his own image[7] . . . —and has instead acquired a deformed or monstrous shape, like a hellish worm or ugly beast. . . .

He must earnestly consider the eternal punishment and torture of the damned; how that in eternal horror they shall suffer torments in their abominations which they had committed here, and may never see the land of the saints[8] to all eternity. . . .

He must consider the course of this world, that all things in it are but a play, wherewith he spends his time in such unquietness. . . . In the deep consideration of these weighty truths, Man shall come to feel in his heart and mind, especially if he at the same time represents and sets before his own eyes his own end, a hearty sighing and longing after the mercy of God, and will begin to bewail his committed sins; and to be sorry he has so wretchedly spent his days so ill. . . .

Such a Man, whom the spirit of Christ thus brings into sorrow and repentance, so that his heart is opened both to know and bewail his sins, is very easily to be helped. He needs but to draw to himself the promise of Christ, that is, that God does not will the death of a sinner but that he wishes them all to come unto him, and he will refresh them. . . . Let such a one but lay hold on the words of Christ and wrap himself up into his meritorious passion[9] and death.

But I will now speak to those who feel indeed in themselves a desire to repent, and yet cannot come to acknowledge and bewail their committed sins; the flesh saying continually to the soul, "stay a while, it is well enough"; or "it is time enough tomorrow"; and when tomorrow is come, then the flesh says again, "tomorrow." The soul in the meanwhile, fighting and fainting, conceives neither any true sorrow for the sins it has committed, nor any comfort. To such a one, I say, I will write a Process, or Way, which I myself have pursued, that he may know what he must do, and how it went with me, if he may perhaps be inclined to enter into and pursue the same; and then he will come to understand what he shall find written afterwards here.

. . . . .

---

7. Genesis 1:27: "So God created mankind in his own image, in the image of God he created them; male and female he created them."
8. Saints: all those who have been saved, and spared the torments of hell.
9. Passion: Christ's *passio*, or suffering, culminating in his crucifixion.

THE PROCESS, OR WAY

A Man must bring a serious mind to this work. He must come before God with sincere earnestness, deep humility, and hearty sorrow for his sins, and with a deliberate and firm resolution, not to enter any more into the old broad way of vanity. And though the whole world should account him a fool, and he should lose both honor and goods, nay, and this earthly life also, for the sake of his new choice, yet he must resolve firmly to abide by it. . . .

The return of all things, when God will be all in all

from Johanna Eleonora Petersen, *Autobiography* (1718)

Based on her close reading of the Bible, especially the Book of Revelation, and the visions her studies inspired, Petersen experienced six revelations that she records in her autobiography: three before she entered, as she put it, her "married state," and three afterward. A major theme of those revelations is the "return of all things,"[10] the effectuation at the end of time of universal salvation: for Jews as well as Christians, for unbelievers as well as believers, and even for those first deprived of the vision of God, the fallen angels expelled from heaven before the world began. That concept of universal salvation, embraced also by many later Pietists, marks a significant departure from the soteriology (doctrine of salvation) entailed in Protestant or Catholic orthodoxy, but points to the cosmopolitanism of the approaching Enlightenment. The passages given here, from her first, second, and fourth revelations, detail Petersen's increasing realization that at the end of time, all creatures will return to God, who will then "be all in all and all would be made new."

In her first revelation experienced while she was yet unmarried, Petersen describes her initial concern about the many of God's creation who would be condemned to hell, and begins to understand that all will in time return to God.

---

10. Petersen expounds the concept at greater length in her 1698 work, *The Eternal Gospel of the Universal Return of All Creatures* (German original 1698), for which see Barbara Becker-Cantarino's description in her edition with translation of *The Life of Lady Johanna Eleonora Petersen, Written by Herself: Pietism and Women's Autobiography in Sixteenth-Century Germany* (Chicago: University of Chicago Press, 2005), 47.

§32. Since my early youth, the ever-faithful God has left me ensnarled in a great struggle to understand why God, who is himself Love Itself, would damn so many, as everyone had always believed, to eternal damnation. So even the luckless children of the infidels,[11] who had never had the chance to know God, were to be trapped in torment forever—that I could not understand, that such could be the effect of divine love, which is Love Itself. But then these words rang in my ears: *whoever does not believe will be condemned.*[12] Yet I could not get rid of the feeling that those were words of hate, not love. So I struggled with that feeling in my heart, saying to myself: "My God is himself Love Itself, so that if I can't quite understand something that seems to me to be contrary to divine love, yet I must still revere him and love him for he is Love Itself." . . .

On the basis of her biblical study, Petersen explores further the possibility that all God's creatures would in time be redeemed.

Based on these verses of Scripture, I was fully reassured that there would be redemption from hell, and that the blood of Christ would be operative also there, and that all would be released from hell excepting only those who had sinned against the Holy Spirit and the fallen angels—for at this time the return of all things had not yet been revealed to me. . . . So I was freed from my long struggle, for such sinners had certainly earned eternal torment, and I praised God that he had given us in Jesus Christ such a mighty redeemer; and God resolved my last doubts when I found in Scripture that all creatures would praise God at the last and that he, when all creation was again made subject to Christ, would be all in all and all would be made new. . . .[13]

In the second revelation experienced when Petersen was still unmarried, she receives reassurance of the eventual conversion of Jews and infidels.

§33. The second secret divulged to me when I was still in my unmarried state is that of the coming conversion of the Jews and the infidels, which the ever-faithful God revealed to me in 1664 by means of a dream. . . . This dream seemed as I slept to convey such deep mysteries that I knew it was something remarkable and I tried with all my strength to awaken, but it went away as quick as lightning. . . . Afterwards I searched again in holy Scripture and found a reference to the conversion of the Jews and infidels that I had never before seen or heard, saying that such a conversion was yet to be

---

11. Petersen uses the German *Heiden*, or "heathen," a word that is in modern English even more grating than "infidel," which has been systematically preferred here.
12. Mark 16:16.
13. A pastiche of allusions to 1 Corinthians 15:22 and 15:28, and Revelation 5:13 and 21:5.

expected.[14] ... I was assured by several spiritual teachers to whom I described this dream at the time, that it had been a dream sent by God.

> *In the second revelation she experienced while in her "married state," Petersen explores in detail, in dialogue with the English visionary Jane Lead, the eventual return of all creatures to God, including even the devil himself.*

§36. The second secret divulged to me when I was in my married state is that of the return of all things, which happened in this way. A noble gentleman sent us a handwritten manuscript entitled *The Eight Worlds* that he had obtained from England, with the request that we give him our opinion of it, each separately, I responding for myself, and my beloved husband responding for himself.[15] I for my part was greatly opposed to the notion contained in that manuscript that the return of the fallen angel was to be expected in the eight thousandth year, since I knew from my reading of holy Scripture that in the eight thousandth year the fallen angel[16] would first be hurled into the fiery pool, where he would be tormented for an eternity of eternities. But in the seven thousandth year, when the wedding of the lamb[17] will occur, the fallen angel will be imprisoned and sealed in the Abyss.[18] And after another thousand years he would be set free for a brief time and to work his last evildoing upon the earth, and thereupon he would be thrown into the fiery pool. So this discussion in the manuscript appeared to me to be quite contrary to holy Scripture. ...

Then I went into my office to heave a sigh and call upon my God to grant me grace and strength to face this task. ... Then behold! I was filled with courage from my prayer, as though all my senses left me and resided with my spirit in the fulfillment of all things, when in my mind I heard with John[19] that at the end of time, God having made all things new and good through Jesus Christ, all creatures will praise God and God will be all in all.

---

14. Petersen elicits this information, although the meaning she infers is not clearly evident, from Romans 2:25, 4:13.

15. Baron Dodo von Knyphausen, who sent to the Petersens a manuscript copy of Jane Lead's book *The Wonders of God's Creation Manifested in the Variety of Eight Worlds* (London, 1695). Lead was an English visionary and leader of the Philadelphian Society, whose ideas inspired William Penn, founder of the province of Pennsylvania and its principal city, Philadelphia.

16. The fallen angel, in the singular, is Satan. His story narrated here, based on Revelation 20:3, unfolds against the background of the notion, based on a pastiche of biblical texts, that some multitude of angels, with their leader the devil, Satan, "fell," or were cast out of heaven by God before the creation of the world.

17. The marriage of Christ to his church, the community of believers, on his triumphal return: Revelation 19:7.

18. Revelation 20:3.

19. John, author of Revelation; the reference is to Revelation 16.

The power and spirit of the Lord Jesus was poured upon them

from Margaret Fell, *Women's Speaking Justified, Proved, and Allowed of by the Scriptures* (1666)

Two admonitions against women speaking in church or teaching religious doctrine, both pronounced in letters of the apostle Paul,[20] had long been formidable barriers to women assuming leadership roles in Christian society. Margaret Fell confronts these directly in her *Women's Speaking Justified*, but only in the second half of that work. In the first part, she adduces scriptural texts showing the acceptance of women as spiritual actors and speakers by God the Father in the Old Testament, and Jesus his Son in the New. The excerpts here argue that God viewed his human creations, male and female, as spiritual equals; that Jesus conveyed to the Samaritan woman, an outcast, and to Martha, the sister and subordinate of his friend Lazarus, the nature of his divine identity; and that through angelic agents, and in his own risen person, he communicated to his female followers the news of his resurrection.

Thereafter, Fell turns to a discussion of the Pauline texts, marking the transition deliberately: "And now to the apostle's words . . . " Here she shows that while Paul did forbid women to speak in church, in his first letter to the Corinthians, when they were in a state of spiritual confusion, he directed the same prohibition to men; and that though he did instruct women, in his first letter to Timothy, not to usurp their husband's authority, he said nothing in that passage to bar them from speaking in church: "of that there is nothing here." "And what is all this to those who have the power and spirit of the Lord Jesus poured upon them," Fell continues, "and have the message of the Lord Jesus given unto them?" They have been uniquely graced by God, and so must speak.

The seventeenth-century text utilized here has been modernized to make it more accessible to contemporary readers.

Since many have objected . . . to women's speaking in the church, it may be inferred that they are condemned for meddling in the things of God. The ground for this objection is taken from the words of the apostle Paul. How far they misunderstand the apostle's intentions in these scriptural passages we shall clearly show when we come to them in their course and order. But first

---

20. 1 Corinthians 14:34–35; 1 Timothy 2:11–12.

let me lay down how God himself manifested his will and mind concerning women, and to women.

And first, consider this . . . : *So God created mankind in his own image, in the image of God he created them; male and female he created them.*[21] Here God joins them together in his own image, and makes no such distinctions and differences as men do; for though they be weak, he is strong. . . . And God has put no such difference between the male and female, as men would make. . . .[22]

Again, Christ Jesus, when he came to the city of Samaria, where Jacob's Well was, where the woman of Samaria was, you may read in how he was pleased to preach the everlasting gospel to her, and when the woman said to him, *I know that Messiah (called Christ) is coming. When he comes, he will explain everything to us.* Jesus said to her: *I, the one speaking to you—I am he.*[23]

Also he said to Martha, when she said, she knew that her brother should rise again in the last day. Jesus said to her, *I am the resurrection and the life. The one who believes in me will live, even though they die; and whoever lives by believing in me will never die. Do you believe this?* She answered, *Yes, Lord, . . . I believe that you are the Messiah, the Son of God, who is to come into the world.*[24] Here she manifested her true and saving faith, when few at that day believed this of him. . . .[25]

Thus we see that Jesus recognized the love and grace that appeared in women, and did not despise it: and by what is recorded in the Scriptures, he received as much love, kindness, compassion, and tender dealing towards him from women, as he did from any others, both in his lifetime, and also after they had exercised their cruelty upon him. . . .[26]

Mark this, you that despise and oppose the message of the Lord God that he sends by women; what would have become of the redemption of the whole body of mankind, if they had not cause to believe the message that the Lord Jesus sent by these women . . . concerning his resurrection? And if these women had not [done] thus, out of their tenderness, . . . [and] if their

---

21. Genesis 1:27.
22. An extended discussion of Eve's action in the Garden of Eden (Genesis 3) is omitted here, as are passages from Isaiah, Jeremiah, and Revelation, where figures of women serve as metaphors for the chosen people or for the church.
23. John 4:25–26.
24. John 11:24–27.
25. The episode of the woman who washed and anointed Jesus's feet (Matthew 26:6–13; Mark 14:3–9; Luke 7:36–50) is omitted here, as are passages about the Galilean women (Matthew 28:55–56; Mark 15:40–41), and women of Jerusalem at Golgotha (Luke 23:27–29).
26. That is, in the crucifixion. There follow the episodes of the three or four women discovering the empty tomb, and the appearances of angels and of Jesus himself telling them to inform the disciples (Matthew 28:1–10; Mark 16:1–10; Luke 24:1–11; John 20:11–18).

hearts had not been so united and knit unto him in love, that they could not depart as the men did, but sat watching, and waiting, and weeping about the sepulcher until the time of his resurrection, and so were ready to carry his message, . . . how should his disciples have known, who were not there? . . .

And now to the apostle's words, which is the ground of the great objection against women's speaking. First, chapter 14 of first Corinthians: let the reader seriously peruse that chapter, and see the end and drift of the apostle in speaking these words: for the apostle is there exhorting the Corinthians to charity, and to desire spiritual gifts, and not to speak in an unknown tongue, and not to be children in understanding, . . . for God is not the author of confusion, but of peace; and then he says, *Women should remain silent in the churches*, etc.[27]

From which it plainly appears, that not only the women, but also some others that were among them, were in confusion: For he says, . . . *If anyone speaks in a tongue, two—or at the most three—should speak, one at a time, and someone must interpret. If there is no interpreter, the speaker should keep quiet in the church and speak to himself and to God.*[28] Here the man is commanded to keep silence, as well as the woman, when in confusion and out of order. . . .

Also [in chapter 2 of first Timothy], where he is exhorting that prayer and supplication be made everywhere, lifting up holy hands without wrath and doubting, . . . he says, *A woman should learn in quietness and full submission. I do not permit a woman to teach or to assume authority over a man; she must be quiet.* [29] . . . Here the apostle speaks particularly to a woman in relation to her husband, to be in subjection to him, and not to teach, nor usurp authority over him. . . . but let it be strained to the utmost, as the opponents of women's speaking would have it, that is, that they should not preach nor speak in the church, of that there is nothing here. . . .

And what is all this to those who have the power and spirit of the Lord Jesus poured upon them, and have the message of the Lord Jesus given unto them? Must not they speak the word of the Lord, because of these indecent and unreverent women that the apostle speaks of . . . in these two scriptures? And how are the men of this generation blinded, that bring these scriptures, and pervert the apostle's words, and corrupt his intent in speaking of them? And by these scriptures, endeavor to stop the message and word of the Lord God in women, by contemning and despising them?

. . . . .

And so let this serve to stop that opposing spirit that would limit the power and spirit of the Lord Jesus, whose spirit is poured upon all flesh, both

---

27. 1 Corinthians 14:34–35.
28. 1 Corinthians 14:27–28.
29. 1 Timothy 2:11–12.

sons and daughters, now in his resurrection; and since that the Lord God in the creation, when he made man in his own image, he made them male and female; . . . and when he was upon the earth, he manifested his love, and his will, and his mind, both to the woman of Samaria and Martha . . . ; and after his resurrection also manifested himself to [women] first of all, even before he ascended to his Father. . . . and so let all mouths be stopped that would limit him, whose power and spirit is infinite, who is pouring it upon all flesh.

God is the joy of his heart, and the desire of his soul

from John Wesley, *The Character of a Methodist* (1742)

Wesley makes a crucial distinction in his brief tract *The Character of a Methodist*, of which the following excerpts constitute nearly half: a Methodist is not characterized by "his opinions of any sort," but by the joy of his heart in God and the desire of his soul for God—by passion, that is, and not by creed. In this, he sums up as well the outlook of the radical Pietism of the seventeenth and eighteenth centuries in its manifold German, Dutch, and English forms, both within and outside of the mainstream Protestant denominations. Here is an evangelical Christianity of a sort that would, not long after Wesley wrote, find a particular home in Anglo-America.

The original text is modified to remove anachronistic language (retained in paraphrased biblical quotations) and Americanize spellings.

1. The distinguishing marks of a Methodist are not his opinions of any sort. His assenting to this or that scheme of religion, his embracing any particular set of notions, his espousing the judgment of one man or of another, are all quite wide of the point. . . . We believe, indeed, that "all Scripture is given by the inspiration of God"; and herein we are distinguished from Jews, Turks, and infidels.[30] We believe the written word of God to be the only and sufficient rule both of Christian faith and practice; and herein we are fundamentally distinguished from those of the Romish

---

30. Wesley's reference to "Turks" denotes the Islamic Ottoman Empire, whose threat to Europe, in force since the fourteenth century, was at this time receding. The term "infidels" refers to the non-Christian peoples of regions beyond Europe and its colonies.

Church.[31] We believe Christ to be the eternal, supreme God; and herein we are distinguished from the Socinians and Arians.[32] But as to all opinions which do not strike at the root of Christianity, we think and let think. So that whatsoever they are, whether right or wrong, they are no distinguishing marks of a Methodist.

2. Neither are words or phrases of any sort. We do not place our religion, or any part of it, in being attached to any peculiar mode of speaking, any quaint or uncommon set of expressions. The most obvious, easy, common words, wherein our meaning can be conveyed, we prefer before others, both on ordinary occasions, and when we speak of the things of God. . . .

3. Nor do we desire to be distinguished by actions, customs, or usages, of an indifferent nature. Our religion does not lie in doing what God has not enjoined, or abstaining from what he has not forbidden. It does not lie in the form of our apparel, in the posture of our body, or the covering of our heads; nor yet in abstaining from marriage, or from meats and drinks, which are all good if received with thanksgiving. . . .

4. Nor, lastly, is he distinguished by laying the whole stress of religion on any single part of it. If you say, "Yes, he is; for he thinks 'we are saved by faith alone'": I answer, You do not understand the terms. By salvation he means holiness of heart and life. And this he affirms to spring from true faith alone. Can even a nominal Christian deny it? . . . We do not place the whole of religion . . . either in doing no harm, or in doing good, or in using the ordinances of God. No, not in all of them together; wherein we know by experience a man may labor many years, and at the end have no religion at all, no more than he had at the beginning. . . .

5. "What then is the mark? Who is a Methodist, according to your own account?" I answer: A Methodist is one who has *the love of God shed abroad in his heart by the Holy Ghost given unto him*; one who *loves the Lord his God with all his heart, and with all his soul, and with all his mind, and with all his strength*. God is the joy of his heart, and the desire of his soul; which is constantly crying out, *Whom have I in heaven but thee? and there is none upon earth that I desire beside thee! My God and my all! Thou art the strength of my heart, and my portion for ever!*[33]

---

31. The Catholic church, based in Rome; the term "Roman Catholic" only became commonly used in England in the nineteenth century.

32. Socinians were a unitarian (that is, anti-trinitarian) sect originating in the sixteenth century; Arians denied that Jesus as Son was consubstantial with God the Father, a position deemed heretical in the fourth century by rival Athanasians, who formulated the doctrine of the Trinity.

33. Quoted passages in this paragraph paraphrase Romans 5:5; Mark 12:33; and Psalm 73:25–26.

6. He is therefore happy in God, yea, always happy, as having in him *a well of water springing up into everlasting life*, and overflowing his soul with peace and joy.... He *rejoices in the Lord always*, even *in God his Savior*; and in the Father, *through our Lord Jesus Christ, by whom he hath now received the atonement*. Having found *redemption through his blood, the forgiveness of his sins*, he cannot but rejoice, ... when he sees *all his transgressions blotted out as a cloud, and his iniquities as a thick cloud*.... Yea, this his joy is full, and all his bones cry out, *Blessed be the God and Father of our Lord Jesus Christ, who, according to his abundant mercy, hath begotten me again to a living hope—of an inheritance incorruptible, undefiled, and that fadeth not away, reserved in heaven for me!*[34]

. . . . .

17. These are the principles and practices of our sect; these are the marks of a true Methodist. By these alone do those who are in derision[35] so called, desire to be distinguished from other men. If any man say, "Why, these are only the common fundamental principles of Christianity!" he has said just what I mean; this is the very truth; I know they are no other; and I would to God both you and all men knew, that I, and all who follow my judgment, do vehemently refuse to be distinguished from other men, by any but the common principles of Christianity—the plain, old Christianity that I teach, renouncing and detesting all other marks of distinction....

18. By these marks, by these fruits of a living faith, do we labor to distinguish ourselves from the unbelieving world, from all those whose minds or lives are not according to the Gospel of Christ. But from real Christians, of whatsoever denomination they be, we earnestly desire not to be distinguished at all.... No: *Whosoever doeth the will of my Father which is in heaven, the same is my brother, and sister, and mother*. And I beseech you, brethren, by the mercies of God, that we be in no wise divided among ourselves ... even as we are called with one hope of our calling; *one Lord, one faith, one baptism; one God and Father of all, who is above all, and through all, and in you all.*[36]

---

34. Quoted passages in this paragraph paraphrase John 4:14; Philippians 4:4; Romans 5:11; Ephesians 1:7; Isaiah 44:22; and 1 Peter 1:3–4.
35. The term "Methodist" was originally a derogatory term.
36. Quoted passages in this paragraph paraphrase Matthew 12:50 and Ephesians 4:5.

Chapter Ten: The Reformation Overseas

The impact of the Protestant and Catholic Reformations, which reconfigured the map of Christendom and the soul of the Western world, were not only European, but also global. These religious movements unfolded concurrently with European expansion abroad: westward to the New World just opened by the first voyage of Christopher Columbus in 1492, and eastward to Asia, where the existence of advanced civilizations had been known since antiquity.

In exploring these new worlds, Catholic and Protestant interests were different. For Catholics, the aim was missionary, an extension of the missionary efforts at home to block the Protestant advance and reclaim the continent for Catholicism. Where Catholic conquerors and administrators went, so too did members of the religious orders—primarily Jesuit, Franciscan, and Dominican—intent on converting new peoples. What these missionaries required of their audiences, whether the indigenous Americans they called Indians who possessed no written religious traditions, or the practitioners of Hinduism, Buddhism, or other Asian religions equipped with sacred texts, was the complete mastery of the rudiments of faith, translated into the languages of those targeted for conversion. The goal, undeniably, was cultural hegemony, as critics today of these missionary efforts often charge. The task here, however, is not to engage that argument, but to note the fierce convictions and unfailing courage of two missionaries who brought Christianity to the non-European peoples they sacrificially served, as well as the cautious and discerning spirit of one theologian's comments on the morality of conversion.

In contrast to the missionary thrust of the Catholics, the Protestants who settled in North America, though they made some few attempts to convert the Indians whose lands they occupied, especially sought the freedom to practice their own faith in a new wilderness setting. Adherents of a gamut of mainstream denominations and radical sects, including Puritans, Baptists, Quakers, Huguenots, Mennonites, and German Pietists, many were seeking refuge from persecution or isolation in the homes they had left (as did also the Catholics from Protestant Britain). The spirit of the Protestant settlement in Anglo-America was determined and defiant, while the religious commitment they sought within their own community was inward, authentic, and demanding.

In this, though, they were alike: both the Catholics who took their faith to the Americas and to Asia, and the Protestants who constructed a better Europe, as they believed, on a new continent, were products of the Reformation. That provenance is evident in the five cases—three Catholics and two Protestants—presented in this chapter.

From his perch as professor of theology at the University of Salamanca (Spain), Francisco de Vitoria (c. 1483–1546) confronted the Spanish occupation of New World territories as a moral and philosophical problem, thereby laying, a century before the Dutch jurist Hugo Grotius, the foundations of modern international law. A Dominican, an instructor of Dominican missionaries, and a follower of his Dominican predecessor, Thomas Aquinas—arguably the greatest of the medieval thinkers who had forged a synthesis of Aristotelian metaphysics and Christian doctrine—Vitoria brought a disciplined conscience to the missionary project central to the Catholic Reformation.

Of interest here is Vitoria's work *De Indis*, literally "on the Indies," as the Spanish termed their South American dominions during Vitoria's lifetime, or "on the Indians," and translated here as *On the Indians of the New World*, to distinguish the subjects from the inhabitants of the Asian subcontinent India. It asks questions such as these: Do the Indians have a right to their own form of life, including property ownership? Must the Indians accept conversion to Christianity under the guidance of missionary instructors? To what extent can wars against the Indians be considered just? What, overall, are the rules of just war?

Vitoria's arguments are read, as are Aristotle's, not in works composed by his hand, but in the lecture notes of his students published after his death. Their methodology is strictly scholastic, producing a spider's nest of arguments, counterarguments, and demonstrations. For the benefit of readers unfamiliar with scholastic terminology, the passages translated here have been extracted from their framework of logical demonstration and presented as plain statements. The conversion to Christianity of Indians under Spanish rule, Vitoria concludes, though it was to be desired, was not to be compelled.

Even as Francisco de Vitoria turned his glance toward the New World, Francis Xavier (1506–1552) looked to Asia, a land of mature civilizations that were ripe, he believed, for the announcement of the Christian message. A Basque-speaking native of the kingdom of Navarre (modern Spain), Xavier was one of the close companions of Ignatius Loyola (see Chapter Eight) and co-founder of the Jesuit order committed to the advancement of Catholic Christianity in Europe and abroad.

In 1541, Xavier sailed from Europe to India, where the Portuguese had established their first settlements in 1500, and labored there from 1542 to 1545, establishing a Jesuit college in the Portuguese capital at Goa, and converting the peoples of the southern tip of India. In 1545, Xavier left India to extend his mission into Malaysia, Indonesia, Japan, and ultimately China; that final destination was before his eyes when he died in 1552.

In his twelve years of missionary work, Xavier acquired several Asian languages, adding to his fund of Basque, Spanish, French, Italian, Portuguese, and Latin, and encountered a welter of Asian religious traditions. His journeys are documented by his more than one hundred letters, mostly in Portuguese or Spanish, to his superiors and fellow Jesuits. Like the 1544 letter excerpted here, sent from southern India where by that date he had converted to Christianity the inhabitants of thirty villages, they speak of his tireless efforts to teach, guide, and heal the native peoples. His extraordinary labors, by which tens of thousands of Asian converts were won for a faith whose fulcrum was then European and Western, were recognized by his canonization in 1622.

Born Marie Guyart (1599–1672), the Ursuline nun Marie de l'Incarnation was one of the first missionaries in New France[1] and the founder of the first school for girls in North America. In 1633, Guyart joined the teaching order of the Ursulines, then resolved to join the new missionary effort in North America. A Jesuit priest introduced Guyart to the wealthy and pious Madame de Chauvigny de La Peltrie (1603–1671), who not only bankrolled her endeavors, but accompanied her on the journey to the New World. There they disembarked on August 1, 1639, and remained until their deaths more than thirty years later.

Guyart's goal was to teach the Indian[2] girls of the region—Huron, Algonquin, and Iroquois—and so integrate them into the Catholic church and European civilization. To do so, she learned the native languages, creating dictionaries and catechisms for the use of her students and colleagues. The Ursuline school she launched still exists, attached to the Ursuline convent in old Quebec City (Canada). After not quite four centuries, the achievement of Marie Guyart de l'Incarnation won the highest possible commendation: on April 2, 2014, she was canonized by Pope Francis as a saint of the Catholic church.

To advance her project, Guyart wrote hundreds of letters, filling more than one thousand pages in their modern edition, reporting on the events not only of her Ursuline convent and school, but also documenting the tumultuous Jesuit effort to convert the Indian population. The letter given here, somewhat abridged, was written just thirteen months after Guyart's arrival in Quebec. It is addressed to a likely patroness of the school, describing the complex lives of her pupils and the sparse little schoolhouse where they learned to pray, to read, and to forget their lives in the forest.

How different are the worlds of the two contemporaries Roger Williams (c. 1603–1683) and Marie Guyart de l'Incarnation! While her mission was

---

1. The region along the Saint Lawrence River in Canada explored by Jacques Cartier in 1534, and settled, with Quebec as capital, by Samuel de Champlain in 1608.

2. The term Guyart applies to the native inhabitants is *sauvage*, "savage," meaning a person living outside the bounds of civilization. Because of its negative connotations to modern readers, not inherent in the original text, it is translated here as "Indian." The even more neutral term "native" does not adequately convey the perception of the indigenous culture as strange and distant.

to bring the Catholic faith to American indigenes neither ready nor eager to receive it, his was to propound, more than a century before Franklin, Jefferson, and Madison, bedrock American principles of religious liberty and the separation of church and state—to be separated, he said, by an impregnable "wall"—now embedded in the First Amendment to the U.S. Constitution.

Founder of the Rhode Island colony, America's first democracy, Williams was in many ways a radical. His own religious views descended from those of radical sectarians of the Reformation, especially the Anabaptists (see Chapter Six), whose opposition to infant baptism he adopted.[3] He was a radical Arminian (see Chapter Nine), who repudiated any test of religious conformity. He was a Radical Pietist (see Chapter Nine), for whom religious experience mattered more than creed. Indeed, of the latter he had none, having successively cast off the Anglican, the Puritan, and the Baptist, to conclude that no true Christian church yet existed on the earth. His ideas have longer roots as well, in the pacifism of Erasmus (see Chapter Two), Luther's cautions against the coercion of conscience by civil authorities (see Chapter Three), and Castellio's repudiation of persecution (see Chapter Six); while they abjure Bucer's vision of the interactive roles of church and state (see Chapter Seven).

In 1644, Williams published his most famous book, *The Bloudy Tenent of Persecution*,[4] of which a small section is given here. Its whimsical framework is a dialogue between the two abstract personalities of "Truth" and "Peace," whose paths, as the speakers wryly observe, rarely cross. But in the moment they have together, they defend religious liberty and decry religious violence, voicing the author's rage at the distortions introduced by vectors of power into the personal experience of faith. Williams' insistence that nothing, and certainly not the state, may impede complete liberty of opinion—"soul freedom," as he called it—mark him as a key progenitor of American society and culture.

So, too, was Jonathan Edwards (1703–1758), writing nearly a century after Williams in a more settled colonial world. Edwards is less concerned with freedom of thought than with intensity of feeling, urging his congregants to a closer commitment to the Christian faith. In this regard, this Calvinist pastor from northwestern Massachusetts resembles his Methodist contemporary John Wesley (see Chapter Nine) on the other side of the Atlantic Ocean. In earnest sermons, without dramatic vocalizations or gestures, Edwards convinced his listeners that they must, to be saved, seek and receive the grace of God. Those who did so were "awakened," undergoing a spiritual experience of conversion.

---

3. At the same time, such other radical Reformation doctrines as unitarianism, universal salvation, and the community of property, were foreign to him.

4. In modern English, "bloudy" is "bloody," and "tenent" is "tenet," or principle; the work is cited in full in Texts and Studies.

Numerous persons experienced that awakening in the town to which he ministered, as he describes in his *Faithful Narrative of the Surprising Work of God in the Conversion of Many Hundred Souls in Northampton* (written in 1736), excerpts from the first section of which are given here. Many thousands more were converted across the Anglo-American colonies during the 1730s and 1740s, transforming the history of the Protestant churches in the United States, where religion became a matter of intense personal experience rather than of ritual and creed. The First Great Awakening was followed by a second, beginning around 1800; others followed, although no consensus has been reached on just how many there were. Christian awakenings and revivals, however, from the time of Jonathan Edwards to our own, have been a major current of American cultural life.

In their new worlds, both Catholics and Protestants saw the legacy of the Reformation develop in ways that could not be foreseen in 1500, before that cataclysm, or the European surge to global dominance, had begun.

War cannot force the Indians to believe, but only to pretend to believe

from Francisco de Vitoria, *On the Indians of the New World*, First lecture, section two: *The false arguments for the subjection by the Spanish of the Indians of the New World* (1539)

In these passages, drawn from articles six through eight and nine through fifteen of sixteen articles, Vitoria destroys one by one the arguments supporting the use of violence against the Indians in pursuit of their conversion: the pope is not their temporal lord, and has no sovereignty over them in spiritual things, as they are not Christians; they have not resisted Christianity, but are simply ignorant of it, not having been informed; they cannot be forced to believe, but only persuaded by tangible evidence or by the example of good life; but the atrocities the Spanish have committed, far from promoting the conversion of the Indians, have discouraged it. In sum, there can be neither justice nor purpose in waging war against the Indians in order to achieve their conversion, for war will not compel them to believe, but only to pretend to believe. Striking in this excerpt is the contrast between Vitoria's systematic presentation of his arguments and the soul-felt protest they make against the compulsion of innocents in matters of faith.

6. *The pope has no temporal power over the Indians nor over any other unbelievers.*

... The pope has no temporal power over those barbarians, nor over any other unbelievers. ... For he has no temporal power unless it serves the cause of his spiritual dominion. But neither does he have spiritual dominion over them;[5] nor consequently, does he hold temporal power.

7. *If the Indians choose not to recognize papal sovereignty, it is not permissible to wage war against them and seize their possessions.*

... Even if the Indians choose not to recognize papal sovereignty, it is not permissible to wage war against them and seize their possessions. ... For ... given that the Indians do not wish to accept Christ as Lord, they must not on that account be coerced by war or harmed in any way. ...

8. *Did the Indians, having not yet heard anything about the Christian faith, commit the sin of unbelief[6] because they did not believe in Christ?*

Before they had heard anything about the Christian faith, the Indians did not commit the sin of unbelief because they did not believe in Christ. ... Those who have never been informed, however much they may have sinned in other ways, are invincibly ignorant,[7] and consequently, their ignorance is not sinful. ... If the faith has not been taught to them, therefore, they are invincibly ignorant, because it is impossible that they should know of it. ...

10. *Should it be expected that the Indians believe in the Gospel of Christ when it is first announced to them, with the result that after only a single announcement has been uttered, they commit a mortal sin[8] by not believing?*

... The Indians must not be expected to believe in response to a first announcement to them of the Christian faith, with the result that they commit mortal sin by not believing in response to this single announcement that Christianity is the one true religion and that Christ is the savior and redeemer

---

5. Vitoria cites 1 Corinthians 5:12: "What business is it of mine to judge those outside the church? Are you not to judge those inside?"

6. The sin of failing to believe; see especially Hebrews 3:12, 11:6.

7. In Catholic doctrine, a person who sins while ignorant, and whose ignorance is involuntary, is "invincibly ignorant," innocent of that sin, however sinful he may be in other regards. In contrast, a person who sins while ignorant, but whose ignorance results from some negligence on his part, such as refusing to accept something of which he has been informed, is "vincibly ignorant," and guilty of the sin he has in his ignorance committed. See Joseph Delany, "Ignorance," *The Catholic Encyclopedia* 7 (New York: Robert Appleton Company, 1910): http://www.newadvent.org/cathen/07648a.htm.

8. Mortal sins rupture a Christian's relationship with God, and condemn the sinner to hell if the sin remains unforgiven.

of the world, since that explanation is made without miraculous signs or any other form of proof or persuasion.... For where neither signs nor any other kind of persuasive mechanism assist in the announcement of the Christian faith, it should not be expected that the Indians will believe.

11. *If the Christian faith is simply announced and proposed to the Indians, and they do not immediately accept it, the Spanish may not wage war against them, for such action would violate the law of war.*[9]

[It follows that] if the Christian faith is proposed to the Indians only once in this way and they do not accept it, the Spanish may not for that reason go to war against them, for such action would violate the law of war.

12. *To what extent, if the Indians are advised and summoned to listen peaceably to those preaching the Christian faith, and they refuse, are they to be deemed to have committed mortal sin?*

If the Indians are advised and summoned to listen peaceably to those preaching the Christian faith, and they refuse to listen, they may possibly be deemed to commit mortal sin.... Therefore, if they are advised to listen to and consider matters pertaining to religion, they can be required at least to hear and to deliberate.... Let them be required to listen, therefore, or else through no fault of their own, they may be deprived of salvation....

13. *Under what circumstances might the Indians be required to accept the Christian faith or suffer the penalty of mortal sin....*

If the Christian faith is proposed to the Indians persuasively, with the provision of forceful and rational arguments, by a person of upright character, ... and if this is done not once and perfunctorily, but diligently and earnestly, the Indians are required to accept the Christian faith under the penalty of mortal sin....

14. *The present author is not convinced that, to this point, the Christian faith has been proposed and announced to the Indians in such a manner that they may be required to believe or commit a sin.*

... It is not sufficiently clear to me that the Christian faith has yet been proposed and announced to the Indians in such a manner that they may be required to believe or commit a sin. I say this because ... they are not required to believe if the faith has not been proposed to them with suitably persuasive arguments: for I hear nothing about miracles or signs or lives of exemplary piety, but I hear rather of a multitude of scandals and cruelty and crimes. Wherefore

---

9. *Ius belli*, the law of war, a concept developed by the Romans and developed by Christian thinkers, especially Thomas Aquinas, meaning that branch of international law, or the law of nations, that pertained under conditions of war.

it is not apparent that the Christian religion has been preached to them with the kindness and decency necessary to persuade them to accept it. . . .

15. *And even if to the greatest possible extent the Christian faith has been patiently and persuasively announced to the Indians, and yet they refuse to accept it, it still would not be permissible to wage war against them and seize their possessions.*

. . . However great the extent to which the Christian faith may have been patiently and persuasively announced to the Indians, and yet they refused to accept it, it still is not permissible to wage war against them and seize their possessions. . . . For never did Christian rulers, whose counselors were the most saintly and learned popes, wage war against the infidels because they refused to accept the Christian religion. Nor is war in any way an argument for the truth of the Christian faith. War cannot move the Indians to believe, therefore, but only to pretend that they believe and accept the Christian faith, which is monstrous and a sacrilege. . . .

So many become Christians, my arms grow weary from baptizing them

from Francis Xavier, *Letter* to his fellow Jesuits in Rome (Cochin,[10] January 15, 1544)

Xavier's 1544 letter to his Jesuit colleagues in Rome paints a vivid portrait of a missionary at work—the first and most successful of the Christian advance into Asia. He immerses himself deeply in the lives of those he aims to convert, learning their customs and language. Studying intensively with tutors who know both the native Malabar, a Tamil dialect, and Portuguese, Xavier acquires the local language, into which he then translates a small canon of texts: the Apostles' Creed, the Ten Commandments, and four basic prayers, including the Our Father (Lord's Prayer). These he memorizes and recites constantly, one sentence at a time, his listeners repeating each one in chorus; and thus twice each day he teaches the boys, charged in turn to teach all in their households, and every Sunday, instructs the whole assembled population. They are made Christians, in Xavier's missionary project, by their

---

10. Kochi, modern India.

verbal mastery of the major tenets of the Christian faith, condensed into the twelve articles of the Creed, the Ten Commandments, and four prayers.

Teaching the faith is Xavier's main goal, but in its service, he also baptizes newborns and buries the dead, and visits in their homes those suffering illness or distress. He attempts, too, to reach the Brahmans, the priestly class, without much success, and to stir up new recruits for the missionary venture from university students primarily intent on advancing their careers. For these latter groups, he has some sharp words; for the poor natives of the Indian coast, not even a hint of condescension.

. . . For more than a year I have been with these Christians, of whom I can tell you there are many, and many more become Christians each day. As soon as I arrived among them. . . , I tried to learn what they knew about Christ our Lord, asking them what it was that they believed. . . . The only response I received was that they were Christians, but since they did not understand our language they did not know . . . what it is they should believe.

As they did not understand me, nor did I understand them, since their native language was Malabar[11] and mine was Basque,[12] I . . . found a few of them who understood both our language and theirs. And after working hard for some time with their help, we translated the prayers from Latin into Malabar. First we taught the people to make the sign of the cross and confess their faith in one God in three persons; then the Creed, the Commandments, the Our Father, the Hail Mary, the Hail Holy Queen, and the Confiteor.[13] Having translated all these into their language and learned them by heart, I went through the town ringing a bell to call all that I could gather together of the boys and men. When they had assembled, twice each day, I taught them. In the space of a month, I had taught them the prayers, and told the boys to teach what they had learned in our school to their fathers and mothers and all of their household, and their neighbors.

On Sundays, I assembled all the inhabitants, men and women, old and young, to recite the prayers in their language, which they were delighted to do, and came with alacrity. Beginning with the confession of faith in one God in three persons, they then repeated after me out loud in their language each article of the Creed. . . . Then I repeated each of the twelve articles of the Creed, one at a time, telling them that to be Christians they need nothing more than to believe firmly, without doubting, in every one of the twelve articles. . . . Then all those gathered, men and women, old and young, responded

---

11. Malabar: a Tamil dialect of southern India.
12. Basque: non-Indo-European language of the Basque region, northern Spain.
13. The Creed or Apostle's Creed; the Ten Commandments (Exodus 20:1–17; Deuteronomy 5:4–21); and prayers regularly recited by Catholics: the Our Father (Lord's Prayer), Hail Mary, Hail Holy Queen (the *Salve Regina*, a hymn to the virgin Mary), and the Confiteor, the prayer of confession.

"yes" with loud voices as I read each article, placing their arms on their chests, one above the other, in the form of a cross. . . .

After the Creed, the next thing I taught them were the Ten Commandments, telling them that Christians had only ten laws. . . . Both Christians and gentiles are impressed to see how holy is the law of Jesus Christ, and how it accords entirely with natural reason. . . .

So many came to call me to their houses during this time, so I might offer prayers for those who were sick . . . that with preaching the Gospel, teaching the boys, baptizing, translating the prayers, answering their questions, I was left no time for other tasks. . . . The result was, in satisfying the needs of those who summoned me or called upon me, I was really overburdened; and yet, lest they lose the faith they had in our Christian faith and law, I could not refuse their holy importunities. . . .

Many conversions of Christians are lost to us in this region because we lack people who will commit themselves to such pious and holy tasks. Often I have thought I should go to your schools and shout, like one who has lost his mind, and especially to the University of Paris, to arouse those at the Sorbonne[14] who possess more knowledge than the will to do something useful with it. . . . I was almost ready to write to the University of Paris . . . to say how many millions of gentiles might become Christians if workers could be had, if they would just exert themselves to locate and encourage some *who will not look out for their own interests, but those of Jesus Christ!*[15] So great is the multitude of those who become Christians in this land where I now work that often my arms grow weary from baptizing, and I lose my voice from having so often recited in their language the Creed and the Commandments and the other prayers. . . . There are days when I baptize an entire village, and on this coast where I labor there are thirty Christian villages. . . .

Among the gentiles in this region is a group called Brahmans,[16] who are supported by all the other gentiles. . . . Whenever the Brahmans are in need of something, they tell the people that the idols are furious because the items requested have not been sent, and that if they do not do so, . . . the idols will kill them, or sicken their bodies, or send demons to invade their houses. And these poor simple people, believing it will be so, fearing the evils the idols will inflict, provide what the Brahmans demand. . . .

One Brahman only did I find in a village on this coast who had some understanding since, as I was told, he had studied in some well-known schools. . . . They have some scriptures that record their commandments. The language in which they are written, which is taught to those who are schooled, is for them what Latin is for us. . . .[17]

---

14. Original college of the University of Paris, founded 1257.
15. Paraphrasing Philippians 2:21.
16. Brahmans: the highest Hindu caste, that of priests.
17. Sanskrit: the language of ancient India in which the sacred Hindu writings were composed.

He asked me to tell him the main principles of Christian doctrine. . . . Accordingly, I said and pronounced with great pleasure these important words from our law: *Whoever believes and is baptized will be saved.*[18] He wrote these words down in his own language, along with their explanation. . . . He told me that one night he had a delightful and joyful dream that he was to become a Christian and be my partner and companion. . . . I told him that he should teach the simple folk to worship one sole God, the creator of heaven and earth, who is in heaven. But he, because of the oath [of loyalty] he had taken, would not do so, for fear that a demon might kill him. . . . .

Are we not of all people on earth the happiest and most fortunate?

from Marie de l'Incarnation, *Letter to a lady of quality* (Quebec, September 3, 1640)

Thirteen months after arriving in New France, Guyart addressed a letter to "a lady of quality," a phrase used at that time to denote a woman of high rank, great wealth, and important social connections. The lady was, most likely, Marguerite Thiersault,[19] a patron of the Jesuit mission and mother of the priest who had introduced Guyart to her lifelong friend Madame de La Peltrie. In polite and persuasive terms, the letter seeks financial support for the school and convent she had founded in Quebec.

To entice her correspondent, Guyart portrays several of her Huron and Algonquin pupils. The images are striking. One girl who longed to return to her native forest fled into the woods, leaving behind her, mutilated, the European costume she had been given to wear. Another was groomed for marriage not to the Frenchman who courted her, but to one of her own people, so that she might "serve as an example to the Indians." Another little girl is depicted devoutly kneeling in prayer, saying the rosary, and singing hymns in her native Indian tongue. Guyart further describes the rickety wooden two-room school, with bunked beds to accommodate both nuns and students, and a view of the stars through the chinks in the roof. "And so,

---

18. Mark 16:16.

19. Oury, *Correspondance*, 100n1; full citation in Texts and Studies. Also Lucien Campeau, "Poncet de La Rivière, Joseph-Antoine," *Dictionary of Canadian Biography*, vol. 1 (University of Toronto/Université Laval, 2003–): http://www.biographi.ca/en/bio/poncet_de_la_riviere_joseph_antoine_1E.html.

Madame," she concludes, "are we not of all people on earth the happiest and most fortunate?"

So we have every reason, Madame, to praise the merciful Father for the bountiful mercies he has bestowed on our poor Indians who are not only willing to accept baptism, but have begun to adopt a sedentary life, settling down and clearing the land. The fervor of the primitive church, it seems, has journeyed to New France and warms the hearts of our good converts, so that if France could help them but a little to build their little cabins in the village they have founded at Sillery,[20] further progress would soon be made. . . .

A great persecution [of our missionaries] has arisen among the Hurons, where it was feared that one of the Fathers had been martyred by the blow of a hatchet; the club broke that was used to beat him on the head out of hatred for the faith he preached. There have been similar designs on the other Fathers, who would be overjoyed to suffer. Yet with all of that, at least a thousand Indians have been baptized. . . .

There is talk about giving us two girls from this Huron nation, along with two Algonquins, in addition to the eighteen who already fill our school. . . . I must tell you, Madame, that there in France, it will be hard to understand how continually God bestows his blessings on our little school. I will report to you a few incidents so that you may share our joy.

The first Indian girl sent to our school, named Marie Negabmat,[21] was so accustomed to running through the woods that we lost all hope of keeping her with us. The Reverend Father Le Jeune[22] who had convinced her father to give her to us sent with her two older Indian Christian girls who stayed here a while in order to settle her in. But that was useless, for she fled into the forest four days later, leaving behind the shreds of the dress that we had given her to wear. Her father, who is an exemplary Christian who lives like a saint, ordered her to return to the school, which she did.

She had not been back two days when a remarkable change took place. She seemed to be quite unlike her former self, so much did she incline to prayer and to the practices of Christian piety. . . . No sooner does she commit a fault, than she comes on her knees to beg forgiveness. . . . In a word, one cannot look at her without being moved, so greatly do innocence and an inner grace radiate from her face.

---

20. A newly founded village, named after its patron Noël Brulart de Sillery; Dale Miquelon, *The Canadian Encyclopedia*: http://www.thecanadianencyclopedia.ca/en/article/sillery/.
21. The god-daughter of Madame de La Peltrie, then ten years old; Oury, 100n9.
22. Paul Le Jeune, superior of the Jesuit mission in New France.

At the same time we received an older girl of seventeen years, named Marie Amiskvian.[23] Never was there seen anyone more docile nor more innocent; nor indeed more honest, for we never found her once to lie, and lying is prized as a virtue by the Indians. . . . Highly intelligent, she easily retains what she is taught, especially the mysteries of our holy faith, which gives us hope that she will accomplish much good when she returns to her life among the Indians. She is courted by a Frenchman, but the plan is to give her to a husband of her own nation,[24] because it is hoped she will serve as an example to the Indians. O, may God inspire some pious donor in France to help her build a little house! For this would certainly be a most meritorious act. This girl has greatly assisted us, as well, in the study of her Indian language, since she speaks French well.

Your god-daughter Marie Magdelaine Abatenau was given to us at not yet six years of age, still covered all over with small pox. At that age she had all alone cared for her father and mother, who were ill with the disease of which they died, with such skill that all who saw her, admired her. No more obedient child could be seen: she does whatever she is told to do with such competence and graciousness that she might be taken for a child of quality; so it is fitting that she is your god-daughter—that is your daughter, I should say gladly, in Jesus Christ.

Marie-Ursule Gamitiens[25] . . . is only five or six years old; yet young as she is, she gives us no trouble when we have her make her Christian devotions, for as soon as she wakes she places herself in the posture of prayer to God. She says her rosary during Mass, and sings the hymns in her Indian tongue.

Agnès Chabdikouechich came to us at the same time. Some time before she entered our school she encountered the Reverend Father de Caën[26] in the forest where she was gathering food, and as soon as she saw him she threw her hatchet to the ground and said: "Teach me." . . . He brought her to the school with a friend, where they both were soon prepared for holy baptism. She has made great progress with us, both in the knowledge of the Christian mysteries and in good manners, needlework, reading, playing the viol,[27] and a thousand other little skills. She is only twelve years old, and made her First Communion[28] at Easter. . . .

---

23. Baptized in Quebec in 1637 or 1638; Oury, 100n11.
24. She was Algonquin; Oury, 100n12.
25. God-daughter of Mademoiselle de Luynes; Oury, 100n13.
26. Jesuit missionary; see Oury, 100n15.
27. Viol: stringed instrument of the era, often played among family and friends gathered for musical recreation.
28. First communion: in the Catholic church and some others, a person's first reception of the sacrament of the Eucharist, often made by children between the ages of seven and twelve.

A description follows of the program of instruction for the girls, of the sufferings caused by a smallpox epidemic, and of the hardships the Ursulines undergo to sustain their school and convent.

To accommodate us all, we have only two small rooms that serve as kitchen, dining room, cloister, classroom, parlor, and choir.[29] We have built a little wooden church whose poverty makes it beautiful. . . . No one would believe the expenses that we have had to make in this little house, though it is so poor that at night we can see the stars shining through the chinks in the roof, and that we can scarcely keep a candle lit because of the wind that rushes through.

I shall tell you how we can hold so many people in so small a place. The ends of each room are divided into alcoves built of pinewood. One bed is placed within near the ground, a second erected like a roof over the first, to be reached by a ladder. Yet with all this, we deem ourselves happier than if we lived in the most opulent monastery in France. . . .

And so, Madame, are we not of all people on earth the happiest and most fortunate?

I hear the cry of the whole earth, drunk with the blood of its inhabitants

from Roger Williams, *The Bloudy Tenent of Persecution* (1644)

This excerpt from the opening exchange between the abstract personages Truth and Peace, the two fey interlocutors of *The Bloudy Tenent of Persecution*, belies that work's seriousness—for it is anything but light-hearted. It is a long and serpentine work, lavishly documented with scriptural exegeses, and in a prose—although it is English prose—presenting formidable difficulties to a modern reader. But the conceptual framework, introduced in the first two chapters of the book, has an eloquent simplicity that underscores the message that will unfold in the two hundred or so pages that follow. Here Peace inquires of Truth the reason for the terrible religious conflicts of their age, and Truth replies, lamenting the tortures of the martyred and "the whole earth, made drunk with the blood of its inhabitants," that people have flung away the "spiritual sword and spiritual artillery" of persuasion and consensus that might be used to quell their quarrels in favor of "an arm of flesh, and sword of steel."

---

29. Cloister: a place of retreat; parlor: a place to entertain visitors; choir: where the liturgy and hymns are sung.

Originally written in seventeenth-century English and laden with apocalyptic allusions and biblical references, this difficult text has been modernized in language, punctuation, and spelling to make it more accessible to contemporary readers.

TRUTH. In what dark corner of the world, sweet Peace, are we two met? How has this present evil world banished me from all its coasts and quarters? And how has the righteous God in judgment taken you from the earth?[30]

PEACE. It is lamentably true, blessed Truth; the foundations of the world have long been out of course, and the gates of Earth and Hell have conspired together to intercept our joyful meeting and our holy kisses. With what a wearied, tired wing have I flown over nations, kingdoms, cities, towns, to find out precious Truth?

TRUTH. The like enquiries in my flights and travels have I made for Peace, and still am told, she has left the earth, and fled to heaven.

PEACE. Dear Truth, what is the earth but a dungeon of darkness, where truth is not?

TRUTH. And what kind of peace is found there but a fleeting dream, your ape[31] and counterfeit?

PEACE. O where is the promise of the God of heaven, that righteousness and peace shall kiss each other?

TRUTH. Patience, sweet Peace, heaven and earth are growing old, and . . . shall melt away, and be burnt up with all the works that the earth contains; and the most high eternal creator shall gloriously create a new heaven and new earth, where righteousness dwells.[32] . . . Until then both you and I must hope, and wait, and bear the fury of Satan's wrath. . . .

PEACE. Most precious Truth, you know we are both harried and pursued. My heart is full of sighs, my eyes with tears. Where can I better vent my full oppressed bosom, then into yours, whose faithful lips may for these few hours revive my drooping wandering spirits, and here begin to wipe tears from my eyes, and the eyes of my dearest children?

---

30. Cf. Revelation 6:4: "Then another horse came out, a fiery red one. Its rider was given power to take peace from the earth and to make people kill each other. . . ."
31. "Ape": that is, an imitation or parody; cf. the verb "to ape," or to imitate.
32. 2 Peter 3:13.

TRUTH. Sweet daughter of the God of peace, begin; pour out your sorrows, vent your complaints: how joyful I am to have these precious minutes to revive our hearts, both yours and mine, and the hearts of all that love the truth and peace.[33] . . . Some few there are, but oh, how few are valiant for the truth, and dare to plead my cause as my witnesses in sackcloth. . . . [34]

PEACE. O how I could spend eternal days and endless years at your holy feet, in listening to the precious oracles of your mouth! . . . But since we must soon part, let us employ these minutes, and . . . revive me with your words, which are sweeter than honey, and the honeycomb.

Dear Truth, I have two sad complaints. First, the most sober of your witnesses, who dare to plead your cause—how is it they are my enemies, contentious, turbulent, seditious? Second, your enemies, though they speak and rail against you, though they outrageously pursue, imprison, banish, and kill your faithful witnesses, yet why must so much blood be shed to overthrow the heretics?[35] Indeed, if they kindle coals and fan the flames of devouring wars that injure both the spiritual and the civil state, . . . how do they pretend that they fight a holy war? He that kills, and he that's killed, they both cry out, it is for God, and for their conscience. . . .

TRUTH. Dear Peace, to answer your first complaint, it is true, your dearest sons, just like their mother, peacekeeping, peacemaking sons of God, have borne and still must bear the faults of those who brought turmoil to Israel, and who turn the world upside down. . . . Yet strife must be distinguished: it is necessary or unnecessary, godly or ungodly, Christian or unchristian, etc. It is unnecessary, unlawful, dishonorable, ungodly, unchristian, in most cases in the world, for there is a possibility of keeping sweet peace in most cases, and if it be possible, it is the express command of God that peace be kept.[36] Alternatively, it is necessary, honorable, godly, etc., with civil and earthly weapons to defend the innocent, and to rescue the oppressed from the violent paws and jaws of oppressing persecuting Nimrods.[37]

But finally, it is as necessary, indeed still more honorable, godly, and Christian, to fight the fight of faith, with religious and spiritual artillery, and to contend earnestly for the faith of Jesus, . . . against all opposers, and the

---

33. Cf. Zechariah 8:19.
34. Cf. Revelation 11:3: "And I will appoint my two witnesses, and they will prophesy for 1,260 days, clothed in sackcloth." A rough textile made of goat's hair or crude fibers, sackcloth was worn as a sign of mourning.
35. The original here reads, "how is all vermilioned over for justice against the heretics?"
36. Cf. Romans 13:1–2.
37. That is, tyrants; Nimrod, great-grandson of Noah, was a hunter. Cf. Psalm 73:3–9; Job 29:17.

gates of earth and hell, men or devils, even against Paul himself, or an Angel from heaven, if he bring any other faith or doctrine.[38]

PEACE. The clashing of such arms never disturbs me. Speak once again, dear Truth, to my second complaint of bloody persecution, and devouring wars, marching under the colors of upright justice, and holy zeal, etc.

TRUTH. My ears have long been filled with a threefold doleful outcry. First, the cry of 144,000 virgins forced and ravished by emperors, kings, and governors.[39] . . . Second, the cry of those precious souls under the altar,[40] the souls of such as have been persecuted and slain for the testimony and witness of Jesus, whose blood has been spilt like water upon the earth, and that because they have held fast the truth and witness of Jesus, against the worship of the states and times,[41] compelling to a uniformity of state religion. . . . Thirdly, the cry of the whole earth, made drunk with the blood of its inhabitants, slaughtering each other in their blinded zeal, for conscience, for religion, against the Catholics, against the Lutherans, etc.

What fearful cries in these past twenty years of hundreds of thousands of men, women, children, fathers, mothers, husbands, wives, brethren, sisters, old and young, high and low, plundered, ravished, slaughtered, murdered, starved? And hence these cries, that men fling away the spiritual sword and spiritual artillery (in spiritual and religious causes) and rather trust for the suppressing of each other's God, conscience, and religion (as they suppose) to an arm of flesh, and sword of steel?

More than three hundred souls were savingly brought home to Christ

from Jonathan Edwards, *A Faithful Narrative of the Surprising Work of God in the Conversion of Many Hundred Souls in Northampton* (November 6, 1736)

A Calvinist theologian who valued "heart religion, and Christian experience," Jonathan Edwards witnessed in his outpost in remote Northampton,

---

38. Cf. Jude 4; Galatians 1:8.
39. A lament for the assault on the wholly innocent because of religion; cf. Revelation 14:1–5.
40. The souls of those martyred for Christ; cf. Revelation 6:9.
41. States and times: the official religions that circumstances have caused to be established.

Massachusetts, some of the earliest revivals of the First Great Awakening that swept Anglo-America in the 1730s and 1740s. Commending his predecessor for his five "harvests"—periods when numerous persons experienced an intense spiritual conviction and relationship with Christ—Edwards began to reap a harvest of his own in 1733, when there arose a tidal wave of conversions. These culminated in the conversion, in 1735, of three hundred persons within a six-month period. The converts, most of them young, became interested in eternal rather than worldly things, participated enthusiastically in worship, and gave expression to powerful feelings of Christian devotion. Edwards describes these events in a restrained tone, presenting himself not as an agent of conversion, but rather as a spectator of what others experienced. He anticipates that in writing his report, he will be found guilty of self-aggrandizement, yet he writes nonetheless, in reply to the request of an unnamed correspondent, so as to publicize the news of the "great work of God" that was achieved in Northampton.

Having seen your letter . . . of July 20, [1736], [in which you take note of] . . . the late wonderful work of God, in this and some other towns in this country, [and also state] . . . your desire to be more perfectly acquainted with it, by some of us on the spot: and having been since informed . . . that you desire me to undertake it, I would now do it, in as just and faithful a manner as in me lies. . . .

The town of Northampton is of about 82 years standing, and has now about 200 families. . . . Take the town in general, and so far as I can judge, they are as rational and intelligent a people as most I have been acquainted with. Many of them have been noted for religion; and particularly remarkable for their distinct knowledge in things that relate to heart religion, and Christian experience. . . .

I am the third minister who has been settled in the town. . . . [The second was the] Rev. Mr. Stoddard,[42] [a man who] was eminent and renowned for his gifts and grace; so he was blessed, from the beginning, with extraordinary success in his ministry, in the conversion of many souls. He had five harvests, as he called them. The first was about 57 years ago; the second about 53; the third about 40; the fourth about 24; the fifth and last about 18 years ago . . . [and] in each of them, . . . the greater part of the young people in the town seemed to be mainly concerned for their eternal salvation. . . .

[Edwards served as assistant to Mr. Stoddard for the two years before the latter's death.] In these two years there were nearly twenty that Mr. Stoddard hoped to be savingly converted; but there was nothing of any general awakening. The greater part seemed to be at that time very insensible of the

---

42. Edwards' grandfather Solomon Stoddard (1643–1729).

things of religion, and engaged in other cares and pursuits. . . . Licentiousness for some years prevailed among the youth of the town; there were many of them very much addicted to night-walking, and frequenting the tavern, and lewd practices, wherein some, by their example, exceedingly corrupted others. It was their manner very frequently to get together, in conventions of both sexes for mirth and jollity, which they called frolics; and they would often spend the greater part of the night in them. . . .

But in two or three years after Mr. Stoddard's death, there began to be a sensible amendment to these evils. The young people shewed more of a disposition to hearken to counsel, and by degrees left off their frolics; they grew observably more decent in their attendance on the public worship, and there were more who manifested a religious concern than there used to be. . . .

Presently upon this, a great and earnest concern about the great things of religion, and the eternal world, became universal in all parts of the town, and among persons of all degrees, and all ages. . . . The minds of people were wonderfully taken off from the world, it was treated amongst us as a thing of very little consequence. They seemed to follow their worldly business, more as a part of their duty, than from any disposition they had to it; the temptation now seemed to lie on that hand, to neglect worldly affairs too much, and to spend too much time in the immediate exercise of religion. . . .

There was scarcely a single person in the town, old or young, left unconcerned about the great things of the eternal world. Those who were wont to be the vainest, and loosest, and those who had been disposed to think and speak lightly of vital and experimental religion, were now generally subject to great awakenings. And the work of conversion was carried on in a most astonishing manner, and increased more and more; souls did come, as it were, by flocks to Jesus Christ. From day to day for many months together, might be seen evident instances of sinners brought out of darkness into marvelous light, and delivered out of a horrible pit, and from the miry clay, and set upon a rock with a new song of praise to God in their mouths.

This work of God, as it was carried on, and the number of true saints multiplied, soon made a glorious alteration in the town: so that in the spring and summer following, [in the year] 1735, the town seemed to be full of the presence of God. . . . Our public assemblies were then beautiful: the congregation was alive in God's service, every one earnestly intent on the public worship, every hearer eager to drink in the words of the minister . . . ; the assembly in general were, from time to time, in tears while the word was preached; some weeping with sorrow and distress, others with joy and love, others with pity and concern for the souls of their neighbors. . . .

This seems to have been a very extraordinary dispensation of providence; God has in many respects gone out of, and much beyond his usual and ordinary way. The work in this town, and others about us, has been extraordinary on account of the universality of it, affecting all sorts, sober and vicious, high and low, rich and poor, wise and unwise. . . .

I am far from pretending to be able to determine how many have lately been the subjects of such mercy; but if I may be allowed to declare any thing that appears to me probable in a thing of this nature, I hope that more than 300 souls were savingly brought home to Christ, in this town, in the space of half a year, and about the same number of males as females. . . .

I am very sensible how apt many would be, if they should see the account I have here given, presently to think with themselves that I am very fond of making a great many converts, and of magnifying the matter . . . , and, for this reason, I have forborne to publish an account of this great work of God, though I have often been solicited. But having now a special call to give an account of it, . . . I thought it might not be beside my duty to declare this amazing work, as it appeared to me to be indeed divine, and to conceal no part of the glory of it; . . . and running the venture of any censorious thoughts which might be entertained of me to my disadvantage. . . .

TEXTS AND STUDIES

The Reformation: Overviews

Recent overviews include Patrick Collinson, *The Reformation: A History* (New York: Modern Library, 2004) and Diarmaid MacCulloch, *The Reformation* (New York: Viking, 2004); also for Reformation thought specifically, Alister E. McGrath, *Reformation Thought: An Introduction*, 4th ed. (Malden, MA: Wiley-Blackwell, 2012). More critical perspectives are offered by Brad S. Gregory, *The Unintended Reformation: How a Religious Revolution Secularized Society* (Cambridge, MA: Belknap Press of Harvard University Press, 2012) and Lee Palmer Wandel, *The Reformation: Towards a New History* (Cambridge: Cambridge University Press, 2011).

Chapter One: In Search of Christ: Steps toward Reformation

John Wyclif. Original text in *John Wyclif's* De veritate sacrae scripturae, *Now First Edited from the Manuscripts with Critical and Historical Notes*, ed. Rudolf Buddensieg, 3 vols. (London: Trübner, for the Wyclif Society; typis J. Abel Gryphiensis, 1905, 1907), 1.15:375–408, excerpts from 375, 377–79, 380, 392, 395–98, 402–3, 405–8. Buddensieg convincingly establishes 1378 as date of completion of the original manuscript in his introduction, at 1:xlviii–liv. Translation consulted: Ian C. Levy, *John Wyclif: On the Truth of Holy Scripture* (Kalamazoo, MI: Consortium for the Teaching of the Middle Ages by Medieval Institute Publications, Western Michigan University, 2001). For Wyclif, see G. R. Evans, *John Wyclif: Myth and Reality* (Downers Grove, IL: IVP Academic, 2005); Anthony Kenny, ed., *Wyclif in His Times* (Oxford: Clarendon Press, 1986); and Stephen E. Lahey, *John Wyclif* (Oxford: Oxford University Press, 2009).

Jan Hus. Original text in Jan Hus, *Tractatus de ecclesia*, ed. Samuel Harrison Thomson (Boulder: University of Colorado Press, 1956), selections from chapters 4, 7, 19, 22, and 23, at pp. 20, 43, 46, 51, 52, 174, 176–77, 182, 214, 216, 227–28, 231–33. Translation consulted: Jan Hus, *De ecclesia: The Church*, trans. David S. Schaff (New York: Charles Scribner's Sons, 1915). For Hus, see Thomas A. Fudge, *Jan Hus* (London: I. B. Tauris, 2010); and for the Hussite aftermath, Craig D. Atwood, *The Theology of the Czech Brethren from Hus to Comenius* (University Park, PA: Pennsylvania State University Press, 2009).

Thomas à Kempis. Original text: *De imitatione christi libri quatuor*, ed. Tiburzio Lupo (Città del Vaticano: Libreria Editrice Vaticana, 1982), excerpts from Book 2: *On the Interior Life*, Chapters 1, 7, 8, 11, 12, at pp. 87, 89, 91, 93, 104–8, 117–19, 121–24. Translation consulted: *The Imitation of Christ*, trans. anonymous (Milwaukee, WI: Bruce Publishing, 1940), online at Christian Classics Ethereal Library (CCEL): http://www.ccel.org/ccel/kempis/imitation.toc.html. For Thomas à Kempis, see the reissued Italian biography by Piergiovanni Bonardi, *L'imitazione di Cristo e il suo autore*, ed. Tiburzio Lupo (Turin: Società editrice internazionale, 1964), and the still older but still useful J. E. G. de Montmorency, *Thomas à Kempis: His Age* *and Book* (London: Methuen, 1906). For the afterlife of *The Imitation of Christ*, see Maximilian von Habsburg, *Catholic and Protestant Translations of the* Imitatio Christi*, 1425–1650: From Late Medieval Classic to Early Modern Bestseller* (Farnham, UK: Ashgate, 2011).

Marguerite de Navarre. Original text of *Le miroir de l'âme pécheresse* in Marguerite de Navarre, *Selected Writings: A Bilingual Edition*, eds. Rouben C. Cholakian and Mary Skemp (Chicago: University of Chicago Press, 2008), lines 1279–1434 (even pages 140–48); the facing English translation by Cholakian and Skemp, *The Mirror of the Sinful Soul* (odd pages 141–49) was also consulted. For Marguerite, see Patricia F. Cholakian and Rouben C. Cholakian, *Marguerite de Navarre: Mother of the Renaissance* (New York: Columbia University Press, 2006); and for her evangelical activity, Jonathan A. Reid, *King's Sister—Queen of Dissent: Marguerite of Navarre, 1492–1549, and Her Evangelical Network* (Leiden: Brill, 2009) and Carol Thysell, *The Pleasure of Discernment: Marguerite de Navarre as Theologian* (New York: Oxford University Press, 2000).

Benedetto da Mantova. Original text of *Il beneficio di Gesù Cristo verso i cristiani* in Benedetto da Mantova, *Il beneficio di Cristo, con le versioni del secolo XVI*, ed. Salvatore Caponetto (Florence: G. C. Sansoni, 1972), 13–85 (chapter 3, lines 1–14; 21–31; 63–84; 102–9; 167–211), with critical study by Caponetto, 469–532. Translation consulted: by Elizabeth Gleason in Gleason, ed., *Reform Thought in Sixteenth-Century Italy* (Chico, CA: Scholars Press, 1981), 110–16. Gleason slightly revises the earlier translation by Ruth Prelowski, *The* Beneficio di Cristo, in *The Proceedings of the Unitarian Historical Society*, XIV, parts I and II (1962–1963) [Italian Reformation Studies in Honor of Laelius Socinus (1562–1962)], ed. John A. Tedeschi, 21–102. For the circulation and condemnation of the text, see also Massimo Firpo, "Il Beneficio di Cristo e il Concilio di Trento, 1542–1546," *Rivista di storia e letteratura religiosa* 31 (1995): 45–72.

Chapter Two: Erasmus: The Egg That Luther Hatched?

The scholarly literature on Erasmus is immense, as are the numbers of editions and translations of his works and anthologies drawn from them. It will be sufficient to note here three of the most useful biographies: C. Augustijn, *Erasmus: His Life, Works, and Influence* (Toronto: University of Toronto Press, 1991); Richard J. Schoeck, *Erasmus of Europe*, 2 vols. (Edinburgh: Edinburgh University Press, 1990, 1993); and James D. Tracy, *Erasmus of the Low Countries* (Berkeley: University of California Press, 1996). Note also the mammoth compilation (in a projected 89 volumes, 1974–2014 and continuing) by the University of Toronto Press of the complete works in English translations: *Collected Works of Erasmus*.

Handbook for the Christian Soldier. Original text in Erasmus, *Ausgewählte Werke*, edited by Hajo Holborn with the assistance of Annemarie Holborn (Munich: Beck, 1933), 22–136, excerpts at 22–24, 28–31, 37–38. Translations consulted: by John P. Dolan in *The Essential Erasmus* (New York: New American Library, 1964), 24–93; and Matthew Spinka, reprinted in Lewis W. Spitz, *The Protestant Reformation* (Englewood Cliffs, NJ: Prentice-Hall, 1966), 23–33, from Spinka, ed., *Advocates of Reform from Wyclif to Erasmus* (London: SCM Press, 1953), 195–305, 308.

Praise of Folly. Original text: *Moriae encomium*, at Latin Library: http://www.thelatinlibrary.com/erasmus/moriae.shtml, selections from ## 53, 54, 57–60, 65–66. Translation consulted:

by Betty Radice, in Erasmus, *Praise of Folly and Letter to Martin Dorp*, 1515 (Harmondsworth, UK: Penguin, 1971).

The Summons. Original text *Paraclesis* in Erasmus, *Ausgewählte Werke*, edited by Hajo Holborn, with the assistance of Annemarie Holborn (Munich: Beck, 1933), 139–49, excerpts at 139–42 and 148–49. Translation consulted: by John C. Olin in Olin, ed., *Desiderius Erasmus: Christian Humanism and the Reformation, Selected Writings* (New York: Harper Torchbooks, 1965), 92–106.

The Complaint of Peace. Original text: *Querela pacis: Undique gentium eiectae profligataeque*, at Latin Library: http://www.thelatinlibrary.com/erasmus/querela.shtml, selections from ## II–III, VIII–IX, XVII–XVIII, XXVIII–XXIX. Translations consulted: by John P. Dolan in *The Essential Erasmus* (New York: New American Library, 1964), 174–204, and Betty Radice in the *Collected Works of Erasmus*, 27 (Toronto: University of Toronto Press, 1986), 293–322, reprinted in Erika Rummel, ed., *The Erasmus Reader* (Toronto: University of Toronto Press, 1990), 288–314.

The Shipwreck. Original texts consulted: *Desiderii Erasmi Roterodami Colloquia familiaria: Nunc emendatiora cum omnium notis*, rev. ed. (Bern: apud Danielem Tschiffeli, 1709), "Naufragium" at 207–16, excerpts at 209–13; *Erasmi Colloquia selecta, or, the Select Colloquies of Erasmus*, Latin text with translation by John Clarke, 20th ed. (Gloucester, UK: R. Raikes, 1782), 1–23, excerpts at 5–15 (1–4 missing from original). Translation consulted: by Craig R. Thompson, in *Collected Works of Erasmus*, 39–40 (1997), reprinted in Erika Rummel, ed., *The Erasmus Reader* (Toronto: University of Toronto Press, 1990), 239–47.

Chapter Three: Luther the Rebel

Biographies of Luther are numberless. Of recent titles, see especially Scott H. Hendrix, *Martin Luther: Visionary Reformer* (New Haven: Yale University Press, 2015); Martin E. Marty, *Martin Luther* (New York: Viking Penguin, 2004); Michael A. Mullett, *Martin Luther*, 2nd ed. (London: Routledge, 2014); Heiko A. Oberman, *Luther: Man between God and the Devil*, trans. Eileen Walliser-Schwarzbart (New Haven: Yale University Press, 1989; reprinted 2006), and Andrew Pettegree, *Brand Luther: 1517, Printing, and the Making of the Reformation* (New York: Penguin, 2015). Much older, but still worth reading, is Roland Bainton's classic *Here I Stand: A Life of Martin Luther* (New York: Abingdon-Cokesbury Press, 1950), frequently reprinted.

Ninety-Five Theses. Original text of the "Disputatio pro declaratione virtutis indulgentiarum," from *D. Martin Luthers Werke: Kritische Gesammtausgabe*, 1 (Weimar: Hermann Boehlau, 1883), 233–38, online at http://faculty.georgetown.edu/jod/texts/95.theses.html. Translations consulted: by Bertram Lee Woolf, in *The Reformation Writings of Martin Luther*, vol. 1: *The Basis of the Protestant Reformation*, ed. Woolf (London: Lutterworth Press, 1953), 32–42, reprinted in *Martin Luther: Selections from His Writings*, ed. John Dillenberger (Garden City, NY: Doubleday, 1961), 489–500; preferred to that in Harold J. Grimm, ed., *Career of the Reformer*, vol. 1 in *Luther's Works*, 26 (Philadelphia: Fortress Press, 1957), 25–33, reprinted in Lewis W. Spitz, ed., *The Protestant Reformation* (Englewood Cliffs, NJ: Prentice-Hall, 1966), 43–50.

On the Freedom of a Christian. Excerpts from the translation (from the German original) and edition of Tryntje Helfferich in *On the Freedom of a Christian with Related Texts* (Indianapolis,

IN/Cambridge, MA: Hackett, 2013), 18–20, 22, 31–34, 36, 41–42. Reprinted by permission of the publisher.

Preface to the Letter of Saint Paul to the Romans. Original text of the *Vorrede auf die Epistel S. Pauli an die Römer* appears in facsimile in *Die gantze Heilige Schrifft deudsch, Wittenberg 1545 [von] Martin Luther: Letzte zu Luthers Lebzeiten erschienene Ausgabe*, eds. Hans Volz with Heinz Blanke, 2 vols. (Munich: Rogner & Bernhard, 1972), 2:2254–68. Translations consulted: by Andrew Thornton, OSB (1983) at Christian Classics Ethereal Library (CCEL), http://www.ccel.org/l/luther/romans/pref_romans.html; and Bertram Lee Woolf, in *The Reformation Writings of Martin Luther*, vol. 2: *The Spirit of the Protestant Reformation*, ed. Woolf (London: Lutterworth Press, 1956), reprinted in John Dillenberger, ed., *Martin Luther: Selections from His Writings* (Garden City, NY: Doubleday, 1961), 19–34.

On the Power of the State. Original text: "Von weltlicher Obrigkeit, wie weit man ihr Gehorsam schuldig sei," in *Luther Deutsch: Die Werke Martin Luthers in neuer Auswahl für die Gegenwart*, ed. Kurt Aland, 7.2 (Göttingen: Vandenhoeck & Ruprecht, 1967), 9–51; online at http://gutenberg.spiegel.de/buch/von-weltlicher-obrigkeit-wie-weit-man-ihr-gehorsam-schuldig-sei-267/1. Translations consulted: by J. J. Schindel in *Works of Martin Luther*, 3 (Philadelphia: A. J. Holman and the Castle Press, 1930), 228–73, reprinted in John Dillenberger, ed., *Martin Luther: Selections from His Writings* (Garden City, NY: Doubleday, 1961), 363–402; and an unattributed translation reprinted in Hans J. Hillerbrand, ed., *The Protestant Reformation*, rev. ed. (New York: Harper Perennial, 2009), 73–91.

The Small Catechism. Original text: "Der kleine Katechismus," in *Luther Deutsch: Die Werke Martin Luthers in neuer Auswahl für die Gegenwart*, ed. Kurt Aland (Göttingen: Vandenhoeck & Ruprecht, 1900–1978), 6:138–59, available online at the University of Paderborn: http://kw1.uni-paderborn.de/fileadmin/kw/institute-einrichtungen/katholische-theologie/Personal/Fenger/Geschichte_und_Theologie_der_Reformation/Der_Kleine_Katechismus__1529_.pdf. The German text is also available in bilingual edition (facing pages), *A Short Exposition of Dr. Martin Luther's Small Catechism* (St. Louis, MO: Concordia Publishing House, 1912), 2–38, with translation authorized by Evangelical Lutheran Synodical Conference of North America. The German text, but lacking Luther's preface or *Vorrede*, is also widely available online, as at, for instance, the website of the Evangelische Kirche in Deutschland: http://www.ekd.de/glauben/bekenntnisse/kleiner_katechismus_1.html_. Of the many English translations available, that of Concordia Publishing House (St. Louis, MO: 1986) is conveniently accessed online at http://bookofconcord.org/smallcatechism.php.

Chapter Four: Luther's Lieutenants

Andreas Karlstadt. The German text is available at Wikisource, http://de.wikisource.org/wiki/Von_abtuhung_der_Bylder: a transcription of Andreas Bodenstein von Karlstadt, *Von Abtuhung der Bylder, und das keyn Betdler vnther den Christen seyn soll* (Wittenberg: Nickell Schyrlentz, 1522). The study of the iconoclast debate of the early Reformation edited by Bryan D. Magrum and Giuseppe Scavizzi, *A Reformation Debate: Three Treatises in Translation* (Toronto: Dovehouse Editions, The Centre for Reformation and Renaissance Studies, 1991), includes translations of three anti-image treatises by Karlstadt, Hieronymus Emser, and Johannes Eck; Karlstadt's at 19–39. A later translation by Edward J. Furcha is available in *The Essential*

Carlstadt: Fifteen Tracts (Waterloo, Ontario, Canada-Scottdale, PA: Herald Press, 1995), at 100–128. For the Karlstadt-Luther relationship, see Ulrich Bubenheimer, "Gelassenheit und Ablösung: Eine psychohistorische Studie über Andreas Bodenstein von Karlstadt und seinen Konflikt mit Martin Luther," *Zeitschrift für Kirchengeschichte* 92, no. 2–3 (1981): 250–68; James S. Preus, *Carlstadt's* Ordinaciones *and Luther's Liberty: A Study of the Wittenberg Movement, 1521–1522* (Cambridge, MA: Harvard University Press, 1974); and Ronald J. Sider, *Karlstadt's Battle with Luther: Documents in a Liberal-Radical Debate* (Philadephia: Fortress, 1978; reprint Eugene, OR: Wipf and Stock, 2001). For Karlstadt, see also Amy N. Burnett, *Karlstadt and the Origins of the Eucharistic Controversy: A Study in the Circulation of Ideas* (New York: Oxford University Press, 2011); Hans-Jürgen Goertz, "Karlstadt, Müntzer, and the Reformation of the Commoners, 1521–1525," in Roth and Stayer, *A Companion to Anabaptism and Spiritualism, 1521–1700* (Leiden: Brill, 2007), 1–44; and Ronald J. Sider, *Andreas Bodenstein von Karlstadt: The Development of His Thought, 1517–1525* (Leiden: Brill, 1974).

Argula von Grumbach. The German text of the letter to the rector and council of the University of Ingolstadt is found in the edition of her German works: Argula von Grumbach, *Schriften*, ed. Peter Matheson (Gütersloh: Gütersloher Verlagshaus, 2010), 64–75. The principal investigations are also by Matheson: see his study "Martin Luther and Argula von Grumbach (1492–1556/7)," *Lutheran Quarterly* 22, no. 1 (2008): 1–15; and the extensive critical introductions to his German and English editions of her works in *Schriften*; and *Argula von Grumbach: A Woman's Voice in the Reformation*, ed. Matheson (Edinburgh: T&T Clark, 1995).

Philip Melanchthon. The *Apologia altera* of the Confession of Augsburg, section II(IV), in Melanchthon, *Opera quae supersunt omnia*, ed. Karl Gottlieb Bretschneider and (rev.) Heinrich Ernst Bindseil, 28 vols. (Halle an der Saale [vols. 1–18] and Braunschweig [vols. 19–28]: C. A. Schwetschke et filium, 1834–1860), reprint New York: Johnson Reprint Corp., 1963, 27 (1859): 429–47. See also the German edition of Horst Geor Pöhlmann, *Apologia Confessionis augustanae* (Gütersloh: G. Mohn, 1967) and the French edition and translation by Pierre Jundt: *La Confession d'Augsbourg: L'Apologie de la Confession d'Augsbourg* (Paris: Cerf, 1989). Also consulted: English translations of Robert Kolb and Timothy J. Wengert, in *The Book of Concord: The Confessions of the Evangelical Lutheran Church* (Minneapolis: Fortress, 2000), 107–294, and of F. Bente and W. H. T. Dau in the *Triglot Concordia: The Symbolical Books of the Evangelical Lutheran Church: German-Latin-English* (St. Louis: Concordia Publishing House, 1921), online at http://bookofconcord.org/defense_4_justification.php. The *Oratio in funere D. Martini Lutheri* is found in Melanchthon, *Opera omnia*, 11 (1843): 726–34. Also consulted: the English translation of James William Richard, *Philip Melanchthon: The Protestant Preceptor of Germany, 1497–1560* (New York: G. P. Putnam, 1898), 381–92. An abridgement is included in the famous ten-volume compilation by William Jennings Bryan of *The World's Famous Orations* (New York: Funk and Wagnalls, 1906), vol. 7, online at http://www.bartleby.com/268/7/9.html. For Melanchthon's importance as a reformer, see Stefan Rhein, "The Influence of Melanchthon on Sixteenth-Century Europe," *Lutheran Quarterly* 12, no. 4 (1998): 383–94; for Melanchthon and Luther, see Robert Kolb, *Bound Choice, Election, and Wittenberg Method: From Martin Luther to the Formula of Concord* (Grand Rapids, MI: Eerdmans, 2005), especially 67–102; and Gü Wartenberg, "Philip Melanchthon: The Wittenberg Reformer Alongside Luther," *Lutheran Quarterly* 12, no. 4 (1998): 373–82; for Melanchthon as educational reformer, see the essays in Reinhard Golz and Reinhard and Wolfgang Mayrhofer, *Luther and Melanchthon in the Educational Thought of Central and Eastern Europe*, trans. Arista da Silva and Alan Maimon (Münster: Lit Verlag, 1998); and Peter Walter, "Melanchthon und die Tradition der 'Studia Humanitatis,'" *Zeitschrift für Kirchengeschichte* 110, no. 2 (1999): 191–208.

Martin Bucer. The text of the *De regno Christi*, ed. François Wendel, appears in vol. 15 of Bucer's *Opera latina* (Paris: Presses Universitaires de France; Gütersloh: C. Bertelsmann, 1955); excerpts here are translated from chapter 2 (*Quae sint regno Christi et regnis mundi communia, quae propria*) at 6–20. The English translation by Wilhelm Pauck, in collaboration with Paul Larkin, appears in his *Melanchthon and Bucer* (Philadelphia: Westminster, 1969), 174–394, with chapter 2 at 179–91. For Bucer, see especially Martin Greschat, *Martin Bucer: A Reformer and His Times*, trans. Stephen E. Buckwalter (Louisville, KY: Westminster John Knox Press, 2004; orig. German Munich: C. H. Beck, 1990). Also useful for the array of issues Bucer encountered are the essays edited by David F. Wright, *Reforming Church and Community* (Cambridge: Cambridge University Press, 1994). For Bucer's stay in England and *De regno Christi*, see the essay by Basil Hall, "Martin Bucer in England," in Wright, *Reforming Church and Community*, at 144–60; Andreas Gäumann, *Reich Christi und Obrigkeit: Eine Studie zum reformatorischen Denken und Handeln Martin Bucers* (Berg: Peter Lang, 2001); and also Greschat, *Martin Bucer*, at 227–50. Other major concerns of Bucer's are treated in separate volumes by Amy Nelson Burnett, *The Yoke of Christ: Martin Bucer and Christian Discipline* (Kirksville, MO: Northeast Missouri State University, 1994); Brian Lugioyo, *Martin Bucer's Doctrine of Justification: Reformation Theology and Early Modern Irenicism* (Oxford: Oxford University Press, 2010); and Nicholas Thompson, *Eucharistic Sacrifice and Patristic Tradition in the Theology of Martin Bucer, 1534–1546* (Leiden: Brill, 2005).

Chapter Five: The Swiss Response

For the Swiss Reformation generally, see Bruce Gordon, *The Swiss Reformation* (Manchester: Manchester University Press, 2002). For Calvinism in Geneva and beyond, Philip Benedict, *Christ's Churches Purely Reformed: A Social History of Calvinism* (New Haven: Yale University Press, 2002); D. G. Hart, *Calvinism: A History* (New Haven: Yale University Press, 2013); and the essays in Andrew Pettegree, A. C. Duke, and Gillian Lewis, eds., *Calvinism in Europe, 1540–1620* (Cambridge: Cambridge University Press, 1994).

Ulrich Zwingli. Zwingli's *Von Erkiesen und Freiheit der Speisen* is found in *Huldreich Zwinglis sämtliche Werke*, vol. 1 (Berlin: Schwetschke, 1905; = Corpus Reformatorum 88), 88–136, available online at http://www.irg.uzh.ch/static/zwingli-werke/index.php?n=Werk.8. I have consulted the English translation of Lawrence A. McLouth in Zwingli, *Early Writings*, ed. S. M. Jackson (New York: G.P. Putnam's Sons, 1912; rpt. Durham, NC: Labyrinth, 1987), 70–112. For Zwingli, see G. R. Potter, *Zwingli* (Cambridge: Cambridge University Press, 1976); Ulrich Gäbler, *Huldrych Zwingli: His Life and Work*, trans. Ruth C. L. Gritsch (Philadelphia, PA: Fortress Press, 1986); and W. P. Stephens, *Zwingli: An Introduction to His Thought* (Oxford: Clarendon Press, 1992).

Marie de Dentière. The excerpt from Dentière's letter to Marguerite de Navarre is taken from its original edition: Marie d'Ennetière [Dentière], *Epistre tres utile faicte et composée par une femme chrestienne de Tornay, envoyée à la Royne de Navarre seur du Roy de France* . . . (Anvers [Geneva]: Jean Gérard, 1539). I have also consulted Mary B. McKinley's translation from the same edition: *Epistle to Marguerite de Navarre and Preface to a Sermon by John Calvin* (Chicago: University of Chicago Press, 2004), 49–87, and made use of McKinley's introduction at 1–48, which presents a study of Dentière's life and the circumstances of her writing the letter. See also McKinley's annotated bibliography, "Marie Dentière," in *Oxford Bibliographies* in Renaissance and Reformation, http://www.oxfordbibliographies.com/view/document/obo-9780195399301/obo-9780195399301-0137.xml.

John Calvin. Calvin's letters to Renée, duchess of Ferrara, and Jeanne d'Albret, queen of Navarre, are from the edition of the Jules Bonnet, *Lettres de Jean Calvin*, 2 vols. (Paris: Librairie de Ch. Meyrueis, 1854), at 1:43–56 and 2:365–68, respectively. Bonnet's edition was translated almost immediately by David Constable in *Letters of John Calvin*, 2 vols. (Edinburgh: Thomas Constable, 1855–1857), which translation I have consulted. For Calvin's relations with these and other prominent women, see the classic article of Catherine Blaisdell, "Calvin's Letters to Women: The Courting of Ladies in High Places," *Sixteenth Century Journal* 13 (1982): 67–84. Selections from Calvin's *Institutes* are taken from the edition by August Tholuck, *Institutio Christiane religionis*, 2 vols. in 1 (Berlin: apud Gustavum Eichlerum [G. Eichler], 1834–1835, liber 3, cap. 21, 129–36). I have also consulted the 1845–1846 translation of *The Institutes of the Christian Religion* (Edinburgh: Calvin Translation Society) by Henry Beveridge (1799–1863), available at http://www.reformed.org/master/index.html?mainframe=/books/institutes/; and that of Ford Lewis Battles, *Institutes of the Christian Religion*, ed. John T. McNeill, 2 vols. (Philadelphia: Westminster Press, 1960), 2:920–32. Recent biographies of Calvin include Jon Balserak, *John Calvin as Sixteenth-Century Prophet* (Oxford: Oxford University Press, 2014) and Bruce Gordon, *Calvin* (New Haven: Yale University Press, 2009). See also the collected essays in Donald K. McKim, ed., *The Cambridge Companion to John Calvin* (Cambridge: Cambridge University Press, 2004); and H. J. Selderhuis, ed., *The Calvin Handbook* (Grand Rapids, MI: William B. Eerdmans, 2009).

Theodore Beza. Excerpts from Beza's *On the Right of Magistrates over Their Subjects* are based on the edition of Robert M. Kingdon, *Du droit des magistrats* (Geneva: Droz, 1970). I have also consulted the translations by Julian H. Franklin in his *Constitutionalism and Resistance in the Sixteenth Century: Three Treatises by Hotman, Beza, and Mornay* (New York: Pegasus, 1969), 97–136, and the translation by Henry-Louis Gonin, edited by Patrick S. Poole, online at Constitution.org: http://www.constitution.org/cmt/beza/magistrates.htm#ques6. See also for context the classic article of Ralph Giesey, "The Monarchomach Triumvirs: Hotman, Beza and Mornay," *Bibliothèque d'Humanisme et Renaissance* 32 (1970): 41–56, and more recently the study of Scott M. Manetsch, *Theodore Beza and the Quest for Peace in France, 1562–1598* (Leiden: Brill, 2000). For Beza's thought more generally, see also Jeffrey Mallinson, *Faith, Reason, and Revelation in Theodore Beza, 1519–1605* (Oxford: Oxford University Press, 2003); and for a portrait of the more than one hundred Calvinist pastors active in Geneva through the early seventeenth century, Scott M. Manetsch, *Calvin's Company of Pastors: Pastoral Care and the Emerging Reformed Church, 1536–1609* (New York: Oxford University Press, 2013).

Chapter Six: The Radical Reformation

For the radical Reformation generally, see the introduction of George H. Williams to *Spiritual and Anabaptist Writers: Documents Illustrative of the Radical Reformation*, eds. George H. Williams and Angel M. Mergal (Philadelphia: Westminster Press, 1957), 19–38, and Williams' subsequent 1962 monograph, *The Radical Reformation*, 3rd ed. (Kirksville, MO: Truman State University Press, 2000). Also useful are anthologies of Lowell H. Zuck, ed., *Christianity and Revolution: Radical Christian Testimonies, 1520–1650* (Philadelphia: Temple University Press, 1975) and Michael G. Baylor, ed., *The Radical Reformation* (Cambridge: Cambridge

University Press, 1991). See also for context John D. Roth and James Stayer, eds., *A Companion to Anabaptism and Spiritualism, 1521–1700* (Leiden: Brill, 2007).

Thomas Müntzer. The translation given here is based on the modern German version in Thomas Müntzer, *Schriften, liturgische Texte, Briefe*, eds. Rudolf Bentzinger and Siegfried Hoyer (Berlin: Union Verlag, 1990), 64–86, abridged version online at GHDI (German History in Documents and Images): http://germanhistorydocs.ghi-dc.org/sub_document.cfm?document _id=4270. The original *Frühneuhochdeutsch* text is available in Thomas Müntzer, *Schriften und Briefe*, ed. Günther Franz (Gütersloh: Gütersloher Verlagshaus G. Mohn, 1968), 241–63. Also consulted: the translation of George H. Williams in *Spiritual and Anabaptist Writers*, 49–70; abridged version online at GHDI: http://germanhistorydocs.ghi-dc.org/sub_document.cfm? document_id=4270&language=english. English-language biographies of Müntzer include Abraham Friesen, *Thomas Müntzer, a Destroyer of the Godless: The Making of a Sixteenth-Century Religious Revolutionary* (Berkeley: University of California Press, 1990); Tom Scott, *Thomas Müntzer: Theology and Revolution in the German Reformation* (New York: St. Martin's, 1989); and Eric W. Gritsch, *Thomas Müntzer: A Tragedy of Errors* (Minneapolis: Augsburg Fortress, 1989). See also Hans-Jürgen Goertz, "Karlstadt, Müntzer, and the Reformation of the Commoners, 1521–1525," in Roth and Stayer, *A Companion to Anabaptism and Spiritualism*, 1–44. For the peasants' revolt viewed as more a social than religious event, see especially Peter Blickle, *The Revolution of 1525: The German Peasants' War from a New Perspective*, trans. Thomas H. Brady Jr. and H. C. Erik Midelfort (Baltimore: Johns Hopkins University Press, 1981).

Maeyken van Deventer and Janneken Munstdorp. The testimonials excerpted here both appear among the hundreds recorded by Theleman Janszoon van Braght in his 1660 compilation, *Het Bloedigh Tooneel der Doops-Gesinde, en Wereloose Christenen* ([Dordrecht]: Voor Jacobus Savry, woonende in 't Kasteel van Gendt), an inaccessible version not, apparently, reissued. It was translated into English the year of its original publication by Joseph F. Sohm with the title *The Bloody Theater, or Martyrs Mirror of the Defenseless Christians*, a translation that has appeared since in many editions and reprints. The work was also translated from the Dutch into German and widely circulated with the title *Der blutige Schauplatz, oder Märtyrer-Spiegel der Taufs-Gesinnten oder Wehrlosen Christen* in editions from 1780 (s.l.: Verlag der Vereinigten Brüderschaft), a complete image of which is available at http://bildsuche.digitale-sammlungen. de/index.html?c=viewer&bandnummer=bsb00066399&pimage=5&v=100&nav=&l=de. The texts given here are translated from the 1870 reprint of the German version (Elkhart, IN: John F. Funk und Bruder), at pages 492–94 and 498–501, consulting also pages 977–9 and 984–7 of the Sohm translation in the 15th edition of 1987 (Scottdale, PA: Herald Press).

For the Anabaptist martyrs, see especially Brad S. Gregory, ed., *The Forgotten Writings of the Mennonite Martyrs* (Leiden: Brill, 2002); Gregory, *Salvation at Stake: Christian Martyrdom in Early Modern Europe* (Cambridge, MA: Harvard University Press, 1999); and Gregory, "Anabaptist Martyrdom: Imperatives, Experience, and Memorialization," in Roth and Stayer, *A Companion to Anabaptism and Spiritualism*, 467–506. For Anabaptism generally, also useful are Roth and Stayer, *A Companion to Anabaptism and Spiritualism*; and J. Denny Weaver, *Becoming Anabaptist: The Origin and Significance of Sixteenth-Century Anabaptism*, 2nd ed. (Scottdale, PA: Herald Press, 2005).

Peter Riedemann. The text given here consists of the chapter *Von der Gemeinschaft der Güter* from Riedemann's *Rechenschaft unsrer Religion, Lehre und Glaubens* (Berne, IN: Huterische Brüder Gemeine, 1902), 84–88. I have also consulted John J. Friesen's 1999 translation, *Peter*

Riedemann's Hutterite Confession of Faith: Translation of the 1565 German Edition of Confession of Our Religion, Teaching, and Faith, by the Brothers Who Are Known as the Hutterites (Scottdale, PA: Herald, 1999), where the chapter appears at 119–22; and the 1950 translation by Kathleen E. Hasenberg (London: Hodder and Stoughton), from which the relevant chapter was reprinted both in Zuck, *Christianity and Revolution*, 128–30, and Hans J. Hillerbrand, ed., *The Protestant Reformation*, rev. ed. (New York: Harper Perennial, 2009), 190–94. Friesen's introduction (at 17–50) offers an invaluable discussion of Riedemann's life and work, for which see also the brief biography by Robert Friedmann at the Global Anabaptist Mennonite Encyclopedia Online: "Riedemann, Peter (1506–1556)," *Global Anabaptist Mennonite Encyclopedia Online*, 1959: http://gameo.org/index.php?title=Riedemann,_Peter_(1506–1556)&oldid=106660; and the Hutterian Brethren website: http://www.hutterites.org/tag/jakob-hutter/. Werner O. Packull provides a biography of Riedemann, *Peter Riedemann: Shaper of the Hutterite Tradition* (Kitchener, ON, Canada: Pandora, 2007), as well as a broader study of Moravian Anabaptist communities, *Hutterite Beginnings: Communitarian Experiments during the Reformation* (Baltimore: Johns Hopkins University Press, 1995).

Michael Servetus. The text given here is based on the Latin text of the *De trinitatis erroribus* (originally published 1531) of the bilingual edition with French translation, *Sept livres sur les erreurs de la Trinité*, trans. Rolande-Michelle Bénin, eds. Rolande-Michelle Bénin and Marie-Louise Gicquel (Paris: Honoré Champion, 2008), 147–59. Also consulted: the English translation (with analytical introduction) by Earl Morse Wilbur, published as special volume 16 in Harvard Theological Studies (Cambridge, MA: Harvard University Press, 1932), reprinted 1969 (New York: Kraus). The *Errors of the Trinity* is also included in Servetus' later *Christianismi restitutio* (1553), available in the English translation of Christopher A. Hoffman and Marian Hillar, *The Restoration of Christianity: An English Translation of* Christianismi Restitutio, *1553* (Lewiston, NY: Edwin Mellen Press, 2007); and also in recent French and Spanish translations. Roland H. Bainton's classic biography, *Hunted Heretic: The Life and Death of Michael Servetus, 1511–1553* (Boston: Beacon Press, 1953) is available in a 1978 reprint (Gloucester, MA: Peter Smith) and a revised edition by Peter Hughes (Providence, RI: Blackstone Editions, 2005). More recent biographies include Jerome Friedman, *Michael Servetus: A Case Study in Total Heresy* (Geneva: Droz, 1978), and Marian Hillar, *The Case of Michael Servetus, 1511–1553: The Turning Point in the Struggle for Freedom of Conscience* (Lewiston, NY: Edwin Mellen Press, 1997). See also the studies of Peter Hughes, "The Present State of Servetus Studies, Eighty Years Later," *Journal of Unitarian Universalist History* 34 (2010/2011): 47–40; and "Servetus and the Quran," *Journal of Unitarian Universalist History* 30 (2005): 55–70.

Sebastian Castellio. Translated here is the Latin text of March 1554 (Magdeburg: per Georgium Rausch), published in facsimile (Geneva: Droz, 1954), with preface of Martin Bellius (Castellio's pseudonym) to Christoph, duke of Württemberg, at 3–28. Also consulted: the English translation by Roland H. Bainton, *Concerning Heretics* (New York: Columbia University Press, 1935). For Castellio, the analytical introductions to the texts just cited, respectively those by Sape van der Woude and by Bainton, have been invaluable. See also the recent biography of Castellio by Hans R. Guggisberg, who also edited the German version of *On Heretics*, available in the English translation of Bruce Gordon, *Sebastian Castellio, 1515–1563: Humanist and Defender of Religious Toleration in a Confessional Age* (Aldershot, UK: Ashgate, 2002). For the emergence of the Western consensus for toleration, see Benjamin J. Kaplan, *Divided by Faith: Religious Conflict and the Practice of Toleration in Early Modern Europe* (Cambridge, MA: Belknap Press of Harvard University Press, 2007); and Perez Zagorin, *How the Idea of Religious Toleration Came to the West* (Princeton: Princeton University Press, 2003). See also the classic work of Stefan Zweig, *The Right to Heresy: Castellio against Calvin*, trans. Eden and Cedar Paul (New York: Viking, 1936; repr., Boston: Beacon Press, 1951).

Chapter Seven: The English Compromise

Useful introductions to the much-contested topic of the English Reformation are Christopher Haigh, *English Reformations: Religion, Politics, and Society under the Tudors* (Oxford: Oxford University Press, 1993); Felicity Heal, *Reformation in Britain and Ireland* (Oxford: Oxford University Press, 2003); and Norman Jones, *The English Reformation: Religion and Cultural Adaptation* (Oxford: Blackwell, 2002).

Simon Fish. The text is from the 1878 reprint (of the original 1529 edition) by Edward Arber: Simon Fish, *A Supplication for the Beggars* (Chilworth and London: Unwin Brothers, The Gresham Press; reprint New York: AMS Press, 1967), 1–14, with a useful historical introduction at vii–xviii, available at Archive.org and Wikisource. Also available (both accessible at Google Books) are earlier editions of 1845 (London: W. Pickering), purporting erroneously to be reprinted from the "original edition of 1524," and 1871, edited by Frederick James Furnivall (London: Kegan Paul, Trench, Trübner; reprint Millwood, NY: Kraus, 1973), 1–15. For Fish, see the article by Mandell Creighton in the *Dictionary of National Biography*, edited by Leslie Stephen and Sidney Lee (London: Smith, Elder, 1885–1901), 19:51–52. For Thomas More's response to Fish, see Rainer Pineas, "Thomas More's Controversy with Simon Fish," *Studies in English Literature, 1500–1900*, 7.1 (The English Renaissance, Winter, 1967): 15–28.

Thomas Cranmer. The text of Cranmer's preface to the Great Bible is most easily accessed from the Bible Researcher website, http://www.bible-researcher.com/cranmer.html, which takes the text from the Chadwyck-Healey Literature Collections: http://collections.chadwyck.com/marketing/about_chadwyck_healey.jsp. Also consulted: the version printed in *Miscellaneous Writings and Letters of Thomas Cranmer, Archbishop of Canterbury*, edited by John E. Cox for the Parker Society (Cambridge: University Press, 1846), 118–125. For Cranmer, see Diarmaid MacCulloch, *Thomas Cranmer: A Life* (New Haven: Yale University Press, 1996).

Jane Grey, Lady. The text is based on the pamphlet-sized collection of Grey's writings entitled *An Epistle of the Ladye Jane* (in London, likely by the press of John Day) published almost immediately after her execution on February 12, 1554, and reprinted in *The Harleian Miscellany*, ed. William Oldys, vol. 1 (London: Printed for J. White, and J. Murray, 1808): 369–72. It is also available, in whole and in part, online, including at the Broadview Anthology of British Literature (reprinting the version found in the 1563 edition of John Foxe's *Actes and Monuments*): http://sites.broadviewpress.com/babl/files/2011/12/Grey_Lady_Jane1.pdf. Biographies (and historical novels) abound: see especially E. W. Ives, *Lady Jane Grey: A Tudor Mystery* (Malden, MA: Wiley-Blackwell, 2009); Leanda de Lisle, *The Sisters Who Would Be Queen: Mary, Katherine, and Lady Jane Grey: A Tudor Tragedy* (New York: Ballantine Books, 2009); and Alison Plowden, *Lady Jane Grey: Nine Days Queen* (Stroud: Sutton, 2003). See also the useful biography online at Tudor Place: http://www.tudorplace.com.ar/aboutJaneGrey.htm.

Edmund Campion. The text is published in the introduction by John H. Pollen to Joseph J. Rickaby's edition and translation of Campion's *Decem rationes: Ten Reasons Proposed to His Adversaries for Disputation in the Name of the Faith* (St. Louis, MO: B. Herder; London: Manresa Press,

1914), at 7–11. It is also found online at Catholic Information Network http://www.cin.org/saints/campion-brag.html, reprinting the version published in "Campion's 'Brag,'" *This Rock: The Magazine of Practical Apologetics and Evangelization* (September 1994). See the classic biographies of Richard Simpson (1867) and Evelyn Waugh (1935), available now, respectively, in the enlarged and revised edition by Peter M. Joseph and George Pell (Leominster, UK: Gracewing, 2010), and in editions of 2005 (San Francisco: Ignatius Press) and 2012 (London: Penguin Classics). Recent studies include Gerard Kilroy, *Edmund Campion: Memory and Transcription* (Aldershot, UK-Burlington, VT: Ashgate, 2005), and the essays collected in Thomas M. McCoog, *The Reckoned Expense: Edmund Campion and the Early English Jesuits: Essays in Celebration of the First Centenary of Campion Hall, Oxford, 1896–1996*, 2nd rev. ed. (Rome: Institutum Historicum Societatis Iesu, 2007; orig. Woodbridge, UK-Rochester, NY: Boydell Press, 1996).

Margaret Hoby, Lady. The original text of Hoby's diary preserved in the British Library, ms. Egerton 2614, of which the digitized version, obtained from Princeton University Library, was consulted and collated with two twentieth-century editions: *Diary of Lady Margaret Hoby, 1599–1605*, ed. Dorothy M. Meads (Boston: Houghton Mifflin, 1930); and *The Private Life of an Elizabethan Lady: The Diary of Lady Margaret Hoby, 1599–1605*, ed. Joanna Moody (Stroud, UK: Sutton, 1998). The editors of the two cited volumes provide ample biographical context, but see also the older study by Evelyn Fox, "The Diary of an Elizabethan Gentlewoman," *Transactions of the Royal Historical Society* 2 (1908): 153–74.

Chapter Eight: Catholic Reform and Renewal

For the Catholic Reformation (or Counter-Reformation) generally, see Robert Bireley, *The Refashioning of Catholicism, 1450–1700: A Reassessment of the Counter Reformation* (Washington, DC: Catholic University of America Press, 1999); R. Po-chia Hsia, *The World of Catholic Renewal, 1540–1770*, 2nd ed. (Cambridge: Cambridge University Press, 2005); Martin D. W. Jones, *The Counter Reformation: Religion and Society in Early Modern Europe* (Cambridge: Cambridge University Press, 1995); and Michael A. Mullett, *The Catholic Reformation* (London: Routledge, 1999).

Gasparo Contarini, Cardinal. The text is based on the edition by John Patrick Donnelly, S.J., of Gasparo Contarini, *The Office of a Bishop (De officio viri boni et probi episcopi)* (Milwaukee, WI: Marquette University Press, 2002), 78–87, 96–99, 104–9, 118–21, 124–27, with Latin text on even-numbered pages; Donnelly's English translation on facing odd-numbered pages has also been consulted. For Contarini, see especially Elizabeth G. Gleason, *Gasparo Contarini: Venice, Rome, and Reform* (Berkeley: University of California Press, 1993), and the essays gathered in Gigliola Fragnito, *Gasparo Contarini: Un magistrato veneziano al servizio della cristianità* (Leo S. Olschki, 1988); and in *Gasparo Contarini e il suo tempo: Atti del Convegno, Venezia, 1–3 Marzo 1985*, eds. Gigliola Fragnito and Francesca Cavazzana Romanelli (Venice: Edizioni studium cattolico veneziano, 1988). See also Constance M. Furey, *Erasmus, Contarini, and the Religious Republic of Letters* (Cambridge: Cambridge University Press, 2006), and, for his youthful spiritual experience, discussed with his peers, J. B. Ross, "Gasparo Contarini and His Friends," *Studies in the Renaissance* 17 (1970): 192–232.

Reginald Pole, Cardinal. The text is taken from the 1587 edition of Pole's work, *Pro ecclesiasticae unitatis defensione, libri quatuor*, with preface of Venetian printer Paolo Manuzio (Ingolstadt:

David Sartorius). I have also consulted the translation of Joseph G. Dwyer: Reginald Pole, *Defense of the Unity of the Church*, ed. and trans. Joseph G. Dwyer (Westminster, MD: Newman Press, 1965). For Pole, see especially Thomas F. Mayer, *Reginald Pole: Prince and Prophet* (Cambridge: Cambridge University Press, 2000).

Ignatius of Loyola, Saint. The letter appears in *Monumenta ignatiana ex autographis vel ex antiquioribus exemplis collecta*, Series prima: *Sancti Ignatii de Loyola Epistolae et instructiones*, t. 12 (Madrid: Typis Gabrielis Lopez del Horno, 1911), Appendix I, Letter 27, 259–62. I have also consulted the translation of William J. Young, S.J., *Letters of St. Ignatius of Loyola* (Chicago: Loyola University Press, 1959), 344–47. Useful biographies of Ignatius include José Ignacio Tellechea Idígoras, *Ignatius of Loyola: The Pilgrim Saint*, trans. and ed. Cornelius Michael Buckley (Chicago: Loyola University Press, 1994); and W. W. Meissner, *Ignatius of Loyola: The Psychology of a Saint* (New Haven: Yale University Press, 1992).

Teresa of Ávila, Saint. The text used, with permission, is Teresa of Ávila, *The Book of Her Life*, translated and edited by Kieran Kavanaugh, O.C.D., and Otilio Rodriguez, O.C.D. (Indianapolis, IN/Cambridge, MA: Hackett, 2008), selections from chapters 32–36 at pp. 228–30, 233, 237, 240, 252–53, 257–59, 268–69. Useful biographies of Teresa include Cathleen Medwick, *Teresa of Avila: The Progress of a Soul* (New York: Knopf, 1999), and Carole Slade, *Saint Teresa of Avila: Author of a Heroic Life* (Berkeley: University of California Press, 1995). See also the important studies of Teresa in her cultural and political context: Gillian Ahlgren, *Teresa of Avila and the Politics of Sanctity* (Ithaca, NY: Cornell University Press, 1996); Jodi Bilinkoff, *The Avila of Saint Teresa: Religious Reform in a Sixteenth-Century City* (Ithaca, NY: Cornell University Press, 1989); and Alison Weber, *Teresa of Avila and the Rhetoric of Femininity* (Princeton: Princeton University Press, 1990).

Francis de Sales, Saint. The text is based on the 1832 edition of the *Introduction à la vie dévote* in *Oeuvres complètes* (Lyon: Perisse Frères, 1832), Part I, chapters 1–3, at 1–12. I have also consulted the English version (from the Library of Spiritual Works for English Catholics, translator not named) available from Christian Classics Ethereal Library (CCEL): http://www.ccel.org/ccel/desales/devout_life. For Francis de Sales, see the biography of André Ravier, *Francis de Sales, Sage and Saint*, trans. Joseph D. Bowler (San Francisco: Ignatius Press, 1988); and for the *Introduction to the Devout Life*, the essays in *Encountering Anew the Familiar: Francis de Sales's* Introduction to the Devout Life *at 400 Years*, ed. Joseph F. Chorpenning, OSFS (Rome: International Commission for Salesian Studies, 2012).

Chapter Nine: The Expanding Reformation

Jacobus Arminius. The text of the fifth oration, the *Oratio de componendo dissidio religionis inter Christianos* (February 8, 1606), is from the 1629 edition of the *Jacobi Arminii ... Opera theologica* (Leiden: Apud Godefridum Basson), 71–91, excerpts from 76–78 and 87–90. Also consulted: the English translation from the Latin of *The Works of James Arminius* by James Nichols in the London edition first published in 1825 (Longman, Hurst, Rees, Orme, Brown, and Green) and frequently reprinted, at 1:92–123; now available at the Wesley Center Online: http://wesley.nnu.edu/arminianism/the-works-of-james-arminius/volume-1/lectures-on-the-study-of-theology/oration-5-on-reconciling-religious-dissensions-among-christians/; and at Christian Classics Ethereal Library (CCEL): http://www.ccel.org/ccel/arminius/works1.ii.vi.

html. For Arminius, see Carl Bangs, *Arminius: A Study in the Dutch Reformation*, 2nd ed. (Grand Rapids, MI: F. Asbury Press, 1985; orig. 1971); Richard A. Muller, *God, Creation, and Providence in the Thought of Jacob Arminius: Sources and Directions of Scholastic Protestantism in the Era of Early Orthodoxy* (Grand Rapids, MI: Baker Book House, 1991); and Keith D. Stanglin and Thomas H. McCall, *Jacob Arminius: Theologian of Grace* (Oxford: Oxford University Press, 2012). See also for Arminianism in broader context, the essays in Theodoor Marius van Leeuwen, Keith D. Stanglin, and Marijke Tolsma, eds., *Arminius, Arminianism, and Europe* (Leiden; Boston: Brill, 2009).

Jacob Boehme (Jakob Böhme). The text is based on the volume introduced and published by G. B. Moreton (Canterbury, UK, 1894) of an eighteenth-century translation, *The Way to Christ, Described in the Following Treatises: Of True Repentance, Of True Resignation, Of Regeneration, Of the Super-sensual Life, written in the year 1622*. The Moreton edition is available through Google books, and digitized at Christian Classics Ethereal Library (CCEL): http://www.ccel.org/ccel/boehme/waytochrist.html, where *Of True Repentance* appears at 3–31, and excerpts are drawn from 2–5 and 12. Also consulted: the 1978 translation of *The Way to Christ* by Peter C. Erb (New York: Paulist Press, 1978). Modern studies of Boehme include John J. Stoudt, *Jacob Boehme, His Life and Thought* (New York: Seabury Press, 1968; reprint of Philadelphia: University of Pennsylvania Press, 1957) and the essays in Ariel Hessayon and S. L. T. Apetrei, eds., *An Introduction to Jacob Boehme: Four Centuries of Thought and Reception* (New York: Routledge, 2014). For Boehme's relations with Blake, see also Bryan Aubrey, *Watchmen of Eternity: Blake's Debt to Jacob Boehme* (Lanham, MD: University Press of America, 1986) and Kevin Fischer, *Converse in the Spirit: William Blake, Jacob Boehme, and the Creative Spirit* (Madison, NJ: Fairleigh Dickinson University Press, 2004). The website Jacob Boehme Online, http://www.jacobboehmeonline.com/, links to Boehme biography, images, and resources, as well as full English versions of his works.

Johanna Eleonora Petersen. The text is based on the original edition: *Leben Frauen Joh. Eleonora Petersen Gebohrnen von und zu Merlau, . . . von ihr selbst mit eigener Hand aufgesetzt, . . .* ([Halle]: Auf Kosten guter Freunde, 1718), 47–51, 56–60 (§§ 32–33, 36), an edition available from SLUB (Die Sächsische Landesbibliothek-Staats-und Universitätsbibliothek Dresden) at http://digital.slub-dresden.de/werkansicht/dlf/32449/1/. The autobiography is reprinted in modern type (but without the original section divisions) in Johanna Eleonora Petersen, *Leben: Eine Selbstbiographie*, ed. Michael Holzinger (Berlin: Holzinger, 2014), based on the reprint of the 1718 version in Werner Mahrholz, ed., *Der deutsche Pietismus: Eine Auswahl von Zeugnissen, Urkunden und Bekenntnissen aus dem 17., 18. und 19. Jahrhundert* (Berlin: Furche, 1921), 201–45, available at Archive.org. I have also consulted the English translation of Barbara Becker-Cantarino, *The Life of Lady Johanna Eleonora Petersen, Written by Herself: Pietism and Women's Autobiography in Sixteenth-Century Germany* (Chicago: University of Chicago Press, 2005), at pages 86–88, 91–93 (§§ 32–33, 36), and Becker-Cantarino's substantial introduction and extensive annotated bibliography of Petersen's works at 1–57. Useful context is provided by the collection of biographies of Pietist theologians edited by Carter Lindberg, *The Pietist Theologians: An Introduction to Theology in the Seventeenth and Eighteenth Centuries* (Malden, MA: Blackwell, 2005), which includes a chapter on Petersen by Martin H. Jung at 147–60. See also the monograph of Ruth Albrecht, *Johanna Eleonora Petersen: Theologische Schriftstellerin des frühen Pietismus* (Göttingen: Vandenhoeck & Ruprecht, 2005).

Margaret Fell. The text of the 1666 pamphlet *Women's Speaking Justified, Proved, and Allowed of by the Scriptures* is available at Quaker Heritage Press: http://www.qhpress.org/texts/fell.html, non-paginated (4,754 words). For Fell, see the biographies by Bonnelyn Y. Kunze, *Margaret Fell and the Rise of Quakerism* (Stanford, CA: Stanford University Press, 1994) and Isabel Ross, *Margaret Fell: Mother of Quakerism*, 3rd ed. (York: Ebor Press, 1996; orig. 1949). See also the concise biography of Fell with full bibliography by Jacqueline Broad, "Margaret Fell," *The Stanford Encyclopedia of Philosophy* (Spring 2012 edition), ed. Edward N. Zalta, http://plato.stanford.edu/archives/spr2012/entries/margaret-fell/. For the context of women's participation in radical religious culture in England, see Teresa Feroli, *Political Speaking Justified: Women Prophets and the English Revolution* (Newark: University of Delaware Press, 2006), and Catie Gill, *Women in the Seventeenth-Century Quaker Community: A Literary Study of Political Identities, 1650–1700* (Aldershot, UK: Ashgate, 2005).

John Wesley. The text is digitized from *The Works of the Rev. John Wesley*, ed. Thomas Jackson, 3rd ed., 14 vols. (London: Wesleyan-Methodist Book-Room, 1872) at Global Ministries: The United Methodist Church: http://www.umcmission.org/Find-Resources/John-Wesley-Sermons/The-Wesleys-and-Their-Times/The-Character-of-a-Methodist; and is available also at Eighteenth Century Editions Online (Gale/Cengage Learning) in numerous eighteenth-century editions. Recent biographies of Wesley include Roy Hattersley, *A Brand from the Burning: The Life of John Wesley* (London: Little, Brown, 2002); Stephen Tomkins, *John Wesley: A Biography* (Grand Rapids, MI: Wm. B. Eerdmans, 2003); and John M. Turner, *John Wesley: The Evangelical Revival and the Rise of Methodism in England* (Peterborough: Epworth Press, 2002). A brief sketch of Wesley by David Hempton appears in *The Pietist Theologians: An Introduction to Theology in the Seventeenth and Eighteenth Centuries* (Malden, MA: Blackwell, 2005), ed. Carter Lindberg, at 256–72. Many valuable resources and links to texts are found at the Wesley Center Online: http://wesley.nnu.edu/john-wesley/.

Chapter Ten: The Reformation Overseas

Francisco de Vitoria. The Latin text, edited by Herbert Francis Wright, is included in *De indis et de ivre belli relectiones*, introduced by Ernest Nys, with English translation by John Pawley Bate, published in the series "The Classics of International Law," edited by James Brown Scott (Washington: Carnegie Institution of Washington, 1917), available at Google Books and elsewhere online. The passages translated here are from "De Indis relectio prior," Section 2, articles 6–8 and 9–15 (of 16), pages 243–51. Translations consulted include the Bate version, a digitized version of which, taken from the 1964 reprint (New York: Oceana Publications; London: John Wiley), is available at Constitution.org: http://www.constitution.org/victoria/victoria_.htm; and that of Anthony Pagden and Jeremy Lawrence in their edition of Vitoria's *Political Writings*, at 265–72. For Vitoria, see André Azevedo Alves and J. M. Moreira, *The Salamanca School* (New York: Continuum, 2010); Annabel Brett, "Francisco de Vitoria (1483–1546) and Francisco Suárez (1548–1617)," in *The Oxford Handbook of the History of International Law*, eds. Bardo Fassbender and Anne Peters (Oxford: Oxford University Press, 2012), 1086–1091, at 1087–1089; Charles Covell, *The Law of Nations in Political Thought: A Critical Survey from Vitoria to Hegel* (New York: Palgrave Macmillan, 2009), chapter 2, "Vitoria, Suarez, Gentili, and Grotius," at 27–62; and Heinz-Gerhard Justenhoven and William A. Barbieri, *From Just War to Modern Peace Ethics* (Berlin: De Gruyter, 2012), especially the chapters by James Muldoon, "Forerunners of Humanitarian Intervention? From Canon Law to Francisco de Vitoria," 99–120, and Justenhoven, "Francisco de Vitoria: Just War as Defense of International Law," 121–35.

Francis Xavier, Saint. The text is from George Schurhammer and Josef Wicki, eds., *Epistolae S. Francisci Xaverii aliaque eius scripta*, rev. ed., 2 vols. (Rome: Apud Monumenta Historica Soc. Iesu, 1944–1945), 1:160–77. Translation consulted: M. Joseph Costelloe, trans., *The Letters and Instructions of Francis Xavier* (St. Louis, MO: Institute of Jesuit Sources, 1992), 63–74. For Xavier, see Georg Schurhammer, *Francis Xavier: His Life and Times*, trans. M. Joseph Costelloe, 4 vols. (Rome: Jesuit Historical Institute, 1973–1982), especially volume 2: *India, 1541–1544*; and the popular biography of Miguel Corrêa Monteiro, *Saint Francis Xavier: A Man for all Others*, trans. Peter Ingham (Lisbon: CTT Correios de Portugal, 2006). See also for Xavier's missionary work the essays edited by Rita Haub and Julius Oswald, *Franz Xavier, Patron der Missionen: Festschrift zum 450. Todestag* (Regensburg: Schnell & Steiner, 2002); and the essays edited by Ignacio Arellano, Alejandro González Acosta, and Arnulfo Herrera, *San Francisco Javier entre dos continentes* (Madrid: Iberoamericana; Frankfurt am Main: Vervuert, 2007).

Marie Guyart de l'Incarnation, Saint. The text is from Marie de l'Incarnation, *Correspondance*, edited by Guy Oury, 2nd ed. (Solesmes: Abbaye Saint-Pierre, 1971), Lettre XLIII at 94–101. Translation consulted: Joyce Marshall, trans. and ed., *Word from New France: The Selected Letters of Marie de l'Incarnation* (Toronto: Oxford University Press, 1967), 70–78. Besides her letters, Guyart authored an autobiography, *The Autobiography of Venerable Marie of the Incarnation, OSU, Mystic and Missionary*, trans. John J. Sullivan (Chicago: Loyola University Press, 1964). Biographies of Guyart include the definitive Guy Oury, *Marie de l'Incarnation* (1599–1672), 2 vols. (Quebec: Presses de l'Université Laval, 1973), and the more recent, in ascending order of year of publication, Anya Mali, *Mystic in the New World: Marie de l'Incarnation, 1599–1672* (Leiden: Brill, 1996); Françoise Deroy-Pineau, *Marie de l'Incarnation: Marie Guyart, femme d'affaires, mystique, mère de la Nouvelle France, 1599–1672* (Montreal: Fides, 1999); and Thérèse Nadeau-Lacour, *Marie Guyart de l'Incarnation: Une femme mystique au coeur de l'histoire* (Paris: Artège éditions, 2015). For Guyart and her missionary role, see the essays edited by Raymond Brodeur, Dominique Deslandres, and Thérèse Nadeau-Lacour, *Lecture inédite de la modernité aux origines de la Nouvelle-France: Marie Guyart de l'Incarnation et les autres fondateurs religieux* (Québec: Presses de l'Université Laval, 2009); and those of Natalie Zemon Davis, "New Worlds: Marie de l'Incarnation," in Davis, *Women on the Margins: Three Seventeenth-Century Lives* (Cambridge, MA: Harvard University Press, 1995), 63–139; and Katherine Ibbett, "Reconfiguring Martyrdom in the Colonial Context: Marie de l'Incarnation," in *Empires of God: Religious Encounters in the Early Modern Atlantic*, eds. Linda Gregerson and Susan Juster (Philadelphia: University of Pennsylvania Press, 2011), 175–90. See also for the Ursuline and Jesuit missions to New France, Guy Oury, *Les Ursulines de Québec, 1639–1953* (Sillery, Québec: Septentrion, 1999) and Takao Abé, *The Jesuit Mission to New France: A New Interpretation in the Light of the Earlier Jesuit Experience in Japan* (Leiden: Brill, 2011). Marie de l'Incarnation was only recently canonized, on April 3, 2014, by Pope Francis.

Roger Williams. The text is based on the first 1644 edition, which has been reproduced and reprinted several times (1848, 1867, 2001), and is available from EEBO (Early English Books Online) and Google books: *The Bloudy Tenent of Persecution* . . . (London: Calvert), 15–18. The 1644 edition was followed by London editions of 1647 (reprinted London: H. Allen, 1972) and 1652, and a much-abridged, partly modernized version is included in James Calvin Davis, ed., *On Religious Liberty: Selections from the Works of Roger Williams* (Cambridge, MA: Belknap Press, Harvard University Press, 2008), 85–156. For Williams, see most recently John M. Barry, *Roger Williams and the Creation of the American Soul: Church, State, and the Birth of*

Liberty (New York: Viking, 2012); Edwin S. Gaustad, *Roger Williams* (Oxford: Oxford University Press, 2005); and Timothy L. Hall, *Separating Church and State: Roger Williams and Christian Liberty* (Urbana: University of Illinois Press, 1998). See also for the importance of the principle of liberty of conscience in American history, Martha C. Nussbaum, *Liberty of Conscience: In Defense of America's Tradition of Religious Equality* (New York: Basic Books, 2008), and Steven Waldman, *Founding Faith: Providence, Politics, and the Birth of Religious Freedom in America* (New York: Random House, 2008).

Jonathan Edwards. The text is based on the version of the *Faithful Narrative* (1736) published in vol. 4 of *The Works of President Edwards with a Memoir of His Life*, ed. Sereno Edwards Dwight (New York: S. Converse, 1830), 17–74, excerpts drawn from 17–19, 22–23, and 27–30. The original 1737 and 1738 editions, published in London and Boston, were followed by several others through the mid-nineteenth century, with little variation. Also consulted: the version published at the website *The Writings of Jonathan Edwards*: http://www.jonathanedwards.org/Narrative.html; and that appearing in *A Jonathan Edwards Reader*, eds. John E. Smith and Harry S. Stout (New Haven: Yale University Press, 1995; digitized by Nota Bene, 2003), 57–87, at 57–66. For Edwards, see especially the biography of George M. Marsden, *Jonathan Edwards: A Life* (New Haven: Yale University Press, 2003). See also the studies Michael J. McClymond and Gerald R. McDermott, *The Theology of Jonathan Edwards* (New York: Oxford University Press, 2012) and Avihu Zakai, *Jonathan Edwards's Philosophy of History: Reenchantment of the World in the Age of Enlightenment* (Princeton: Princeton University Press, 2003), and the essays in Gerald R. McDermott, ed., *Understanding Jonathan Edwards: An Introduction to America's Theologian* (New York: Oxford University Press, 2009) and Stephen J. Stein, ed., *The Cambridge Companion to Jonathan Edwards* (New York: Cambridge University Press, 2007).

INDEX

Act of Supremacy (1534), 125, 145
Acts of the Apostles, biblical book, 43, 73, 88, 89, 115
Adam, 20, 22, 28n7, 41, 58, 77, 79, 114, 120
Albertus Magnus, 29n11
Alexander V, Antipope, 10n21
Algonquins, xv, 184, 192, 193, 194n24
Ambrose, Saint, Church Father, 56
Amish, 106
Amsterdam, 108
Anabaptist, Anabaptism, xiii, 84, 101, 103–7, 111–17, 185, 208–10
angels, xv, 24, 29, 36, 107, 118, 173–76, 177n26, 198
Anglicanism, xiv, xv, 126–28, 165–67, 185
Anglo-America, xi, xv, 103, 164, 179, 182, 186, 199
Antichrist, 9
anti-trinitarianism, 13, 180, 185n3
Antwerp, 105, 111, 124
apocalypse, apocalypticism, xv, 18, 104, 108, 166, 171n6, 173, 175, 196
apostles, 4, 6, 17, 18, 20, 25, 27–31, 40, 43, 56, 60, 67, 72, 73, 77–79, 88, 89, 92, 96, 104, 109, 111, 112, 114, 118–20, 133, 176, 178; Apostles' Creed, 60, 61, 106, 189–91
Aquinas, Thomas, Saint. *See* Thomas Aquinas, Saint
archbishops. *See* bishops, archbishops
Arians, Arianism, 106, 180
Aristotle, Aristotelian, 1n1, 2, 76, 148, 183
Arminius, Jacobus (Jakob Hermanszoon), Arminianism, xiv, 164, 165, 167–70, 185, 213–14
Asia, xv, 182, 183, 184, 189
Athanasian Creed, 106, 117, 180n32
atonement, 3, 19, 20, 21, 48, 75, 76n34, 77, 136, 171, 181. *See also* crucifixion, justification by faith, redemption
Augsburg Confession, xii, 66, 74–77

Augustine, Saint, Church Father, 2, 56, 79, 108
Augustinian Order, 42, 85
autobiography, genre, xi, xiv, xv, 147, 157–60, 165–66, 173–75, 214, 216

baptism, 9, 25, 26, 33, 58, 82, 92, 105, 126, 135, 136, 141, 142, 171, 181, 189–94; of adults ("believer baptism"), 104n2, 105; of infants, 84, 104, 105, 128, 185
Baptists, 182, 185
Basel, 84, 107, 108
Basil of Caesarea, Saint, Church Father, 79
Bayle, Pierre, 108
Bellius, Martinus. *See* Sebastian Castellio
Benedetto da Mantova, xii, 3, 19–22, 203
Benedictine Order, 3, 126
Bernard of Claivaux, Saint, 79
Beza, Theodore, xiii, 87, 88, 95, 96n22, 100–102, 107, 108, 208
Bible, xii, xiii, xiv, xvi, 1–3, 14, 19, 32, 33n20, 43, 53–56, 70n15, 71n21, 72, 73, 74n27, 77n37, 78, 79n42, 91, 97, 104, 108–12, 125, 128, 132–34, 141, 142, 166, 173, 174, 175n16, 179, 196, 211; Authorized (King James) Version (1611), 125; Bishops' Bible (1559), 125; Great Bible (1539), 125–26, 132–34, 211; Hebrew Bible, 19, 43, 71n21. *See also* Gospel, New Testament, Old Testament, Scripture
bishops, archbishops, xi, xiv, 6, 9, 28, 30, 37, 61, 67, 77n37, 125, 129–31, 144–52, 153n12, 161, 162, 169
Blake, William, 165
Boehme, Jacob (Jakob Böhme), xiv, xvi, 164–66, 170–73, 214
Boleyn, Anne, 124, 145
Bonhoeffer, Dietrich, 2
Book of Common Prayer (1549, 1552, etc.), 125, 126
born again, experience. *See* Great Awakening; regeneration, experience of

219

Bourbon, Henri de (Henry of Bourbon).
   See Henry IV, king of France
Braght, Theleman Janszoon van, 105, 209
Brahmans, 190–92
Brenz, Johann, 108,
Bucer, Martin, xiii, 67–68, 80–83, 185, 207
Buddhism, 182
bull, papal, 6, 9, 10, 64
Bullinger, Heinrich, 84

Calvin, John, xiii, 67, 84–88, 92n12,
   94–99, 103, 106–8, 109n9, 114, 124,
   147, 164, 165, 198, 207, 208
Calvinism, Calvinist. See Reformed
   Protestantism
Campion, Edmund, xiv, xvi, 127–28,
   138–40, 153, 211–12
Canisius, Peter, xiv, 146, 155–57
canon law, 4, 43, 46,
Capuchin, 162
cardinals, xi, xiv, 7, 8, 30, 124, 144–46, 148
Carthusian Order, 162
Castellio, Sebastian, xiii, 107–8, 120–23,
   167, 185, 210–11
catechism, xii, 43, 44, 60–63, 155, 156,
   184, 205
Catherine of Aragon, queen consort of
   England, 124, 145
Catholic, Catholicism, xi, xiin1, xiii–xv,
   1n3, 2, 3, 5n12, 7, 8, 30n16, 46n6, 65,
   68, 84, 87–89, 92, 94, 95, 103, 105–7,
   115n22, 125–28, 134–35, 138–40,
   144–64, 173, 180n31, 182–95, 203,
   211–13, 215–16. See also Reformation:
   Catholic
charity. See love of God, divine love
Charles V, Holy Roman Emperor, 66, 75
children, xii, 9, 20, 22, 24, 31–34, 38, 40,
   44, 60, 61, 63, 66, 69, 82, 84, 85, 104,
   105, 111–14, 116–18, 120, 128, 131,
   143, 152, 156, 174, 178, 185, 194n28,
   196, 198
China, 183
Christoph, Duke of Württemberg, 121–23
Christos ("anointed one"). See Messiah
Chrysostom, John, Saint, Church Father,
   108
Church Fathers, 56n17, 76n33, 77, 79, 83,
   108, 118

Cicero, 30, 32
circulation of the blood, pulmonary, 107
clergy, clerics, xi, xii, xiv, 1, 2, 9, 23, 24, 28,
   37, 43, 50, 64, 84, 91, 92, 94, 97, 103,
   109, 124, 125, 129, 130nn9 and 10,
   131n12, 144–50, 157, 158, 166, 167,
   169. See also bishops, cardinals, friars,
   monks, papacy, pastors, prelates, priests
clerical corruption, critique of, xii, 2, 9, 23,
   24, 28, 92, 109, 124, 125, 129–31, 144,
   145, 150, 157
Colloquy of Marburg (1529), 84
Colloquy of Regensburg (Ratisbon; 1541),
   144
Columbus, Christopher, 182
commandments, 8, 9, 52, 60, 61, 62, 68,
   69, 71, 75, 78, 100, 115, 131, 161, 162,
   171, 189–91. See also Law of God, Ten
   Commandments
common people. See laity
Communion, 9, 64, 135, 158; First
   Communion, 194. See also Eucharist,
   Lord's Supper, Mass
confession, confessor, 9, 38, 41, 46, 74,
   130, 158, 159, 190. See also Augsburg
   Confession
Constantine, Roman emperor, 5n13
Contarini, Gasparo, Cardinal, xiv, 144–46,
   148–52, 212
convent, conventual life. See enclosure,
   religious
conversion, converts, xiv, xv, 23, 44, 65, 67,
   68, 86, 87, 94–96, 105, 127, 147, 174,
   182–86, 189, 191, 193, 198–201
Council of Constance, 2
Council of Trent, xiv, 144, 145, 147
Counter-Reformation. See Reformation:
   Catholic
Coverdale, Myles, 125
Cranmer, Thomas, Archbishop of Canterbury, xiv, xvi, 67, 125–26, 132–34, 146,
   211
cross of Christ, 3, 10, 12–15, 19–22, 28–31,
   36, 39, 45, 48, 49, 56, 75, 96, 113, 127,
   135–37, 190, 191. See also crucifixion of
   Christ, passion of Christ
crucifixion of Christ, xiii, 19, 24, 43, 172n9,
   177n26. See also cross of Christ, passion
   of Christ

cult of saints. *See* saints: cult of
Curio, Coelius Secundus, 108
Cynics, 32

Daniel, biblical book of, 104, 108–11
death, dying, 9, 10, 12n22, 13, 15, 18, 21, 31, 34, 37–41, 46, 47, 49, 58, 65, 67–69, 72, 75-78, 81–83, 85, 92, 93, 95, 97, 99, 105, 107, 112–14, 116, 120, 126–28, 135, 152–54, 164, 171, 172, 183, 184, 199, 200
Decalogue. *See* Ten Commandments
decretal, papal, 4–6, 73
Demosthenes, 30
Dentière, Marie, xiii, 85, 86n2, 91–94, 207–8
d'Este, Ercole, duke of Ferrara, 86
devil, 21, 28, 63, 121, 123, 143, 171, 175n16, 196, 198
devotio moderna, 2
devotion, devout life, xiv, 148, 160–63, 199
dialectic, dialectical, 4, 5, 76
diary, genre, xi, xiv, 128, 140–43
Discalced Carmelites, Order of, xiv, 147, 157–60
discord, religious, 92, 167–70, 195–98
Divine Office, 149n6, 160, 195n29. *See also* psalms
Dominican Order, xv, 41, 42, 150n9, 159, 182, 183
Duns Scotus, 29n11

Eck, Johann, 64, 103
Edict of Nantes (1598), 87
education, 24, 32–35, 37, 44, 57, 60-63, 66, 68, 73n24, 82, 85, 88, 105, 111–14, 134, 146–47, 149, 155–57, 184, 189–95
Edward VI, king of England, 67, 124, 126
Edwards, Jonathan, xv, xvi, 185–86, 199–201, 217
Elect, election, 10n21, 82, 97–99, 104, 108–11, 115n22
Elizabeth I, queen of England, xiv, 124, 127–28, 138, 139
enclosure, religious, 147, 149, 157–60
end of time, doctrine. *See* apocalypse, apocalypticism
English Mission, 127. *See also* Jesuits
English Reformation. *See* Reformation: English

Enlightenment, xvi, 108, 164, 166, 173
Epicurus, Epicurean, 32 78
Episcopalian, 126. *See also* Anglicanism
Erasmus, Desiderius, xii, 23–41, 43n2, 45, 46n4, 57, 67, 107–8, 125, 185, 203–4
Eucharist, 1n3, 64, 84, 135, 194n28. *See also* Communion, Lord's Supper, Mass
evangelical, evangelicalism, xii, 3, 23, 57, 58, 65, 85, 86, 94, 95, 179, 195; Evangelical Rationalism, 103
Evangelist, 5. *See also* Gospel, New Testament
excommunication, 2, 7, 9, 131, 168
external man, 51–52

faith, in God, xi–xiii, 3, 4, 9, 11, 14, 15, 18, 20, 22, 25, 27, 33, 38, 41–44, 46, 49, 51–57, 60, 61, 63–67, 73, 75, 77, 79, 80, 88, 90–93, 95, 97, 105, 112, 122, 125–27, 132, 135–40, 148, 150, 161, 166, 170, 171, 177, 179–81, 182, 184–91, 193, 194, 197, 198. *See also* justification by faith
fallen angels. *See* angels
Farel, William, 85
fathers, 40, 60, 62, 63, 71-73, 78, 86, 92, 112, 113, 114, 126, 145, 149, 150, 190, 193, 194, 198. *See also* Church Fathers
Feckingham, John, 126–27, 134–37
Fell, Margaret, xv, xvi, 166, 176–79, 214–15
feminism, 166
Fifth Monarchy, 109, 111
First Amendment, of U.S. Constitution, 185
First Great Awakening. *See* Great Awakening
Fish, Simon, xiii, xvi, 124–25, 128–31, 211
Fisher, John, Bishop, 145, 152–54
Flaminio, Marcantonio, 3
flesh, 46, 48, 50, 51, 53–56, 58, 63, 69, 70, 73, 82, 110, 112, 117, 118, 136, 162, 170–72, 178, 179, 195, 198
folly, foolishness, 24, 27–31, 203–4
food prohibitions, 84
foreknowledge, 99
Fox, George, 166
Foxe, John, *Acts and Monuments*, 127
Francis de Sales, Saint. *See* Sales, Francis de, Saint

Francis I, king of France, 3, 85, 86n2, 91, 93
Francis, Pope, 184
Franciscan Order, 74n29, 150n9, 162n24, 182. *See also* Observants
Franck, Sebastian, 108
Franklin, Benjamin, 185
Frederick the Wise, Elector of Saxony, 104, 108n5
free will, 19, 20, 23, 76n34, 120, 121, 148, 165
freedom, Christian, religious freedom, xii, xv, xvi, 42–44, 49–52, 57–60, 65, 67–68, 88–91, 100–102, 103, 106–8, 165, 168, 182, 185–89, 195–98. *See also* free will, separation: of church and state, toleration
French Wars of Religion. *See* Wars of Religion, French
friars, 41, 42, 47, 74, 129, 130, 150, 162n24. *See also* Augustinian, Capuchin, Dominican, Franciscan, mendicants, monks, Observants

Geneva, xiii, 67, 84–88, 91, 95, 96, 106–8, 147
German Reformation. *See* Reformation: German
good works. *See* works
Gospel, 4–6, 9, 20, 24, 25, 29, 33, 34, 37, 43, 45, 48, 51, 53, 55, 56, 58, 69, 72, 73, 76–80, 88, 89, 91, 93, 96, 97, 104, 109, 111, 115, 131, 138, 139, 150, 151, 173, 177, 181, 187, 191. *See also* Bible, Evangelists, New Testament, Scripture
government. *See* state power, in relation to church
governors, 111, 198. *See also* kings, magistrates, princes, rulers
grace of God, 8, 15, 17, 20, 45, 48, 49, 52–57, 63, 74–76, 89, 91, 93–95, 97–99, 112, 140, 161, 164, 170, 171, 175–77, 185
Great Awakening, xi, xv, 186, 198–201
Great Peasants' War. *See* Peasants' War, German
Grey, Jane, Lady, xiv, xvi, 126–27, 134–37, 211

Grotius, Hugo, 183
Grumbach, Argula von, xii, 65–68, 71–74, 206
Guyart, Marie, de l'Incarnation, Saint, xv, 184, 192–95, 216

Harvey, William, 107
heathen. *See* infidels
heaven, 9, 10, 12, 13, 14–17, 19, 27, 28, 32, 35, 39, 46, 47, 49, 51, 52, 55, 60, 63, 69, 79, 81, 82, 89, 98, 112, 116, 138–40, 150, 168, 173, 175n16, 180, 181, 192, 196, 198. *See also* salvation
Hegel, Georg W. F., 165
Heidegger, Martin, 165
Heidelberg Disputation (1518), 67
hell, 12, 15, 21, 41n34, 46, 47, 49, 74, 171–75, 187n8, 196, 198
Henry IV, king of France, 3, 86, 87
Henry VIII, king of England, xiii, xiv, 124–31, 145–46, 152–54
heresy, heretic, xii, 2, 28, 72–73, 103, 105, 107–9, 111, 120–27, 130, 131, 140n27, 144, 150, 155–57, 163, 167–68, 180n32, 197, 210
Hildegard of Bingen, 166
Hinduism, 182, 191
Hoby, Margaret, Lady, xiv, xvi, 128, 140–43, 148, 212
Holy Ghost. *See* Holy Spirit
Holy Spirit, xiii, 6, 11, 54, 55, 58, 63, 76, 79, 82, 99, 104, 106, 107, 110, 117, 118, 133, 134, 166, 169, 174, 176–79
hope, 13, 15, 18, 19, 25, 27, 38, 41, 47, 54, 56, 95, 98, 109, 112, 143, 153, 164, 167, 181, 194, 196, 201
Hugh of St. Victor, 79
Huguenots, xiii, 87, 88, 95, 182
Hurons, xv, 184, 192, 193
Hus, Jan, xi, 1, 2, 7–10, 103, 109n9, 144, 202
Hutter, Jakob, 105
Hutterites, 104–6, 114, 210
hypostasis, hypostases, 117–18

idol, idolatry. *See* images, cult of
Ignatius of Loyola, Saint, xiv, 2, 146–48, 155–57, 183, 213
illumination, by God, 5, 110

images, cult of, xii, 23, 32, 34, 38, 64, 68–71, 79, 84, 90, 109, 110, 126, 150
Incarnation, doctrine of, 28n8, 81, 106, 117, 118n47
Incarnation, Marie de l'. *See* Guyart, Marie, de l'Incarnation, Saint
India, Catholic mission to, xv, 183–84, 189–92
Indians, American, xv, 182–84, 186–89, 192–95
indigenous peoples. *See* Indians, American
indulgences, xii, 42, 45–49, 144
infidels, xv, 24, 36, 71, 92, 109, 110, 139, 164, 174, 179, 189. *See also* unbelief, unbeliever
Ingolstadt, 65, 68
Inquisition, 107; Roman Inquisition, 3
instruction. *See* education
interdict, 2, 5, 7, 9, 10, 168
inwardness, interiority, 2, 11, 23, 46, 50–56, 85, 149, 162, 166, 182
Iroquois, 184

James I, king of England, VI of Scotland, 125
Jeanne de Chantal, Saint, 148
Jeanne d'Albret, queen of Navarre, 86, 94–97
Jefferson, Thomas, 185
Jerome, Saint, Church Father, 56, 108
Jesuits, xiv, xv, 127, 138–40, 146, 155–57, 182–84, 189–92, 193n22, 194n26
Jews, xv, 107, 164, 173, 174, 179
John Frederick, son of John, Duke of Saxony, 104, 108, 109
John of the Cross, Saint, 147
John the Baptist, 20, 79, 119
John, Duke of Saxony, 104, 108, 109
Judas, 91, 94, 119
just war, theory of, 183, 186–89
justice, of God. *See* justification by faith
justification by faith, doctrine, xii, 3, 21, 44, 53–57, 66, 67, 74–79, 92, 96, 104, 122, 134–36, 144, 148, 161, 170, 180

Karlstadt, Andreas, xii, 64–65, 67–71, 84, 95, 103, 205–6
Kempis, Thomas. *See* Thomas à Kempis
King James Version (of the Bible). *See* Bible: Authorized Version
kingdom of Christ, xiii, 12, 13, 67, 80–83, 94, 109. *See also* kingdom of God

kingdom of God, 10, 11, 21, 31n17, 58, 63, 103, 104. *See also* kingdom of Christ
kings, 33, 37, 39. 58, 81–83, 113, 198
Knyphausen, Dodo von, Baron, 175n15

La Peltrie, Mme de Chauvigny de, 184, 182, 193n21
laity, laypersons, xiv, 2, 5, 9, 70n15, 74n28, 135, 137, 144–52, 155–60, 169
Last Judgment, 171
Last Supper, 1n3, 12n22
law, canon. *See* canon law
law, international, 183, 186–89
Law of God, 8, 9, 19–21, 27, 43–44, 49, 51–58, 68, 71, 75–79, 92, 101, 110, 116, 191, 192. *See also* commandments, Old Testament, Ten Commandments
Lead, Jane, 175
Leipzig Debate (1519), 64, 103
Lent, xiii, 84, 88
liberty. *See* freedom
Liturgy of the Hours. *See* Divine Office
Lollards, 1
Lord's Prayer. *See* prayer: Lord's Prayer
Lord's Supper, 61, 64, 92, 94, 95, 126, 135–37. *See also* Communion, Eucharist, Mass
Louis XII, king of France, 86
Louise de Marillac, Saint, 148
love of God, divine love, xii, 9, 11–18, 21–23, 26, 32, 34, 36, 49, 51, 52, 54–56, 62, 68, 76–78, 80, 89, 92, 116n32, 135, 147–49, 151, 153, 160–63, 171, 174, 177–80, 200
Luther, Martin, xi–xiv, xvi, 1, 3, 23, 42–69, 72, 73, 75, 77–80, 84–88, 103–4, 108, 114, 124, 125, 144, 148, 161, 164, 165, 170, 185, 204–6
Lutheranism, xi–xiv, 3, 44, 60, 64–68, 71, 74, 75, 79, 84, 85, 88, 165, 167, 170, 198. *See also* Reformation: German

Madison, James, 185
Maeyken van Deventer, xiii, 105, 111–13, 209
magistrates, magisterial, xiii, 44, 61, 64, 65, 87, 100–103, 108, 120, 124, 169
Marguerite de Navarre, xii, xiii, 3, 14–19, 85, 86n2, 91–94, 203

Martha, sister of Lazarus and Mary, 176
martyr, martyrdom, xi, xiii, xv, 2, 18, 79, 83, 84, 101, 104, 105, 107, 111–14, 120, 127, 145n1, 146, 152, 154, 167, 193, 195, 198n40, 209, 216
Mary I (Tudor), queen of England, xiv, 124, 126, 146
Mary Magdalene, follower of Jesus, 94
Mary, Virgin, mother of Jesus Christ, 38, 39, 94, 106, 116, 119, 190
Mass, 1n3, 76, 84, 94–96, 130, 150, 194. *See also* Communion, Eucharist, Lord's Supper
Massacre of St. Bartholomew's Day (1572), 87
Melanchthon, Philip (Schwarzerdt), xii–xiii, 66–68, 72–80, 87, 106, 206
mendicants, mendicancy, 29, 41n34, 124, 129
Mennonites, 104, 106, 182
Messiah ("anointed one," Greek *Christos*), 14n23, 118–19, 177
Methodism, Methodist, xi, xv, 2, 164–67, 179–81, 186, 215
missionary, missionizing, xv, 127, 138–40, 146–48, 155–57, 182–84, 189–95, 216
monks, monasticism, xii, 1–3, 23, 28, 29, 111, 124, 129, 130, 150, 162n23. *See also* Benedictine, Carthusian, friars, mendicants
More, Thomas, Sir, Saint, 124, 125, 145, 152, 153n12
Moses, 79, 93
mothers, xv, 3, 37–41, 66, 71, 86, 92–94, 105, 106, 111–14, 124, 142, 145, 146, 165, 166, 190, 192, 194, 197, 198
Munstdorp, Janneken, xiii, 105, 111–14, 209
Münster, Münsterites, 104
Müntzer, Thomas, xiii, 103–4, 108–11, 209
Muslims, 33n22, 107. *See also* Saracens, Turks
mystic, mysticism, xiv, 3, 7, 79, 103, 144, 147, 166

Native Americans. *See* Indians, American
Nebuchadnezzar, king of Babylon, 109
New France, 184, 192, 193
New Jerusalem, 104
New Testament, 6, 15, 23, 24, 30, 31, 43, 46n4, 48n9, 53, 57, 58, 69, 71, 73, 75, 79n42, 88, 104, 106, 120, 125, 176. *See also* Bible, Evangelist, Gospel
New World, xv, 182–84, 186
Nietzsche, Friedrich, 165
nobles, nobility, xi, xii, 2, 28, 37, 68, 71, 74n60, 85–87, 108, 131, 137n24, 144, 146, 147, 162. *See also* princes
North America. *See* Anglo-America
Northampton (Massachusetts), xv, 186, 198, 199
nuns, xi, xiv, xv, 148, 158, 160, 184, 192

oath-taking, 105, 106
obedience, 6–8, 49, 51, 52, 56–59, 72, 76, 78n38, 82, 83, 100, 101, 119, 120, 130, 131, 134, 139, 145, 157–60, 194
Observants, Franciscan friars (Friars Minor), 74
Old Testament, 6, 14, 19, 30, 43, 68, 71n21, 75, 78n38, 79n42, 91, 93, 104, 114, 125. *See also* Bible, Law of God
Origen, 56
Original Sin, doctrine, 28, 82, 114
Our Father. *See* prayer: Lord's Prayer

pacifism. *See* peace
pamphlet, xi, xiii, xv, 111, 124, 125, 126n2, 127, 129, 155, 157, 166, 167
papacy, pope, xiii, xiv, 2, 4–10, 28, 30, 37, 42, 45–48, 61, 72, 127n5, 128, 144–46, 153, 184, 186, 187, 189, 216
passion of Christ, 10, 12, 14, 24, 70, 95, 171, 172. *See also* cross of Christ, crucifixion of Christ
pastors, xi, xiii, xv, 2, 44, 48n8, 60, 61, 78, 84, 86, 87, 103, 104, 120, 185
Paternoster. *See* prayer: Lord's Prayer
Paul, Saint, apostle, xii, 6, 15, 17–21, 25, 27–29, 33, 40, 43–44, 50, 53–58, 66, 73, 79, 88, 90–91, 92n12, 96, 115–20, 135, 148, 176, 198, 205
peace, pacifism, xii, 24, 34–37, 106, 137, 167–69, 185, 195–98, 204
Peasants' War, German (1524–1525), 104
penitence, 46, 79, 82, 161. *See also* repentance
Penn, William, 175n15
Peripatetics, 32
persecution, 86, 105, 106, 108, 122, 127, 138, 158, 160, 164, 167, 268, 182, 185, 193, 195–98

Peter, Saint, apostle, 4, 6, 56, 89–90, 119; basilica of, 42, 45, 47, 48
Petersen, Johanna Eleonora, xv, 165–66, 173–75, 214
philosophia christi. *See* philosophy: of Christ
philosophy, 76, 150, 156; of Christ, 23, 24, 32–34. *See also* Aristotle, Plato, scholastic, Stoics
Pietism, Radical Pietism, xiv, xv, 165, 166–67, 173, 179, 182, 185, 214, 215
Plato, Platonism, 32, 76n35, 148
Pole, Margaret Plantagenet, 146n2
Pole, Reginald, Cardinal, 145–46, 152–54, 212–13
political authority. *See* State power, in relation to church
Polycarp, Saint, 79
poor. *See* poverty
pope. *See* papacy
poverty, poor relief, 12, 30, 32, 42, 45, 47, 48, 70n15, 94, 110, 129, 130, 133, 145, 147–49, 151, 152, 158, 159, 161, 162, 166, 171, 190, 191, 193, 195, 201
prayer, 24, 25, 27, 31, 40, 48, 102, 128, 140–42, 146, 147, 149, 158, 160n22, 162, 170, 171, 175, 178, 184, 189–94; Ave Maria (Hail Mary), 190; Confiteor (prayer of confession), 190; Lord's Prayer (Our Father, Paternoster), 40, 60–63, 70, 189, 190; Salve Regina (Hail, Holy Queen), 38, 190
preacher, preaching, 1, 6, 9, 10, 29, 36, 37, 41n34, 48, 51, 60, 61, 73, 76, 77, 92–94, 97, 107, 111, 120, 131, 138, 139, 141, 149, 150, 151, 156, 177, 178, 188, 189, 191, 193, 200
predestination, xiii, 2, 7, 8, 86, 87, 97–99, 109n9, 120, 121, 164. *See also* Elect, election
prelates, 7, 9, 23, 34, 36, 66. *See also* bishops, cardinals
priests, xi, xiv, xv, 1, 2, 6n17, 23, 28, 30, 31, 37, 38, 41, 46, 50, 66, 106, 111, 126, 127, 129–31, 137, 138, 145–47, 149, 150, 155, 156, 166, 144, 190, 192
princes, xi–xiii, 30, 32, 34, 36, 58, 59, 67, 69, 72, 74, 83, 86, 100, 102–4, 108–11, 120–24, 152, 154, 162, 163, 169. *See also* kings, rulers

Privy Council (English), xiv, 127, 138–40
property: common ownership of, 105–6, 114–17; private, 183, 185n3, 187, 189; repudiation of, 147, 158, 159
prophets, 5, 14, 19, 33, 49, 57, 67, 72, 74–79, 104, 109, 112–14, 133
Protestant, Protestantism, xi–xv, 3, 44, 64–66, 89, 97, 101, 105–7, 115, 124–28, 134, 138, 139, 144–47, 155, 164, 167, 173, 179, 182, 186, 202
psalms, 14, 29, 109, 126
purgatory, 46, 47, 125, 161
Puritans, Puritanism, xiv, 100–101n24, 128, 148, 166, 182, 185
Pythagoras, 32

Quakers, Quakerism, xv, 165–66, 182
Quebec (Canada), xv, 184, 192, 194n23

Radical Reformation. *See* Reformation: Radical
real presence, doctrine, 84
reason, rationality, xiii, 5, 16, 31, 35, 56, 75, 76, 103, 134, 136, 149, 167, 188, 191, 199
redemption, 31, 81, 95, 135, 136, 143, 174, 177, 181, 187. *See also* atonement, justification by faith
Reformation: Catholic, xiv, 144–63, 182, 183, 202, 212; English, xiii, xiv, xv, 67, 81, 124–43, 145–46, 152–54, 164–66, 175, 176–81, 211–12; German, xii–xv, 42–83, 103–6, 108–11, 114–17, 125, 146, 155–57, 164–66, 170–75, 204–7, 209–10, 214; Radical, xi, xiii, xiv, 101, 103–23, 182, 185, 208–9; Scandinavian, xiii, 81; Swiss, xiii, 65, 84–103, 104, 105, 147, 207–8. *See also* Protestant, Protestantism
Reformed Protestantism (Calvinism), xi, 84–103, 147, 198
regeneration, experience of, xiv, 74–77, 81, 82, 136, 165, 170, 185, 200
relics, cult of, 23, 24, 32, 34, 38, 134, 150
Remonstrants, 164
Renata di Francia. *See* Renée de France
Renée de France, duchess of Ferrara, 86, 94–96
repentance, 41, 45–49, 92, 102, 165, 170–73

resurrection, 21, 34, 71n21, 92, 94, 119, 120, 176–79
return of all things, doctrine, 166, 173–75. *See also* salvation: universal
Reuchlin, Johann, 66
Revelation, biblical book, 43, 73n26, 120, 121, 173, 177n22
Rhode Island, xi, xv, 108, 185
riches, the rich. *See* wealth
Riedemann, Peter, xiii, 105–6, 114–17, 209–10
righteousness, of God, xii, 3, 9, 21, 51, 54–56, 76, 78n38, 81, 100, 109, 111, 171, 196. *See also* justification by faith
Roman College, 157
rulers, xiii, 24, 37, 57, 69, 72, 83, 88, 100n23, 101n25, 102, 167, 189. *See also* magistrates, nobles, princes, state power
Ruth, foremother of Jesus, 93

sacrament, 2n5, 9, 46, 60, 61, 64, 82, 135, 136, 138, 139, 144, 150, 194n28
saints, sainthood, 14, 67, 77n37, 115, 116, 126, 172, 184, 200; cult of, xii, 23, 24, 32, 38–41, 79n41, 144, 149–51. *See also* Elect, images
Sales, Francis de, Saint, xiv, 147–48, 160–63, 213
salvation, xii, xiv, xv, 2, 3, 7–10, 13, 17, 19, 21, 28, 32, 36, 39, 45, 47, 49, 50, 52, 60, 67, 70, 72, 75, 81, 82, 91, 95, 97–99, 109, 113, 114, 117, 120, 130, 134, 136, 140, 148, 165, 169, 170, 172, 180, 185n3, 188, 199; universal, doctrine of, 165, 173–75
Samaritan woman (John 4:1–26), 94, 176
Saracens, 33. *See also* Muslims
Satan. *See* devil
savages. *See* Indians, American
Schleitheim Articles (1527), 105
scholastic, scholasticism, 1, 3, 4n9, 29, 66, 75, 76, 78, 88, 120n64, 183
Schopenhauer, Arthur, 165
Schutz, Katharina, 65
Scripture, xi, xv, 1–9, 23–27, 32–34, 39, 50, 56, 66, 67, 69, 70, 72–76, 78, 79, 83, 85, 87–89, 91–94, 96–99, 101n25, 104, 106, 110, 114, 117–19, 132–36, 144, 150, 151, 152, 156, 166, 174–79, 191, 195, 202. *See also* Bible, Gospel, New Testament, Old Testament
Seehofer, Arsacius, 65, 71–73
separation: from established church or civil society, 105, 106, 147; of church and state, 106, 185, 198
separatism. *See* separation
sermon. *See* preacher, preaching
Servetus, Michael, xiii, 106–8, 117–20, 210
sin, sinners, xii, 3, 9, 11, 14, 15, 19–21, 25, 26, 28, 31, 40, 42, 45–49, 52–56, 59, 61, 75–77, 81, 82, 85, 95, 102, 110, 114, 116n30, 119, 135, 136, 138, 139, 141, 149, 151, 167, 168, 170–74, 181, 200; mortal sin, 187, 188
Society of Jesus. *See* Jesuits
Socinianism. *See* anti-trinitarianism
Socrates, 76
Son of God, 15, 19, 22, 24, 28, 34, 36, 40, 56n15, 72n23, 75, 79, 80, 92, 94, 97, 106, 109, 115, 118, 119, 134, 135, 166, 176, 177, 180n32
Sophia (wisdom), 166
Spalatin, Georg (Georg Burkhardt), 66, 73
spirit, spiritual, xi, 2, 4, 10, 13, 21, 23, 26, 27, 30, 33, 36, 45, 49–56, 59, 69, 71, 74, 78n38, 80, 88, 89, 92, 94, 96, 111, 112, 115–17, 127, 139, 144–49, 151, 154, 160–62, 164–67, 172, 175, 176, 178, 179, 182, 185–87, 195–99; Spiritualism, 103, 109. *See also* Holy Spirit, inwardness
state power, in relation to church, xii, xiii, 43, 44, 57–60, 67–68, 78n38, 79, 80–83, 87–88, 100–102, 105, 106, 184–85, 205, 208, 216–17. *See also* separation: of church and state
Stoddard, Solomon, Dr., 199, 200
Stoics, 32
Strasbourg, 65, 67, 85
Swiss Brethren, 104, 105

Table or Tablet, First or Second. *See* Ten Commandments
Tauler, Johannes, 79
Ten Commandments, 60–62, 71, 75n31, 100, 189–91. *See also* commandments

Teresa of Ávila, Saint, xiv, xvi, 147–48, 157–60, 213
Tertullian, Church Father, 119
Tetzel, Johann, 47, 48n7
theology, theologians, xi, xv, 1, 2, 4, 5, 7, 14, 19, 23, 24, 28, 33, 37, 41n33, 42–45, 53, 60, 64, 66, 76n33, 77n37, 85–88, 103, 106–8, 117, 120, 126, 134–37, 146, 148, 155–59, 164, 170, 182–83, 198
Thiersault, Marguerite, 192
Thomas à Kempis, xi, 2, 10–14, 166, 170, 202–3
Thomas Aquinas, Saint, 29, 78, 148, 183, 188n9
toleration, religious, 103, 106, 120–23, 164, 167–70, 185, 195–98
translation, xii, xiv, xvi, 1, 2, 14n24, 24, 31–33, 42n1, 43, 46n4, 70n15, 72, 78–80, 87, 100, 108, 125, 132–34, 165, 170, 182, 183, 184n2, 189–91
transubstantiation, doctrine, 1, 136
Treasury of Merits, 45, 48
Trinity, trinitarianism, xiii, 28n8, 106, 107, 117–21, 134, 135, 166, 180n32, 190. *See also* Athanasian Creed
Turks, 33, 36, 37, 92, 169, 179. *See also* Muslims
Tyburn, 127, 128, 140
Tyndale, William, 125
tyrant, tyranny, 21, 72, 74, 83, 88, 100–102, 130, 197n37

unbelief, unbeliever, xv, 54, 56, 73, 91, 107, 181, 187. *See also* infidels
unitarianism. *See* anti-trinitarianism
University: of Ingolstadt, xii, 65, 71–74; of Leiden, xiv, 164, 167–70; of Oxford, 1; of Paris, 191; of Prague, 1; of Salamanca, 183; of Wittenberg, 42, 64, 66
Ursuline, teaching order of nuns, xv, 184, 195

vernacular, 24, 32, 33, 74n28, 125, 132
Vincent de Paul, Saint, 148

Virgin Mary. *See* Mary, Virgin, mother of Jesus Christ
Vitoria, Francisco de, xv, 183, 186–89, 215
vulgar tongue. *See* vernacular
Vulgate, 24, 46n4, 70n16

Waldensians, 103
war: xii, xiv, 2, 24–27, 34–37, 82, 87, 92, 95, 104, 129, 139, 164, 168, 169, 183, 186–89, 195–98. *See also* discord, religious; just war; peace
Wars of Religion, French, 87, 95
wealth, xiv, 5n13, 18, 22, 30, 36, 37, 39, 48, 115, 124, 125, 128–31, 139, 151, 152, 162, 166, 169, 184, 192, 201; ecclesiastical, management of, 45, 47–48, 124–25, 128–31, 149, 151–52. *See also* property
Wesley, John, xv, xvi, 2, 164, 166–67, 179–81, 185, 215
Wesley, Susanna, 166
William of Ockham, 29n11
Williams, George H., 103, 208, 209
Williams, Roger, xv, xvi, 108, 184–85, 195–98, 216
Wittenberg, xii, 64–68, 88, 103
Wolsey, Thomas, Lord Chancellor, 124
women, as Christian advocates, xii–xv, 65, 71–74, 85, 92–94, 105, 111–14, 126, 134–37, 147, 157–60, 165–66, 173–79. *See also* feminism
word of God, 1, 4, 5, 10, 51, 59, 61, 63, 67, 71–74, 78, 82, 90, 93, 97, 98, 109–11, 118, 120, 132–34, 137, 149, 150, 169, 179
works, effectiveness of, 19–22, 50n14, 51, 52, 54–57, 74, 76, 78, 122, 134, 136, 161, 165
Wyclif, John, xi, 1–6, 23, 103, 144, 202

Xavier, Francis, Saint, xv, 183–84, 189–92, 216

Zell, Matthew, 65
Zeno of Elea, 76
Zurich, xiii, 84, 85, 104, 109
Zwingli, Ulrich, xiii, 84–85, 88–91, 95, 103, 104, 124, 207